Fragile Lands
of Latin America

Published in cooperation with the
Roger Thayer Stone Center for Latin American Studies
of Tulane University

Fragile Lands of Latin America

Strategies for Sustainable Development

EDITED BY

John O. Browder

Westview Press
BOULDER, SAN FRANCISCO, & LONDON

Westview Special Studies in Social, Political, and Economic Development

Published in 1989 in the United States of America by Westview Press, Inc., 5500 Central Avenue, Boulder, Colorado 80301, and in the United Kingdom by Westview Press, Inc., 13 Brunswick Centre, London WCIN IAF, England

Library of Congress Cataloging-in-Publication Data
Fragile lands of Latin America : strategies for sustainable
    development / edited by John O. Browder.
      p. cm.—(Westview special studies in social, political, and
economic development)
    Includes bibliographies and index.
    ISBN 0-8133-7705-6
    1. Land use, rural—Latin America. 2. Soil conservation—Latin
America. 3. Soil degradation—Latin America—Case studies.
4. Sustainable agriculture—Latin America. I. Browder, John O.
II. Series.
HD320.5.Z63F68 1989
333.76'13'098—dc19   88-20803
                                                                                          CIP

Printed and bound in the United States of America

The paper used in this publication meets the requirements of the American National Standard for Permanence of Paper for Printed Library Materials Z39.48-1984.

10   9   8   7   6   5   4   3

Contents

Contents

PART FIVE
RESEARCH IN PROGRESS

Foreword

Although we may never know whether the summer of 1988 was a first manifestation of the greenhouse effect or not, it gave us an arresting preview: Drought stunted harvests in the American Midwest; the normally copious Mississippi dwindled to a trickle, leaving barges stranded; and the Caribbean and Mexico were devastated by Hurricane Gilbert, the worst tropical storm on record in the Western Hemisphere. The altered composition of the atmosphere is affecting the basic physics and chemistry of the planet. The message is clear: We live on a fragile planet, the capacity of which we have begun to exceed.

In addition, in 1988 the report of Alberto Setzer of the Brazilian Institute of Space Research revealed that deforestation in Brazilian Amazonia was greater than anyone had feared. In 1987 some 178,000 fires, each greater than one 1 square kilometer in extent, were detected by satellite. This destruction covered 20 million hectares (ha), of which 8 million had been primary forest (*mata densa*). Brazilian deforestation *alone* was equal to 15 ha/minute—a level which, just a few years ago, was widely considered to reflect the *world* rate of deforestation. That forest loss inevitably meant species extinctions and hence a quantum, if unmeasured, reduction in biological diversity. Biological communities, among the richest known on earth, vanished into enormous smoke plumes and a pall that hung over western Amazonia for weeks. Setzer estimates that about 620 million tons of carbon were released into the atmosphere, which is equivalent to 20 percent of the excess CO_2 accumulated in the atmosphere in 1987. Tropical deforestation has thus become a reality for everyone—it is no longer a matter of obscure and anonymous vanishing species in some distant place. The problems of tropical deforestation, biological impoverishment, and the greenhouse effect (which will engender further species loss) must now be seen as an enormous global problem. We are all locked in the greenhouse together.

The dilemma is an ecological Gordian knot on a planetary scale, yet the reality and the difficulty of it is that it is the consequence of myriad small decisions about land use. Each decision seems utterly reasonable within its own context; the aggregate is the problem. Just as the genesis of the problem is this set of prolific individual decisions about the land, so must the solution constitute an equally prolific, but in the end wiser, set of decisions.

The problem of the greenhouse effect is as much a matter of how the fragile lands of the planet are used as it is a matter of use of fossil fuels. Management of forests, while not a solution in itself, can nonetheless contribute measurably to bringing the annual increment of carbon added to the atmosphere from three billion tons down to zero. The sustainable management of fragile lands thus becomes a topic not just of hemispheric but also of global importance.

This volume provides a beacon of hope in a time of ecological darkness. There is serious evidence here that there *are* ways to use the variety of fragile lands from wet tropical forest to semi-desert in a fashion that is both sustainable in terms of the environment and of modest economic return. There are down-to-earth calculations of monetary return from these systems—returns that, by and large, at least over the longer term, exceed those from more destructive forms of land use. How markets might respond to extensive use of these systems is probably anyone's guess, but in the end, sustainable use of the land is in everyone's interest whereas destructive land use is in no one's interest.

It is of significance that many of the preferable alternate systems of land use chronicled here have bases in pre-Columbian practices. It is largely unrecognized that there were considerable Amerindian populations in Latin America prior to European discovery, many inhabiting lands considered fragile and marginal.

All too much like changing hemlines, fashion seems to vacillate between the equally false notions of the noble savage in exquisite tune with the environment and of "only modern is good." It is certainly true that there are numerous examples of primitive peoples having exceeded the carrying capacity of the land. The mysterious collapse of the Mayan civilization will always be tantalizing in that regard. It is also clear that slash and burn agriculture, while ecologically sound at low densities, is disastrous at high ones.

Indigenous peoples were and are inevitably closer to the land and its ecology. They are more likely to learn from their ecological errors than modern people who can migrate from one end of the continent to another with ease or can call on subsidies from a distant national treasury to muddle through. Neither extreme, the Luddite technophobia or blind technophilia, is the answer. Rather, there is everything to be gained by judiciously combining what we can learn from the traditional systems with what we can gain from the new.

An interesting theme runs through this volume, namely the quest for less wasteful systems. This is not just seeking agriculture that is permanent and sustainable to the point of precluding the periodic need to abandon the land and move on. It is also a matter of systems less dependent on and less wasteful of external ingredients and of systems that better approach closed ones. It is the leakiness of industrial society, both the industry itself and its agriculture, that contributes in greater degree to local, regional, and global pollution. To the extent that fragile land management can reduce leakage, particularly by massive burning of organic matter, it will simultaneously benefit those who live on those lands and the world in general.

Paradoxically, ecology and economy share a common etymology: the Greek word for house, *ecos*. The reality has largely been that the two have been in terrible conflict, as we have assiduously worked at pulling the ecological rug from beneath ourselves. Perhaps within the context of this book the two are coming at last in concert. As the composition of the atmosphere testifies, this cannot happen soon enough.

Thomas E. Lovejoy
Washington, D.C.

Acknowledgments

This book is a collection of revised papers originally presented at the Symposium on Fragile Lands of Latin America: The Search for Sustainable Uses, sponsored by Tulane University's Center for Latin American Studies and held during the Fourteenth Congress of the Latin American Studies Association on March 17–19, 1988, in New Orleans. The Fragile Lands Symposium and this book were made possible with the generous support of several organizations and individuals.

I thank the Tinker Foundation for its financial support of the Mesoamerican Ecology Institute of Tulane University, which provided substantial funding for this project. The Latin American Studies Association (LASA) under President Paul Drake, and its 1988 program committee under Charles Bergquist, favored my proposal to include the Fragile Lands Symposium as a "special event" in the program of the Fourteenth Congress, while the LASA executive council approved my proposal to form a new LASA Task Force on Natural Resources and the Environment. I thank them and LASA for this support and for travel grants furnished to LASA by the Inter-American Foundation and the Ford Foundation for two symposium participants. The World Wildlife Fund and Conservation Foundation, the Agency for International Development, and Mr. and Mrs. Stanley Day all provided valuable financial assistance to the project. The Roger Thayer Stone Center for Latin American Studies, under its director, Richard E. Greenleaf, provided vital logistical and staff support for the production of this volume. I especially thank Martha Peters-Hernandez who skillfully and patiently handled the tedious work of manuscript production from beginning to end. She is the champion of this volume.

In addition to the authors, who graciously tolerated the usual badgering of an anxious editor and complied with editorial deadlines and requirements in good humor, I am also grateful to Thomas Lovejoy, for his thoughtful foreword, and to Julie Denslow, Arturo Gomez-Pompa, and B. L. Turner II, who, in addition to volume contributors Gerardo Budowski and Ghillean Prance, gave thoughtful commentary on the papers presented at the Fragile Lands Symposium.

John O. Browder
New Orleans and Blacksburg

About the Editor and Contributors

Janis B. Alcorn is a specialist in indigenous ethnobotany and agroforestry. Her research has focused on Bora (Peru) and Huastec Maya (Mexico) resource management. Presently she serves as an American Association for the Advancement of Science Fellow in the Agency for International Development.

Anthony B. Anderson is a tropical botanist and a specialist in tropical ecology and agroforestry systems of the Brazilian Amazon. He is an Associate Researcher at the Museu Goeldi, Belem, Brazil.

John O. Browder (editor) is a regional development planner and a specialist in Brazilian Amazon development policy analysis. He teaches international development planning at the Virginia Polytechnic Institute and State University in Blacksburg, Virginia.

Gerardo Budowski is a specialist in tropical agroforestry and comparative farming systems. He serves on the faculty of the Universidad para la Paz, in San Jose, Costa Rica.

Kay L. Candler is a cultural anthropologist and a specialist in cognition and symbolism of the Quechua of highland Peru. She is presently a graduate student at the University of Illinois.

Wil de Jong is a tropical forester and specialist in agroforestry and ethnobotany of the Peruvian Amazon. He recently served as Research Associate in the Institute of Economic Botany in New York.

William M. Denevan is a cultural ecologist and historical geographer and a specialist in Amazonian biogeography and pre-Columbian agriculture. He serves on the faculty of the University of Wisconsin, Madison.

William E. Doolittle is a cultural ecologist and historical geographer and a specialist in the pre-Columbian agro-ecosystems of northern Mexico. He serves on the faculty of the University of Texas, Austin.

Clark L. Erickson is an archaeologist and specialist in the pre-Columbian agriculture of the Andes. He serves on the faculty of the University of Pennsylvania, Philadelphia.

David Gow is a social anthropologist and development practitioner who has worked in numerous foreign countries on various development planning and management projects. He serves with Development Alternatives, Inc., in Washington, D.C.

Gary S. Hartshorn is a tropical forest ecologist and a specialist in neotropical forest management, land-use, and conservation. He serves with the World Wildlife Fund.

Susanna B. Hecht is a geographer and a specialist in tropical deforestation, agro-ecology, and development in the Brazilian Amazon. She serves on the faculty of the University of California, Los Angeles.

Flavio Coello Hinojosa is a tropical ecologist and specialist in tropical biology and park management. He is Chief of Conservation and Wildlife, Ecuadorian Amazon, for the Departamento de Areas Naturales y Recursos Silvestres of Ecuador's Ministerio de Agricultura.

Mário Hiraoka is a geographer and a specialist in indigenous tropical agriculture and human ecology of tropical South America. He serves on the faculty of the Millersville University of Pennsylvania.

Mário Augusto G. Jardim is a tropical forester and specialist in commercial palm ecology and is associated with the botany department at the Museu Goeldi in Belem, Brazil. He is also pursuing his masters degree in the forestry program at the University in Piracicaba, São Paulo.

James D. Nations is a human ecologist and specialist in appropriate technology and sustainable land use in the tropics. He is affiliated with the Center for Human Ecology, Austin, Texas.

Christine Padoch is an anthropologist and a specialist in traditional resource use patterns, agroforestry, and the social and environmental aspects of economic development in the neotropics and south Asia. She is Associate Scientist for the New York Botanical Garden, Bronx, New York.

Ghillean T. Prance is a tropical botanist and specialist in the tropical forest ethnobotany, systematics, and economic botany of Amazonia. He is Director of London's Royal Botanic Gardens at Kew.

Carlos Reiche is a rural economist and specialist in economic and financial analysis of agroforestry systems. He is Professor-Researcher with the Centro Agronómico Tropical de Investigacion y Enseñanza (CATIE), Turrialba, Costa Rica.

Stephan Schwartzman is a cultural anthropologist and a specialist in the rubber tappers' movement of the Brazilian Amazon. He serves as Staff Anthropologist for the Environmental Defense Fund.

John M. Treacy recently completed his Ph.D. in geography at the University of Wisconsin, Madison. His research focuses on pre-Columbian Andean farming systems.

Gene C. Wilken is a cultural geographer and specialist in natural resources and farming systems of Latin America and Africa. He serves on the faculty of the Colorado State University, Fort Collins.

Fragile Lands
of Latin America

Research Sites of Contributing Authors

1 Hiraoka
2 Padoch & de Jong
3 Anderson & Jardim
4 Hartshorn
5 Nations & Hinojosa
6 Schwartzman
7 Treacy
8 Erickson & Candler
9 Alcorn
10 Doolittle
11 Hecht

Introduction

John O. Browder

Latin America's forests are being leveled. Its soils—some worked to exhaustion and some underutilized—are eroding. The potential contributions of its waters, including the shining Caribbean and the aortal Amazon and its life-giving arteries, to balanced and healthy economic development are being jeopardized. High population growth rates overwhelm the modest accomplishments of Latin America's own "Green Revolution." Unprecedented megalopolises threaten to topple out of control and skewed patterns of land distribution—plus, now, the debt crisis—defeat steady, balanced, sustainable development in city and countryside alike."

—James Gustave Speth (1986)

That Latin America today faces an unprecedented environmental crisis on several fronts is an assertion we hear with increasing regularity. We read or see images in the popular press of the disaster following the indiscriminate dumping of carcinogenic dioxin, used as a defoliant, at Tucurui, Goiania, and elsewhere in Brazil. We confront almost daily reports of the alarming destruction of Amazonian rain forests, the erosion of denuded slopes in Hispanola and elsewhere in the Antilles, land slides onto hillside towns and villages in the Andes of Colombia, Ecuador, and Peru, choking air pollution in Mexico City, and the despoliation of renewable fisheries, forests, and other biotic resource systems throughout the region. In spite of over forty years of modern economic "development," to which many of these environmental tragedies are linked, "one-third of Latin America's population, about 130 million people, are now living in extreme poverty" (Cockburn, 1989). In their Introduction to *Bordering on Trouble,* editors Maquire and Brown assert:

> The degradation of Latin America's natural resource base is threatening Latin welfare and hemispheric political security. In the name of devel-

opment, and all to often to line the pockets of a few, forests and fertile
soils are destroyed and the seas and fresh water supplies contaminated—
on a scale that will make it impossible to support Latin America's growing
number (Maquire and Brown, 1986).

What can be done to arrest the rising tide of natural resource
destruction in Latin America? Are there strategies for non-destructive
development? Admittedly there are very few shining success stories of
large-scale development of Latin America's abundant natural resources.
The audacious 16,000 km² Jari silviculture project in Brazil's northern
Amazon, created by Daniel Ludwig in 1968, today operates in the red;
in 1985 operating deficits reached an estimated $47 million, equivalent
to $2,900 per hectare (ha) (Fearnside, 1988). Brazil's mamouth mineral
extraction and agro-silvicultural complex, the Grande Carajas program,
also has come under increasing criticism for both its expected environmental impacts and extraordinary economic costs (Fearnside, 1986).
Costly subsidies to Amazon beef cattle producers have transformed at
least 800,000 km² of Brazilian natural rain forest into short-lived
pastures without ameliorating Brazil's long-term dependence on foreign
beef (Browder, 1988a). A growing number of researchers now agree that
cattle ranching on neo-tropical soils is viable only with substantial
subsidies (Browder, 1988a, 1988b; Fearnside, 1986; Hecht, 1982, 1985;
Norgaard et al., 1986; Shane, 1986). Meanwhile, peasant farmers, encouraged by the Brazilian government to colonize the rain forests of
western Amazonia have razed an estimated 60,000 km² of natural
vegetation since 1973; yet fewer than one-half of these colonists remain
on their government land grants for more than one year (World Bank,
1987; Browder, 1988c). Ambitious fuelwood plantations are replacing
large areas of natural vegetation in Brazil with fast-growing Eucalyptus
monocultures to feed Brazil's steel industries. One such endeavor projects a rate of return on investment of 15% (Spears, 1985), or a net
return of only $45 per ha. Rice monocultures promoted by the Brazilian
government on the fertile Amazon floodplains, according to one study,
generate net returns of only $50 per ha at a rate of 16% on investment
(Hiraoka, this volume).

Along the arid Pacific coastline, from Mexico to Chile, expensive
irrigation projects designed to transform barren deserts into farmbelts
have had mixed results. Some initiatives have been stymied by unan-
ticipated problems such as salination, rendering irrigated water useless
for agriculture (Doolittle, this volume). Large scale land reclamation
and agricultural development projects in the Peruvian Andes offer little
hope of benefiting the rural poor, while threatening to undermine efforts
to revive potentially sustainable pre-Columbian methods of raised field

and terrace farming (Erickson and Candler; and Treacy, both this volume). Some development planners and economists have become increasingly skeptical of "conventional" solutions to the seemingly intractable problems posed by efforts to manage the complex and fragile biotopes that dominate the Latin American landscape. As a result, there is growing interest in the little-known potential of traditional and indigenous resource management strategies. For example, management of a single natural resource (the acai palm) by traditional inhabitants of the Amazon floodplains produces net returns of about $110 per ha, offering workers a daily income that is five times greater than what they could expect to earn as urban wage laborers (Anderson and Jardim, this volume). More intensive indigenous natural forest management practices produce yields of fruits, timber, gums, resins, and crops worth between $434 per ha (Peters et al., cited in Prance, this volume) and over $800 per ha (Padoch and de Jong, this volume). In many cases, however, inadequate marketing facilities and the conversion of rain forests to less productive uses prevents the full realization of the rain forest's immense economic potential.

This volume of selected research papers, originally presented at the "Symposium of Fragile Lands of Latin America—The Search for Sustainable Uses," presents some fresh evidence of the viability of a few "non-conventional" strategies for natural resource development and management. Taken together, these papers do not converge on a single integrated approach to sustainable land development for Latin America, although several common themes are evident. Rather, this volume is a composite of several disparate but promising strategies that warrant closer study. What may make this volume unique is the type of analysis undertaken by the authors. Each author attempted to demonstrate the financial viability of a particular strategy or important strategy component within a general cost-benefit framework. Although detailed financial analyses were not possible in all cases, in most cases sufficient information was presented to permit one general conclusion: Many non-conventional land use strategies satisfy conventional criteria of financial viability. Within the varied social and cultural contexts in which they are practiced, these strategies warrant serious attention by broad-minded development planners and lending institutions.

Content and Organization

This book is organized into five parts. The first part includes three chapters that discuss the theoretical contexts for the empirical research that follows. Denevan's paper defines "fragile lands" and outlines their geographic distribution and extent in Latin America. The chapter by

Gow further develops the conceptual discussion of fragile land development with reference to a specific development program created by the Agency for International Development (AID). The chapter by Wilken proposes a fundamental revision of conventional wisdom about the direction of technology flows and outlines a procedure to enable the transfer of "traditional" technology. Together these three chapters broadly define some of the critical boundaries to the debate on what constitutes "sustainable development."

The second part consists of nine chapters that address various aspects of tropical rain forest management, derived mainly from research undertaken in the Amazon. Rain forest strategies are emphasized in this book; rain forests comprise the largest general fragile land biotope in Latin America (about 44% of the region's area). An overview of the economic importance of rain forest products is presented by Prance. Such products raised over US $1 billion in foreign exchange for Brazil in 1985 (Prance, this volume). Three chapters focus on rain forest floodplain strategies (Anderson and Jardim, Hiraoka, and Padoch and de Jong). Wetlands, of which floodplains are an important part, comprise only 3% of Latin America's area, but are widely believed to offer the greatest potential for large-scale agricultural production in Latin America's tropical lowlands (Meggers, 1977 cited in Barrow, 1985). In consequence of the dynamic rhythms of rain fall, flooding, and soil deposition, the floodplains are among the most complex and unstable environments for conventional cultivation and uniform resource management. While programs have been initiated to tap the agricultural potential of the Amazon's floodplains through mechanized cash crop monocultures, the three authors represented here explore alternative production systems that evolved from traditional riverine communities. These *cabóclos* or *ribereños* form a "living bridge" between a rapidly disappearing indigenous tradition and the modern world. Here are found a variety of land use adaptions that blend natural resource management with agriculture and reflect the innate symbiosis between floodplain society and its dynamic habitat.

Three chapters explore potential development strategies for the tropical forests (mainly *terra firme*) based on the concept of restricted use zones or "reserves." Hartshorn presents some initial findings from a timber production forest in the Peruvian Amazon indicating potential returns on investment of $3,500 per ha and a rate of return of about 50%. Nations and Hinojosa examine a wildlife production reserve established in the Oriente of Ecuador and demonstrate its potential as a profit-making enterprise. Schwartzman describes the rubber tappers' movement to create extractive reserves in western Brazil and outlines the structure of this adaptive and largely subsistent economy.

Two chapters examine indigenous rain forest land uses. Present knowledge suggests that continuous cultivation on typically nutrient-deficient neotropical soils using artificial soil fertilization can be cost-efficient (Nicholaides, et al., 1984; Sanchez, et al., 1982). The underlying assumption that artificial fertilizers are necessary is challenged by Hecht, who proposes that the soil management practices of the Amazonian Kayapó offer promising possibilities for sustained cultivation of rain forest soils without artificial fertilizers. Departing from Amazonia, Alcorn describes the indigenous land management strategies of the Huastec Maya in Mexico and the importance of their farm forests (te'loms). By Alcorn's preliminary estimates, the Huastec land use system produces a cash return of about $455 per ha. Here, again, another conventional development assumption is challenged and the natural forest is shown to significantly contribute to the economic and social wellbeing of indigenous human communities on an indefinitely sustainable basis.

The third part comprises two chapters that explore potentially sustainable farming strategies on Andean highlands where efforts to revive pre-Columbian techniques of hill-side terrace farming (Treacy) and raised field farming (Erickson and Candler) are being pursued by Peruvian peasant communities. The authors present evidence of the potentially superior productivity of these pre-Columbian techniques over conventional large-scale agricultural development projects. For instance, the costs of new terrace construction ($2,000 per ha) compare favorably to the initial costs of opening coastal desert land to irrigated agriculture ($2,500 to $6,000 per ha). Moreover, new bench terraces produce yields 45% higher (4-crop average) than non-terraced land in the same Andean locality (Treacy). Meanwhile, the complementary technology of raised fields could turn the Lake Titicaca region of Peru from a periodic potato importer to a self-sufficient food producer capable of supporting nearly twice its current population (Erickson and Candler), a prospect that has important implications for the conservation of Peru's lowland rain forests.

The fourth part is a single chapter on an adaptive farming system in arid northwestern Mexico. Doolittle presents a study of intermittent farming of desert streambeds (*arroyos*) as an example of a low-cost, appropriate alternative to costly large-scale irrigation schemes on fragile arid lands.

The final part of the book presents two short reviews of promising research in progress on a development strategy for a region of high rainfall, the Chocó of Colombia (Budowski) and an ambitious project to examine the financial performance of agroforestry systems on small demonstration farms in Central America (Reiche).

Common Themes

Three common themes characterize the resource management strategies examined in considerable detail through this volume. First, they tend to be well adapted to the natural environments in which they are found. Such strategies are, in essence "adaptive" in character, and it is this quality of adaptiveness that fundamentally distinguishes them from most of the "conventional" development schemes highlighted in the first part of this Introduction.

This adaptiveness is reflected, particularly in the case of the tropical rain forest strategies presented, by the large number of species that contribute to household production; e.g. at least 53 known species are managed by floodplain inhabitants of the Amazon's estuary (Anderson and Jardim, this volume), some 50 species by traditional rubber tappers in the western Amazon (Schwartzman, this volume), and 300 species by the Huastec Maya of Mexico (Alcorn, this volume). In shocking contrast, modern tropical agriculture, which typically entails forest removal, is often based on biologically depauperate and short-term monocultural communities that rapidly degrade into economic wastelands.

The diversity and biological richness of "traditional" production systems are supported by seemingly complex agroecological land use zones that together "mimic," rather than replace, the natural environment. Whereas a typical Amazon cattle rancher may recognize only one agroecological zone, pasture grassland, the Kayapó Indians of Amazonia recognize at least 10 ecological zones, and manipulate most of the plant species found in their habitat to support the productive functions of these zones (Posey, 1985). By adapting production to their environment, the Kayapó obtain superior yields of plant and animal protein than do either colonist farmers or commercial ranchers (Hecht, this volume). The same may be said of Andean terraces and raised fields (Treacy; Erickson and Candler, both this volume), *arroyo* agriculture in northern Mexico (Doolittle, this volume), and riberiño farming systems on the Amazon flood plains (Hiraoka, this volume); the physical structures of these diverse agroecosystems blend into, and are sustained by the dynamics of the natural environment.

The second common theme extends from the first. The adaptive natural resource management strategies presented in this volume, by virtue of their biological diversity and structural congruity with the natural environment, function indefinitely in the ecological and cultural contexts in which they are found; they are, in essence, indefinitely "sustainable." In contrast to colonists in Rondonia who remain on their farm lots for 2 to 7 years (Browder, 1988c), two diverse groups of traditional "forest managers," the rubber tappers of western Amazonia (Schwartzman, this volume) and the Huastec Maya of Mexico (Alcorn, this volume), follow distinct land use strategies that have documentable histories of continuous production ranging from 50 to 60 years. In the case of the Huastec Maya, managed forest groves may go back 3,000 years, and continue today to provide an important supplement to household production.

The third common theme is found in the preliminary efforts of this diverse group of distinguished authors to quantify the financial costs and benefits of the strategies they have studied. While some economists may ponder the analyses presented here, I venture that all who read with an open mind will learn from these efforts. The research presented in this volume challenges "conventional" wisdom; many "pre-modern" or otherwise "adaptive" strategies withstand the test of modern financial profitability and *also* conserve fragile natural resources in Latin America. There are financially and economically promising alternatives to resource-destructive land development in Latin America, many are potentially very profitable.

Beneath the ecological diversity of Latin America's remarkable and largely "fragile" landscape (Denevan, this volume), there are a myriad of potential strategies for meeting the growing challenge of sustainable management of fragile lands. Humans have dwelled upon this world region for at least the last 10,000 years. Before the past disappears, let us consider some of its opportunities for the future.

References

Barrow, C.J., 1985. "The Development of the *Varzeas* (Floodplains) of Brazilian Amazonia," in John Hemming (ed.), *Change in the Amazon Basin, vol.1, Man's Impacts on Forests and Rivers.* Manchester University Press, Manchester.

Browder, John O., 1988a. "The Social Costs of Rain Forest Destruction," *Interciencia* 13(3):115–120.

———, 1988b. "Public Policy and Deforestation in the Brazilian Amazon," in Robert Repetto and Malcolm Gillis (eds.) *Government Policy and the Misuse of Forest Resources.* Cambridge University Press, New York.

———, 1988c. "The Economics of Small Farmer Settlement and Deforestation in Rondonia, Brazil." Paper presented at the Symposium on Fragile Lands of Latin America: The Search for Sustainable Uses, Fourteenth Congress, Latin American Studies Association, March 17–19, New Orleans, Louisiana.

Cockburn, Alexander, 1989. "Brazil's Poor Get Hungrier on Bare-Bones IMF Menu," *Wall Street Journal,* Thursday, March 23, p. A25.

Fearnside, Philip M., 1986. "Agricultural Plans for Brazil's Grande Carajas Program: Lost Opportunity for Sustainable Local Development?" *World Development* 14(3):385–409.

Hecht, Susanna, B., 1982. "Cattle Ranching Development in the Eastern Amazon: Evaluation of a Development Strategy." Ph.D. dissertation, University of California, Berkeley.

_____, 1985. "Environment, Development and Politics: Capital Accumulation and the Livestock Sector in Eastern Amazonia," *World Development* 13(6):663–684.

_____, 1988. "Jari at Age 19: Lessons for Brazil's Silvicultural Plans at Carajas," *Interciencia* 13(1)12–24.

Maguire, Andrew and Janet Welsh Brown (eds.), 1986. *Bordering on Trouble: Resources and Politics in Latin America*. Adler and Adler, Bethesda, Maryland.

Meggers, B.J., 1977. *Amazonia: a Illusão de um Paraiso*. Giv. Brasileira, Rio de Janeiro.

Nicholaides, J.J., III, D.E. Bandy, P.A. Sanchez, J.H. Villachica, A.J. Coutu, and C.J. Valverde, 1984. "Continuous Cropping Potential in the Upper Amazon Basin," in Marianne Schmink and Charles H. Wood (eds.), *Frontier Expansion in Amazonia*. University of Florida Press, Gainesville.

Norgaard, Richard B., Giorgio Possio, Susanna B. Hecht, 1986. "The Economics of Cattle Ranching in Eastern Amazonia. Manuscript.

Posey, Darrell, A., 1985. "Native and Indigenous Guidelines for New Amazonian Development Strategies: Understanding Biological Diversity Through Ethnoecology," pp. 156–181 in John Hemming (ed.), *Change in the Amazon Basin, vol. 1, Man's Impact on Forests and Rivers*. Manchester University Press, Manchester.

Sanchez, P.A., D. Brandy, J. Villachica, and J. Nicolaides. 1982. Soils of the Amazon and Their Management for Continuous Crop Production. *Science*. 216:821–827.

Shane, Douglas R., 1986. *Hoofprints on the Forest: Cattle Ranching and the Destruction of Latin America's Tropical Forests*. Institute for the Study of Human Values, Philadelphia.

Spears, J., 1985. "Deforestation Issues in Developing Countries: The Case for an Accelerated Investment Programme," *Commonwealth Forestry Review* 64(4):313–343.

Speth, James Gustave, 1986. "Forward," in Andrew Maguire and Janet Welsh smith (eds.), *Bordering on Trouble: Resources and Politics in Latin America*. Adler and Adler, Bethesda, Maryland.

World Bank, 1987. "Brazil: Northwest I, II, and III Technical Review, Final Report. Washington, D.C.

PART ONE

Fragile Lands and Technology Transfer: Conceptual Frameworks

1

The Geography of Fragile Lands in Latin America

William M. Denevan

Introduction

The nature and problems of fragile lands in relation to agriculture in Latin America recently have been brought into focus by international development institutions (see Gow, this volume). What I want to do here is to define, categorize, and map fragile lands in Latin America, and briefly present some relevant concepts and comments.

Definition

"Fragile Lands" are lands that are potentially subject to significant deterioration under agricultural, silvicultural, and pastoral use systems. Indicators of deterioration include both short-term and long-term declines in productivity, negative off-site impacts, and slow recovery of water, soil, plant, and animal resources following disturbance (based on Bremer et al., 1984:3).

I have added the word "potential" in the definition to emphasize the fact that land is not naturally fragile. It is only fragile in terms of (1) specific types of use systems, and (2) specific intensity and frequency levels of usage. For example, steep slope lands are not particularly vulnerable to erosion if they have been terraced. And a small plot of tropical forest is not very fragile if it is only farmed one year out of one hundred by slash and burn methods. There are only potential fragile lands, with the degree of fragility varying with the nature of use in relation to the type of environment. Otherwise we get into deterministic ways of thinking about the environment (as with the concept of "agricultural potential," which does not exist independent of culture). The environment is neutral. It is human beings who give it attributes through the ways they interact with it.

Fragility is a relative concept. All environments are subject to deterioration under human use. Thus it is more appropriate to refer to "less fragile lands" rather than "non-fragile lands." Also, different components of environments are potentially more fragile than others. Finally, environments are not naturally stable but change both slowly and very rapidly, and degree of fragility varies accordingly.

The concept of fragility is related to but different from that of "marginality," which refers to lands which have significant environmental constraints (requiring special environmental management technology) and/or low productivity or accessibility.

Tropical lands tend to be particularly fragile because process rates for productivity, decomposition, mineral cycling, succession, erosion, etc. are generally higher in the tropics than in temperate regions (Farnworth and Golley, 1974:x–xi). On the other hand, cold lands are potentially very fragile for the opposite reason—very slow process rates.

Classification, Distribution, and Extent

Setting these points aside, I have attempted a simple classification consisting of seven categories of fragile lands based on slope, climate, and vegetation (Table 1). The main stress factors are indicated for each (see photographs).

Figures 1–4 show the approximate geographic distribution of the seven categories of fragile lands. Only large units are shown. One is immediately impressed by the fact that most of Latin America can be considered fragile. The largest non-fragile, or less fragile, lands are the temperate grasslands and forests of southern South America.

The approximate areas covered by each fragile land category are shown in Table 2. Fragile lands account for 87% of the total land area of Latin America. Within this area there are unmeasured pockets of less fragile land, which amount to only a small percentage of the total. The less fragile temperate lands of southern Brazil, the Argentine pampas, and Uruguay total only about 13% of the land area of Latin America.

The only non-usable lands considered here are the cold lands above the tree and grass lines where frost is too severe for crops, pasture, or trees. These areas are scattered in the Andes and southern tip of South America and are not mapped. It may appear to be an extreme statement to maintain that all other lands are usable, but such is indeed true, depending on the technology and crops available and the labor or capital expenditures people are willing or able to make for subsistence

Table 1
Categories of Fragile Lands and Their Stress Factors

Category	Stress Factors

First group: Flat to gently sloping terrain (primarily lowlands)

Category	Stress Factors
1. Tropical forests (tierra firme or interflueve)	Soil fertility (low initially; readily depleted once forest is removed) Pests (weeds, animals, insects, diseases; can cause field abandonment even on superior soils)
2. Tropical savannas (well drained)	Soil fertility and structure Pests
3. Wetlands (subject to seasonal or permanent flooding: savannas, floodplains, swamps, lake edges; not always particularly fragile)	Excessive flooding (height and/or duration)
4. Dry lowlands	Aridity (highly variable) Salinization (salt accumulation under irrigation) Inadequate flooding (height and/or duration in river valleys) Desertification (from vegetation degradation)

Second group: Moderate to steeply sloping terrain (primary highlands)

Category	Stress Factors
5. Montane tropical forests	Slope (vulnerability to erosion especially great due to high rainfall) Soil fertility (extremely variable) Pests
6. Dry highlands	Slope Frost Aridity
7. Rainfed highlands	Slope (vulnerability to erosion especially great due to high rainfall) Frost

Plate 1   Tropical forest along the Amazon near Iquitos, Peru (M. Hiraoka, 1983; reprinted by permission).

Plate 2   Tropical savanna (well drained), Orinoco Llanos, Venezuela (W. M. Denevan, 1972).

Plate 3   Flooded savanna, Llanos de Mojos, northern Bolivia (W. M. Denevan, 1962).

Plate 4   Coastal desert, northern Peru, showing a section of the Moche-Chicama inter-valley, pre-Inca canal (James S. Kus; reprinted by permission).

Plate 5   Montane tropical forest, eastern Bolivian Andes (W. M. Denevan, 1961).

Plate 6   Dry highlands, Colca Valley, Peruvian Andes; note abandoned terraces on center slope (W. M. Denevan, 1983).

Plate 7   Rainfed highlands, largely cleared of forest, Colombian Andes (W. M. Denevan, 1977).

Figure 1   Map of mountains 1,000-plus meters in elevation (modified from Cole, 1965:31).

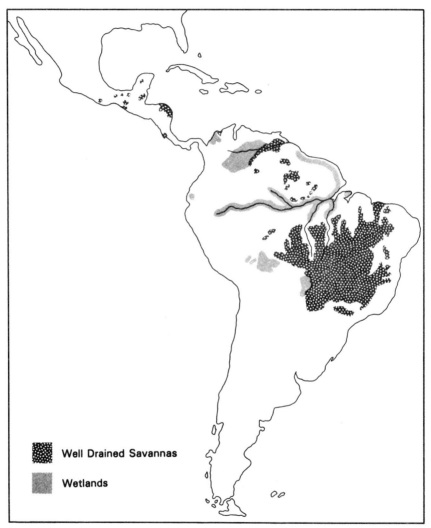

Figure 2   Map of well-drained savannas and wetlands (wet savannas and floodplains) (modified from Sarmiento and Monasterio, 1975:225).

Tropical Forests

Figure 3 Map of tropical forests (modified from Cole, 1965:42).

Figure 4   Map of dry lands: highland and lowland, including dry forest, cactus scrub, and desert (modified from Cole, 1965:42).

Table 2
Extent of Fragile Lands

Category	Area Covered[a] (km^2)	Percentage of Latin America
1. Tropical forests	7,970,000	39
2. Tropical savannas	2,375,000	11
3. Wetlands	665,000	3
4. Dry lowlands	5,225,000	25
5. Montane tropical forests	340,000	2
6. Dry highlands	590,000	3
7. Rainfed highlands	760,000	4
Less fragile	2,650,000	13
Total	20,575,000	100

[a] Modified from Cole, 1965:49. More recent estimates show lower figures for tropical forests and tropical savannas, which could raise the less fragile total to as much as 20%.

or for market. All forest can be used. Deserts can be irrigated, depending on water availability. Steep slopes can be terraced. Swamps can be drained. And infertile soils can be fertilized. The costs, of course, may be prohibitive for permanent, sustained systems, or systems may be used which are sustainable only on a periodic basis.

Figures are not available, but certainly a much lower percentage of the more fragile lands is cultivated compared to the less fragile lands. Furthermore, the more fragile lands are dominated by small farmers, whereas the less fragile lands are dominated by large farmers, haciendas, plantations, and corporate farms.

Management of Fragility

All the fragile land categories can be utilized under extensive management systems (shifting cultivation, sectorial fallowing, agroforestry, low density grazing) with minimal deterioration. However, all are subject to deterioration under intensive use systems. Sustained, intensive productivity generally requires significant landscape and soil modification (terracing; raised and sunken fields; water control canals, reservoirs, and embankments; and soil additives) in order to manipulate resource conditions and stress factors (slope, water availability, temperature, pests, soil fertility). Under traditional land-use systems such modifications are usually labor intensive; they are usually responses to population or market pressure; and they usually include risk-minimizing strategies which may lower productivity. By manipulating natural stress factors, such systems render fragile lands less fragile and more sustainable, many having been in place for hundreds, even thousands of years.

Modern land-use systems (based on fossil fuel inputs), in contrast, are capital intensive and the costs of landscape and resource management are often excessive in relation to economic returns (irrigation is a major exception). As a result, fragile lands may not be utilized under modern systems. Development of fragile lands needs to draw upon traditional knowledge, on labor rather than on expensive fossil fuel energy, on management improvements which increase productivity without threatening sustainability, on risk avoidance, and on environmental stability (Denevan, 1980a). Traditional knowledge is location specific, however, "and only arrived at through a unique co-evolution between specific social and ecological systems" (R.B. Norgaard quoted in Redclift, 1987:151).

A large portion of the fragile land area of Latin America is excessively dry, subject to flooding, or consists of steep slopes. As a result, special landscape engineering techniques are required before effective cultivation is possible. Three traditional techniques, each highly varied, have been utilized throughout the Americas: terraces, irrigation canals, and raised fields. All of these were important in Pre-Columbian times (Denevan, 1980b). Terrace and irrigation systems continue to the present, but raised field cultivation is now rare. Vast areas with these agriculture landforms are now abandoned for reasons that are not altogether clear, but the fragile nature of the environments involved and demographic change are clearly central factors.

Most of the papers in this volume concern land systems in tropical forests, which are particularly fragile environments since most, not just one or two, components of the ecosystem are adversely affected once forest is cleared for agriculture or pasture: soil structure, organic matter, mineral content, biota, surface temperatures, humidity, runoff, and evapotranspiration.

Relevant Concepts

Perception. People's attitudes towards fragile lands and how and whether they are used depend on perceptions which vary culturally and individually and change over time. Some attributes of fragile lands may be perceived so positively as to outweigh the negative aspects which are then controlled by technology and high labor inputs. Alfred Siemens (1977:21) has discussed this for the wetlands of the Mayan region, considered to be miserable, disease ridden, useless swamps since early colonial times. The Maya, in contrast, found these lands to be sources of water, wildlife, and organic muck for constructing raised fields and hence prime settlement locations. The areas of prehistoric raised fields around Lake Titicaca were mapped as only usable for fishing and totora reeds by a recent land-use survey, reflecting current scientific perceptions of what is usable or fragile, and what is not.

Carrying Capacity. A difficult concept to apply, refers to the number of people that can be supported by a given environment, with a given land use system, and a given standard of living, without environmental deterioration. Fragile lands presumably have lower carrying capacities because they are readily susceptible to deterioration. This is not necessarily the case, however. Some fragile lands have some of the highest food productivities in the world, for example the chinampas in wetlands in Mexico, rice paddies on tropical soils in Southeast Asia, and irrigation systems in the deserts of Peru. However, input costs needed to farm fragile lands are often very high. Such farming may be feasible if the fragile aspects of the environment are complemented by very positive aspects, such as low rainfall (requiring costly irrigation) being complemented by flat terrain, warm temperatures, and good soil. On the other hand, fragile lands include the most degraded lands in Latin America and the worst poverty, particularly areas of steep slopes (Posner and McPherson, 1982). (For a recent discussion and application of carrying capacity to Amazonia, see Fearnside, 1986.)

Risk Avoidance. Fragile lands tend to be characterized by a high degree of environmental risk. Subsistence strategies are favored which minimize risk, especially by diversification of crops and habitats, usually at the expense of productivity. Commercial systems, in contrast, tend to maximize productivity at the cost of greater risk, which is then compensated for through economic institutions. More frequent failure of commercial systems on fragile lands, however, may make input costs prohibitive.

Fragility of the Production System. This volume focuses on the fragility of environments. We should keep in mind, however, that the agroecosystem is also fragile to greater or lesser degrees depending on technology and knowledge availability. And these, in turn, may reflect social fragility in terms of organization, markets, prices, income, social relationships, politics, etc. These other types of fragility can be more critical than environmental fragility, which may be more manageable or more readily adapted to.

Conclusion

These brief comments provide some perspective on the nature of fragile lands. We might ask whether the concept of fragile lands is useful, especially in Latin America where most land is seriously fragile. On the other hand, I believe that a focus on fragility does help concentrate attention on agroecological components of land-use systems—the interaction between crop, technology, and environment—whereas development planning in the past has been dominated by socioeconomic thinking. Both approaches are, of course, essential.

We do need some serious new thinking about managed agricultural change because agricultural development, for the most part, has been a dismal failure for the small farmers of the Third World, who to a large extent have been pushed onto the most fragile lands.

References

Bremer, J., A. Babb, J. Dickinson, P. Gore, E. Hyman, and M. Andre. 1984. Fragile lands: a theme paper on problems, issues, and approaches for development of humid tropical lowlands and steep slopes in the Latin American region. Development Alternatives, Inc., Washington, D.C.

Cole, J.P. 1965. Latin America: an economic and social geography. Butterworths, Washington, D.C.

Denevan, W.M. 1980a. Latin America. Pages 217–244 in G.A. Klee (ed.), World systems of traditional resource management. Edward Arnold, London.

Denevan, W.M. 1980b. Tipología de configuraciones agricolas prehispanica. América Indígena 40:619–652.

Farnworth, E.G., and F.B. Golley (eds.). 1974. Fragile ecosystems: evaluation of research and applications in neotropics. Springer-Verlag, New York.

Fearnside, P.M. 1986. Human carrying capacity of the Brazilian rainforest. Columbia University Press, New York.

Posner, J.L., and M.F. McPherson. 1982. Agriculture on the steep slopes of tropical America: current situation and prospects for the year 2000. World Development 10:341–353.

Redclift, M. 1987. Sustainable development: exploring the contradictions. Methuen, London.

Siemens, A.H. 1977. Some patterns seen from the air. Journal of Belizean Affairs 5:5–21.

Sarmiento, G., and M. Monasterio. 1975. A critical consideration of the environmental conditions associated with the occurrence of savanna ecosystems in tropical America. Pages 223–250 in F.B. Golley and E. Medina (eds.), Tropical ecological systems. Springer-Verlag, New York.

2

Development of Fragile Lands:
An Integrated Approach Reconsidered

David Gow

Introduction

In this chapter I attempt to synthesize an integrated approach to the sustainable development of fragile lands. While fully realizing that such terms as "sustainable development" and "fragile lands" are often emotion-laden and value-ridden, I shall nevertheless try to clarify their definition and use. This paper is divided into three sections. In the first section, I briefly describe why "fragile lands" are resources at risk. In the second section, an approach to fragile land development which has evolved from the Development Strategies for Fragile Lands project (DESFIL), financed by the Agency for International Development (AID), is presented and discussed, drawing on recent experience in Latin America and the Caribbean. In the final section, I attempt to synthesize these various strands of thought and provide a set of guidelines for an integrated approach to resolving fragile lands issues—specifically the sustainable development of such lands.

Terminology

Sustainable Development

There is no general consensus regarding the meaning of "sustainable development." Indeed, a keynote speaker at a recent World Bank symposium side-stepped the issue this way:

> The temptation is to begin with a definition of "sustainability." To ask: What is it? Frankly, I don't think I can define it without unduly constraining the free flow of my thought. In other words, I don't know what

it is. As it is something that is "sustained," it obviously has a time dimension (Hopper 1987:5).

Nevertheless, there is a rich and stimulating literature on the topic. Douglass (1984) identifies three schools of thought. The first regards sustainability as food sufficiency: agriculture is primarily an instrument for feeding the world, guided by conventional cost-benefit analysis. Sustaining the natural resource base is secondary. If the introduction of new technology leads to greater soil erosion, the costs of fertility and soil losses may be compensated by increased yields. However, this view is strictly short-term.

A second school regards agricultural sustainability primarily as an ecological question. An agricultural system which needlessly depletes, pollutes, or disrupts the ecological balance of natural resource systems cannot be sustained, and should be replaced by one which is adapted to longer-term biophysical constraints. Hence, a crucial measure of agricultural sustainability is the sustained yield capacity of renewable agricultural resources, such as croplands, pastures, and forests. Instead of taking population as a given, this group tends to espouse policies which limit population to those levels which can be sustained by a finite physical environment.

Closely related to this "stewardship" school is agroecology which, like sustainability itself, has come to mean many things. According to Hecht (1987), the term loosely incorporates ideas about a more environmentally and socially sensitive approach to agriculture, one that focuses not only on production, but also on the ecological sustainability of the production system. It has roots in the agricultural sciences, in the environmental movement, in ecology, and in the ecological analysis of indigenous farming systems.

While agroecology has produced many detailed technical recommendations (Altieri 1987; Harrison 1987; Tull, Sands, and Altieri 1987), it has also elaborated some emerging principles of general interest to those concerned with sustainable development (Dover and Talbot 1987:50–52). First, there is no substitute for detailed knowledge of the specific environment being developed or managed. One way this can be obtained is through agroecosytem analysis, which focuses on what Conway calls the four properties of ecosystems—productivity, stability, sustainability, and equitability:

Productivity is the yield or net income per unit of resource. Stability is the degree to which productivity is constant in the face of small disturbances caused by the normal fluctuations of climate and other environmental variables. . . . Sustainability is the ability of a system to maintain productivity in spite of a major disturbance, such as is caused by a rare drought or flood or a new pest. Finally, equitability expresses how evenly the products of an agroecosystem are distributed among its human beneficiaries . . . (Conway 1985:35).

Equally important may be understanding one agroecosytem's dependence on—or autonomy from—other agroecosytems. In many areas of the world, lowland agriculture often depends heavily on the washing of nutrients from higher altitudes for its fertility. Thus, one ecosystem may be able to maintain its productivity only as another degrades (Rambo 1985).

Another property of ecosystems that may be of considerable importance is energy efficiency and finding ways to substitute structure for energy in the maintenance of the ecosytem. For example, multi-storied plant canopies can capture greater amounts of sunlight, which in turn can produce larger amounts of biomass that might otherwise need fertilizer. The addition of animals to the farming system means that more plant material is turned into usable food. Finally, increased diversity in the ecosytem may serve ecological, economic, and nutritional ends by increasing biomass productivity and spreading risk, giving farmers more products to sell at different times of the year, and improving diets by providing a wider array of vitamins and minerals.

The final school, identified by Douglass as the "alternative agriculturalists," resemble the ecologists in their desire to husband the carrying capacity of renewable agricultural resources. But they also differ in their emphasis on sustainable human communities. Not only must human beings establish a stewardship of the earth, they must also establish this sense in their relationships with each other, particularly as it affects justice and participation.

In its more extreme form, "alternative agriculture" has come to be known as Deep Ecology which, according to its adherents, is metaphysical at base and represents a search for a sustaining metaphysics of the environment (Redclift 1987:43). Deep ecology rejects the anthropocentric view that humankind lies at the center of all that is worthwhile and that other creatures are valuable only as long as they serve us:

> In a nutshell, its basic tenet is that all living things have a right to exist—that human beings have no right to bring other creatures to extinction or to play God by deciding which species serve us and should therefore be allowed to live. Deep ecology maintains that all living things have an inherent value—animals, plants, bacteria, viruses—and that animals are no more important than plants and that mammals are no more valuable than insects (Nations 1988:79).

From my perspective, development includes a long-term concern for the future, and the principal objective of development initiatives should be to generate self-sustaining improvements in human capability and well-being. But however one defines sustainable development, two interrelated issues must be examined—energy and population:

> First, we need to consider to what extent we use energy efficiently within agriculture at the present time, since the development of more sustainable options may depend critically upon making better use of the resources we already command. Second, we need to consider population, together with ecological sustainability and energy efficiency, since the prospect of a decline in fertility in most parts of the South provides an incentive for more sustainable agricultural practices (Redclift 1987:22).

Historically, economic development has been linked to a progressive increase in energy consumption, and this is nowhere more apparent than in the case of agricultural development and intensification. Agricultural intensificiation refers to the use of new technologies, of a biological, chemical or mechanical nature, or some combination of these, that will increase per unit yields of plant or animal production (Wilcock and Ndoreyaho 1986:39). The conversion of energy has been the principal means through which, first, food production has kept ahead of population growth and, second, the number of people working in agriculture has been reduced. Fossil fuels have been used to drive agricultural machinery, produce agrochemical inputs, and transform agricultural production through food-processing and marketing. The uses to which energy is put in the process of agricultural development is only one of several dimensions of sustainability (Redclift 1987:22–29).

The second crucial issue that must be faced is population and the impact of rapid population growth on the natural resource base. World population approached four billion in 1975 and is expected to double by 2025. In terms of sustainability, what matters most is not so much the net increase in population at the global level, but the rate of change in population in the most critical regions. For example, population growth rates tend to be highest where basic needs are not met, particularly in Africa where per capita food production has declined 10 percent since 1970 (Redclift 1987:30).

Sustainability is not static. Neither is development. Both are dynamic. The question that must always be borne in mind is the following: "Is it possible to undertake environmental planning and mangement in a way that does minimum damage to ecological processes without putting

a brake on human aspirations for economic and social improvement?"
(Redclift 1987:33).

Fragile Lands

Bremer et al. (1984:3) define fragile lands as lands that are highly
subject to deterioration under common agricultural, silvicultural, and
pastoral use systems and management practices, as demonstrated by:

- Declining short-term production.
- Loss of the long-term potential productivity of the resource base.
- Serious off-site impacts resulting from environmental degradation.
- Slow recovery of the soil, water, plant, and animal resources after
  human or natural disturbance.

All lands are fragile if mismanged. Fragile lands do not pose a
problem in and of themselves; it is only when destructive patterns of
land use are combined with a delicate natural resource base, subject
to deterioration, that the problem arises. In other words, fragile lands
are vulnerable, they are lands at risk (Little, Horowitz, and Nyerges
1987).

Moran (1987) has argued for less vagueness and more precision when
discussing fragile ecosystems. While some may use fragile lands and
environmental degradation interchangeably, disciplinary specialists do
not. Discussing a 1974 conference on fragile ecosystems, Moran comments:

> Participants emphasized the importance of working toward a sustained
> yield of products useful to man without degradation of the productivity,
> richness, and viability of ecosystems. This is the ecologists' meaning of
> environmental degradation: a loss of natural habitat, whether to agricul-
> ture, pasture, mines or settlement. It is not the meaning I nor many
> others follow in talking about degradation. It is best always to clarify
> whether the subject is "environmental degradation," "fertility degrada-
> tion" (the meaning used . . . [here]), or "soil degradation" (referring to
> compaction, erosion, etc.) (Moran 1987:71).

For the purposes of this chapter, however, fragile lands are those
lands which are prone to environmental degradation, leading to both
soil and fertility loss, and concomitant decrease in productivity.

Why Fragile Lands Are at Risk

There is a growing consensus, at least on the part of biological and social scientists, that the underlying factors responsible for the creation of lands at risk are complex and interrelated. According to Leonard (1984:53), two broad assumptions have dominated the development community's perspective:

- Traditional systems of land-based production are inherently consumptive of soil fertlity and other natural resource stocks and can only be perpetuated under low population densities.
- Rapid population growth in the second half of the twentieth century has fundamentally undermined the viability of pastoralism, shifting cultivation, and other traditional land-use systems heavily dependent on renewable resources; that is, population growth has inexorably pushed rural people to exceed the carrying capacity of the land under their traditional technologies.

But this perspective has often ignored an increasing body of historical evidence that many societies, under a wide range of population densities, ecological conditions, and technical sophistication, prospered as a result of community-based management of crops, pasture, forests, and water that permitted intensive exploitation without inducing degradation (Brokensha 1983).

Increasingly, however, social scientists have demonstrated that environmental degradation is often the result of much broader causal factors than a simplistic imbalance between the natural resource base, the level of technology, and the population density. Among the more important causal factors are the following:

Poverty: Recent work on deforestation has indicated that the real cause is poverty, a consequence of skewed land distribution and low agricultural productivity (Caufield 1984: World Resources Institute 1985). Large farmers tend to own land in fertile valleys, which are less prone to erosion, they have ready access to government-supplied development resources, and they have alternative sources of employment and income. In contrast, small farmers on the hillsides usually have few such options, and must continue exploiting marginal resource bases (Hansen and Erbaugh 1987:84).

Policy: There is growing evidence, particularly for Central America and Latin America, that government policies in such areas as credit, land titling, and marketing work against sustained yield production systems and force farmers to orient production toward short-term gain.

There are few incentives to encourage sustainable land use (Collins 1986; Collins and Painter 1986).

Technology: Research and testing to develop improved agricultural technologies have focused heavily on flat areas most resembling the temperate zones. The technologies developed for these areas are rarely relevant to either steep hillsides or the humid tropics. Worse, their use may lower production and promote rapid deterioration of the productive resource base (Bremer et al. 1984; Hansen and Erbaugh 1987). But this situation is changing. In specific cases, suitable technologies are available as a basis for action (Hanrahan 1988). In addition, indigenous methods offer a wealth of technical approaches with potentially broader applicability.

Institutions: The long history of neglect of fragile lands has not fostered strong institutions for fragile lands management. Often multiple local, regional, and national institutions with conflicting or overlapping roles are active in a single location (Bremer et al. 1984). The problem is that national and local institutional capabilities to mobilize and induce people to promote, implement, and maintain the sustainable use of their natural resource base are lacking. Some commentators believe that the technical capability to manage and improve renewable natural resource systems threatens to outstrip the ability of institutions to organize people to apply improved techniques at the local level (Leonard 1984:49).

The Development Strategies for Fragile Lands Project (DESFIL)

DESFIL in Theory: The 1984 Concepts Paper

At the present time I am working on a project entitled "Development Strategies for Fragile Lands" (DESFIL), funded by the United States Agency for International Development. The principal objective of DESFIL is to improve ways of addressing fragile lands issues at the policy, strategy, planning, design, and implementation levels (Plunkett 1987). The ideas for this project evolved from needs identified by AID field missions. One of the important milestones was a review paper on the problems, issues, and approaches for sustainable development of fragile lands (Bremer et al. 1984). The most interesting section deals with alternative approaches to solving fragile lands problems. The interventions proposed are divided into three broad categories (Bremer et al. 1984:61-87):

- *Direct Interventions in Fragile Lands:*
  - Investments in land maintenance
  - Investments in land productivity
- *Indirect Interventions in Fragile Lands:*
  - Technology generation
  - Measuring and monitoring of resource status
  - Planning and reform policy
  - Tenure reform
- *Interventions Outside of Fragile Lands:*
  - Alternatives to fragile lands use
  - Measures to reduce off-site impacts

Direct Interventions

The classic approach to slowing land degradation is through investments in land maintenance, a term that covers all expenditures to preserve, protect, or restore land productivity, including, but by no means limited to, soil conservation. Many of these measures increase production and some, such as reforestation, are themselves production methods. On-farm land maintenance investments consist primarily of constructing land and water-control structures to limit erosion and maintain soil productivity, such as: terracing; vegetative barriers; repair of gullies; placement of water control structures; and planting of grasses on fallow land or waterways.

Off-farm investments include: control of waterways (an expensive necessity in any comprehensive watershed program); land-conserving construction techniques, particularly for roads that may reduce maintenance costs in the future and limit downstream impacts; reforestation programs and the creation of reserves that can also maintain the productivity of lands and other resources downstream.

A second category of investments comprises those intended to raise the productivity of land-use systems, including agricultural, silvicultural, and pastoral systems. Defined broadly, such interventions include all the technical approaches to increasing traditional agricultural production, such as introduction of improved crop systems, improved agroforestry and livestock systems, and mixed systems. It is important to point out that many techniques for raising short-term productivity increase environmental degradation. Without a parallel increase in land-maintenance efforts, measures to promote gains in short-term production may be off-set by the costs of diminished long-term production and stability. At the same time, many land maintenance technologies cannot be implemented economically in the absence of other measures to increase production in the short term.

Indirect Interventions

The first approach recommended is technology, and approaches to technology generation for fragile lands. These approaches focus on four closely related, but different technological issues:

- What is the state of the resource base and our knowledge of it?
- Do technologies exist for controlling erosion and productivity loss that are profitable under prevailing economic conditions?
- Do technologies exist to raise the sustainable productivity and net income that can be achieved from the land resource base?
- Do research systems exist that can continue to develop the necessary information and technologies in ways that ensure their relevance to fragile lands users?

The last question may be the most important. Without a recognition of why research has failed to address fragile lands needs and what the special requirements of this research are, it is not possible to establish operational priorities for action. Strengthening or redirecting the research establishment itself may be a priority.

The second approach emphasizes the measurement and monitoring of natural resources. The need to improve information on changes in the resource base, particularly in critical areas such as important watersheds, creates numerous openings for government or donor-supported programs, including strengthening of organizations charged with natural resource monitoring and introduction of cost-saving monitoring techniques.

The third element discusses the role of planning and policy reform— particularly land-use planning, land development policies, regional planning, agricultural sector policies, and macroeconomic policies. Emphasis is often placed on strengthening a government's capacity for policy analysis and formulation to permit full consideration of the economic and environmental implications of proposed policies. Since the institutional responsibilities for fragile lands programs are typically spread across numerous agencies, this makes it unlikely that funds allocated to fragile lands will be applied in an effective manner. Concentration of efforts in high-priority areas will require coordination among national agencies and donors.

Finally, the specific ways in which land is owned and used can have a significant impact on land use, including investment behavior and land management in general. One approach to encouraging desired management behavior is to improve the tenure situation of fragile lands users, by making it more secure, regularizing it legally, making it easier to sell and buy land, or changing the structure of land rents, taxes, and other payments. This may involve actions such as titling and registration, improvement of land markets and related credit markets, and restructuring of incentives created by existing tenure, legal, and tax systems.

Nevertheless, there is a growing body of knowledge that questions the causal assumptions of some of these actions. For example, the evidence for Central America indicates that land titling may be counterproductive, leading to an increase in the price of land, land speculation, and land concentration, all of which combine to drive the small farmers off the land (Collins and Painter 1986).

Outside Interventions

Historically, only two situations have led to a reduction in the intensity of land use: destruction of the land and transfer of resources to more attractive uses. Land users cannot be convinced to reduce land-use intensity without an alternative that yields a greater income, since reduced intensity nearly always means reduced income. Possible alternatives include:

- Resettlement and colonization (which have a very checkered track record in Central and Latin America).
- Increased transformation of local products that can provide an alternative to agricultural work and encourage use of less intensive farming systems, with fruit trees and cattle, over potentially more damaging systems based on annual crops.
- Off-farm employment, which may call for seasonal migration.
- Land reform in other areas where lands are less fragile.

The second intervention outside of fragile lands requires measures to reduce off-site impacts. In some cases, it may be more practical to limit the downstream impact of fragile lands misuse than to try to stop the destructive practices at their source. These measures, however, do not help fragile lands users. They encourage further delay in addressing fragile lands problems and tend to provide only a temporary solution, possibly at considerable cost.

DESFIL in Practice

STAB in Haiti

In the 15 months that DESFIL has been in operation, several activities have been undertaken that all shed light on the problems of fragile lands development, specifically in Haiti and Peru. The most ambitious activity, that unfortunately was aborted, was support to STAB, the Technical Secretariat for Watershed Management, a small division within the Haitian Ministry of Agriculture, Natural Resources, and Rural Development. STAB was established to develop a concerted, effective approach, both technically and institutionally, for reversing the degradation of Haiti's upper watersheds.

Although a Division of Natural Resources already existed within the Ministry, its principal preoccupation was the daily management of natural resource projects. Little time and few resources were available to address major policy issues. Nor was there time to develop a national strategy for addressing the problem or establishing a comprehensive data base for sound management decisions. Hence, STAB was created to improve:

- The effectiveness of watershed management projects through technical inputs and evaluations;
- The institutional capacity within the government for addressing these problems through coordination and resolution of conflicting policies and development of both a strategy and a data base (Pierce and Tremblay 1988).

In essence, STAB was designed to meet the need for information exchange, evaluation, conflict resolution, and strategy. It pursued a coordinated approach and included activities undertaken by non-governmental organizations and the private sector. In February 1987, DESFIL placed two long-term personnel with STAB, a natural resources adviser and an agricultural economist. One of STAB's first tasks was to find out what was already known about hillside agriculture and watershed management. Given that development assistance from the government was virtually non-existent in the rural areas, non-governmental organizations of various hues and stripes stepped in to fill the gap. As a result, there was, and still is, a multitude of development projects, large and small, often independently pursuing their own strategies and objectives.

STAB created an inventory of 116 watershed management projects, developed a project tracking system, and established tangible measures for project evaluation. Other activities included evaluation of ongoing projects, identifying their impact and reasons for success or failure, and development of new fragile lands and watershed management project ideas and designs.

Equally important, however, was the creation of a workable network to disseminate sound technical approaches and innovations. For this to be effective, the information developed by STAB had to be packaged effectively and distributed. The following actions were undertaken:

- Production of maps indicating the location of watershed management and hillside agriculture projects.
- Preparation of technical bulletins for fragile lands and watershed management.
- Creation of a documentation center to collect and disseminate relevant information, reports, bulletins, and audio-visual materials.

The development of a strategy had to include participation and acceptance by representatives of all major organizations involved in watershed management in Haiti. This was done by establishing the Committee of Reflection, which served as the institutional forum for discussing and resolving watershed issues within the public and private sectors, and also for sharing technical approaches and information. Strategy development was part of its mandate. The project inventory represented the first step in establishing priorities based on geographic, technical, and socioeconomic considerations. For the first time, the ministry knew what work was being done and where. Maps were developed to identify areas where watershed activities were under way as well as areas without projects. Based on these maps, STAB was able to advise on the location of new projects.

The success of STAB, shortlived as it was, owes much to the simplicity and directness of its pragmatic approach. The Secretariat wanted to become the institutional memory for watershed management in Haiti by investigating what was actually happening on the hillsides, what had worked and where, what had been learned from these experiences, and making this information available in a simple, straightforward format to all interested parties. In this initial phase of consolidating and disseminating information that was already available, STAB was not seen as a threat.

Several lessons from the STAB experience may be applicable to similar situations in other countries, which include the following (Pierce 1988:31–34):

- *Strong Institutional Support.* The idea of the Secretariat was not something superimposed by donors but grew from a need recognized within the Ministry.
- *Creation of Institutional Credibility.* By the time STAB personnel were ready to set policy, they had established a credible project information data base, had developed strong personal ties with the key actors in watershed management, and knew more about what

was happening in the country's watershed than any other institution.

- *Program Versus Project Management.* Unlike other units in the Ministry, STAB had no daily project management responsibilities, thereby allowing it to focus solely on the longer-term issues associated with developing a rational watershed management program.

Biological Diversity in Peru

The 1986 Amendments to the Foreign Assistance Act, Sections 118 and 119, dealing with tropical deforestation and biological diversity, require that each AID mission provide the following information in its country development strategy statement, its major planning document:

- The status of host country efforts to conserve biological diversity and tropical forests.
- Actions that the AID mission could take to conserve biological diversity and tropical forests.

Conservation of biological diversity and tropical forests is important to the world scientific community, to growing numbers of the public in developing and developed countries, and to local populations. In addition, it is a basic assumption that such efforts will improve the possibility of economic development in the long run.

Although there is some debate about which neotropical country is biologically the richest in Latin America, there is little doubt that Peru is among the top three, along with Colombia and Brazil. In Peru, the threat to individual rare or endangered species, and to a certain extent natural and agronomic ecosystems, originates from a complex mixture of social, economic, demographic, political, and ethical factors. Although not all commentators are in agreement, the principal causes are poverty, inadequate policies, inappropriate development strategies, and lack of resources (Gow et al. 1988).

In terms of development of the high selva and the resulting deforestation, structural factors have played a crucial role. In the specific case of southern Peru, the Tambopata Valley has been the site of coffee cultivation by seasonal migrants from the sierra since the 1940s. Extremely steep slopes, rarely less than 40 percent grade, make the region highly susceptible to erosion. Farmers producing coffee in the valley face a variety of production and marketing constraints, including a lack of access to credit and to inputs such as fertilizers and pesticides, poor transport, insecure titles, and a government-backed monopsony on the purchase of coffee. These constraints mean that farmers have neither the time nor the resources to invest in land maintenance technologies (Collins 1986).

Another factor aggravating the problem of deforestation has been the shifting political commitments of the government. Under the previous administration, development of the high selva was a top priority. President Belaunde subscribed to the last frontier perception of the Amazon—as a vast, underexploited region that could help solve Peru's economic problems (Smith 1982). From this belief followed the development paradigm pursued in most government-sponsored development efforts in the high selva: high-input agriculture with an emphasis on short-term gains. Such an approach is difficult to maintain over the long run because of the high costs—both financial and environmental— that are involved.

In making recommendations to AID, attention was paid to the comparative advantage that Peru enjoys in terms of biological diversity and environmental awareness, as demonstrated by the following:

- Peru's rich ecological diversity, ranking first in the world in life zones.
- Peru's young, but very active and growing non-governmental environmental conservation movement.
- Peru's position as a major stakeholder in the selva of western Amazonia, a region commanding world attention because of the critical social and ecological issues which converge there.
- Peru's germplasm base as one of the world's historically outstanding sources of wild plants and animals for domestication and commercialization.

The recommendations made to AID/Peru all involve information and the uses to which that information could be put. Briefly, the four proposed program areas encompass the following:

- *Conservation Policy and Education:* To enhance conservation policy making capabilities and increase efforts to promote public awareness of environmental issues in Peru, especially those most closely related to biological diversity.
- *Conservation and Development:* To establish and enhance activities which show that economic enterprise is consistent with economic diversity.
- *Research:* To expand current taxonomic, ecological, and economic knowledge of Peru's wildlands, especially as related to the status of threatened and endangered species.

- *Training and Institution Building:* To assist with the strengthening of Peru's data centers and conservation units within the national park system, and to improve the research and managerial capabilities of wildlands conservation and protection of biological diversity (Gow et al. 1988).

An Integrated Approach:
Wishful Thinking or Practical Reality?

The DESFIL experience to date, together with a review of the recent, relevant literature, indicates that enough is known to sketch the broad outlines of an integrated approach to the sustainable development of fragile lands. Such an approach would include the following:

Political Commitment, Policy, and Planning. If such an approach is to have any chance of success, then there has to be a commitment on the part of national governments (Heaver and Israel 1986). Such commitment must be demonstrated through the enactment of relevant policies and development strategies, as well as the provision of the necessary resources to implement them (Gow 1987). Without these, plans for sustainable development will never move beyond the drawing board. This was possible for STAB in Haiti, until the political climate changed. The work in Peru has not yet moved beyond the planning phase and will not until there is this political commitment, not only by the national government, but also by the respective donor agency.

Technological Interventions, Adaptive Research, and Monitoring. Enough is known about technological interventions, using both Western and indigenous models, to greatly improve the sustainability of present land-use systems. Many of the possible technical interventions are site-specific and must be adapted to the prevailing environmental conditions. There is no standard technical package that can be extended willy-nilly—just as there is no standard way in which these interventions can be disseminated, since they must be adapted to prevailing social and political conditions. Hence, the interest in Haiti is finding out more about what had actually worked and why, and then disseminating the results to those interested. Equally important, however, is the need to monitor how effective these technological interventions are and, where necessary, make the necessary modifications.

Institutional Strengthening and Coordination. Public sector institutions dealing with fragile lands issues are often weak and fragmented—whether they be in the Ministry of Planning, the Ministry of Agriculture, or the Ministry of Natural Resources. The necessary conditions for their strengthening include political commitment and availability of resources, as well as the required technical competence. In Haiti, STAB met all three conditions.

Enhancing Local Organizational Capacity. Local organizations of farmers and their families can play important roles in the sustainable development of fragile lands by acting, according to Honadle and VanSant (1985:53), as vehicles for:

- Adapting project activities to local conditions, particularly proposed technical interventions.
- Marshaling local resources.
- Sustaining project benefits.
- Achieving greater political and economic leverage for local people by exercising influence over local administrators and asserting claims on government.
- Managing the natural resource base in a rational manner through education and training, and by enforcing rules, incentives, and penalties.

Equally important in this context are the non-governmental organizations (NGOs) working in natural resource management which often play an intermediary role as indigenous grassroots support organizations (Carroll and Baitenmann 1987). In Haiti, STAB worked closely with the NGO community. Much of the interest and initiative in biological diversity and conservation in Peru has been fueled by the NGOs.

Environmental Education and Extension. This is the most realistic and practical way of disseminating what is known about fragile lands issues to those most affected by them. It is also the first step in translating this knowledge into practical action—an important component of DESFIL's planning activities in Peru. In addition, it reinforces Friedmann's (1987:306) admonition to planners that they resist the tendency to concentrate information, knowledge, and decision making in a small leadership elite and that they share their expertise with those most likely to be affected.

Conservation and Development. There is no essential contradiction between sustainable economic development and conservation of the natural resource base. The environmental community increasingly realizes and accepts that conservation and economic development are complementary concerns, particularly in the case of those people, often already marginal, who are trying to live off fragile lands. The development community does not yet fully accept this necessary complementarity. In Peru and elsewhere, local expectations were built up when national parks and reserves were declared, but these quickly turned into frustrations when it was perceived that few or no economic benefits were forthcoming. A whole set of issues depend on rectifying this problem and helping local enterprises derive their income from the existence of protected lands. Potential activities include nature tourism, natural-forest management, game cropping, and sustainable extraction of minor forest products (Gow et al. 1988).

Acknowledgments

This paper was prepared under the Development Strategies for Fragile Lands Project, financed by the U.S. Agency for International Development, through the Office of Rural Development, Science and Technology Bureau, and the Office of Development Resources, Latin America/Caribbean Bureau. The conclusions are mine alone and do no necessarily reflect the views of either AID, DESFIL, or Development Alternatives, Inc. (DAI).

References

Altieri, M.A., ed. 1987. Agroecology: The Scientific Basis of Alternative Agriculture. Boulder: Westview Press.

Bremer, J., A. Babb, J. Dickinson, P. Gore, E. Hyman, and M. Andre. 1984. Fragile Lands: A Theme Paper on Problems, Issues, and Approaches for Development of Humid Tropical Lowlands and Steep Slopes in the Latin American Region. Washington, D.C.: Development Alternatives, Inc.

Brokensha, D. 1983. Community-Based Natural Resource Management. Natural Resource Management Workshop: Collected Papers. Edited by E. Berry and B. Thomas. Pp. 87–103. SARSA. Binghampton, NY: Institute for Development Anthropology/Clark University.

Carroll, T.F. and H. Baitenman. 1987. Organizing Through Technology: A Case from Costa Rica. Grassroots Development 11(2):12–20.

Caufield, C. 1984. In the Rainforest: Report from a Strange, Beautiful, Imperiled World. Chicago: University of Chicago Press.

Collins, J.L. 1986. Smallholder Settlement of Tropical South America: The Social Causes of Ecological Destruction. Human Organization 45(1):1–10.

––––– and M. Painter 1986. Colonización y Deforestación en America Central: Discusion sobre Matérias de Desarrollo. SARSA. Binghamton, NY: Institute for Development Anthropology/Clark University.

Conway, G.R. 1985. Agroecosystem Analysis. Agricultural Administration 20(1):31–55.

Douglass, G.K. 1984. The Meanings of Agricultural Sustainability. Agricultural Sustainability in a Changing World Order. Edited by G.K. Douglass. Pp. 3–29. Boulder: Westview Press.

Dover, M. and L.M. Talbot 1987. To Feed the Earth: Agro-Ecology for Sustainable Development. Washington, D.C.: World Resources Institute.

Friedmann, J. 1987. Planning in the Public Domain: From Knowledge to Action. Princeton: Princeton University Press.

Gow, D.D. 1987. Sustainable Development of Fragile Lands: The Case of Extensive Livestock Production in Africa. Agricultural Administration and Extension 24:3–32.

Gow, D., K. Clark, J. Earhart, M. Fujita, J. Laarman, and G. Miller 1988. Peru: An Assessment of Biological Diversity. A report submitted to AID/Peru. Washington, D.C.: DESFIL.

Hanrahan, M. 1988. Sustainable Uses for Steep Slopes: Workshop Proceedings, Vol. 2. DESFIL Report. Washington, D.C.: Development Alternatives, Inc.

Hansen, D.O. and J.M. Erbaugh 1987. The Social Dimension of Natural Resource Management. Sustainable Resource Development in the Third World. Edited by D.D. Southgate and J.F. Disinger. Pp. 81–94. Boulder: Westview Press.

Harrison, P. 1987. The Greening of Africa: Breaking through in the Battle for Land and Food. International Institute for Environment and Development-Earthscan. New York: Penguin Books.

Heaver, R. and A. Israel 1986. Country Commitment to Development Projects. World Bank Discussion Papers Number 4. Washington, D.C.: World Bank.

Hecht, S.B. 1987. The Evolution of Agroecological Thought. Agroecology: The Scientific Basis of Alternative Agriculture. Edited by M.A. Altieri. Pp. 1–20. Boulder: Westview Press.

Honadle, G. and J. VanSant 1985. Implementation for Sustainability: Lessons from Integrated Rural Development. West Hartford: Kumarian Press.

Hopper, W.D. 1987. Sustainability, Policies, Natural Resources and Institutions. Sustainability Issues in Agricultural Development: Proceedings of the Seventh Agriculture Sector Symposium. Edited by T.J. Davis and I.A. Schirmer. Pp. 5–16. Washington, D.C.: World Bank.

Leonard, H.J. 1984. Socio-Economic Aspects of Natural Resource Management: A Framework for Policy Research. Priorities for Rural Development Research. Edited by M.S. Grindle and S.T. Walker. Pp. 42–96. Cambridge: Harvard Institute for International Development. Pierce, T. and A. Tremblay 1988 Watershed Management in Haiti: A Final Report. The DESFIL Newsletter 1(2)7–9.

Little, P.D., M.M. Horowitz, and A.E. Nyerges, eds. 1987 Lands at Risk in the Third World: Local-Level Perspectives. Boulder: Westview Press.

Moran, E.F. 1987. Monitoring Fertility Degradation of Agricultural Lands in the Lowland Tropics. Lands at Risk in the Third World: Local-Level Perspectives. Edited by P.D. Little, M.M. Horowitz, and A.E. Nyerges. Pp.69–91. Boulder: Westview Press.

Nations, J.D. 1988. Deep Ecology Meets the Developing World. Biodiversity. Edited by E.O. Wilson and F.M. Peter. Pp.79–82. Washington, D.C.: National Academy Press.

Pierce, T. and A. Tremblay 1988. Watershed Management in Haiti: A Final Report. The DESFIL Newsletter 1(2):7–9.

Pierce, T.H. 1988. Watershed Management in Haiti: The STAB Experience. DESFIL Technical Report. Washington, D.C.: Development Alternatives, Inc.

Plunkett, H.S. 1987. U.S.A.I.D.'s Fragile Lands Initiative in Latin America. Mountain Research and Development 7(2):173–174.

Rambo, A.T. 1984. Human Ecology Research on Human Development. Ecosystems Models for Development. Edited by A.T. Rambo, J.A. Dixon, and W. Tsechin. Pp. 6–27. Honolulu: East-West Center, Environment and Policy Institute.

Redclift, M. 1987. Sustainable Development: Exploring the Contradictions. New York: Methuen.

Smith, R.C. 1982. The Dialectics of Domination in Peru: Native Communities and the Myth of the Vast Amazonian Emptiness. Cambridge, Massachusetts: Cultural Survival.

Tull, K., M. Sands, and M.A. Altieri 1987. Experiences in Success: Case Studies in Growing Enough Food Through Regenerative Agriculture. Emmaus: Rodale International.

Wilcock, D. and V. Ndoreyaho 1986. The Rwanda Social and Institutional Profile. Volume Two: Agriculture at a Watershed. Report prepared for AID/Rwanda. Washington, D.C.: Development Alternatives.

World Resources Institute 1985. Tropical Forests: A Call for Action. Part 1: The Plan. Washington, D.C.: WRI/WB/UNDP.

3

Transferring Traditional Technology: A Bottom-Up Approach for Fragile Lands

Gene C. Wilken

Introduction and Definitions

The phrase *technology transfer* usually implies transfer of equipment and skills from more- to less-technically advanced societies. But unlike flows in nature, technology transfers are not controlled by gradients. Instead, transfers can take place in any direction as users adopt particular technologies to solve problems and achieve goals.

Defining problems and goals involves individual or social choice. Thus instead of relative high- and low- or advanced- and less-advanced qualities, technology should be evaluated on its appropriateness for achieving identified goals. This broader definition is not limited to technical appropriateness but also includes economic and social or cultural appropriateness as well (Samli 1985).

Characterizing traditional technology as appropriate is not new. But appropriate technology has come to mean technology that is "decentralized, small in scale, labor intensive, amenable to mastery and maintenance by local people, and harmonious with local cultural and environmental conditions" (Shaikh 1981). This definition is somewhat circular: traditional technology is appropriate to traditional systems. It is also misleading since it presupposes the criteria by which technologies are evaluated. It is not technology *per se,* but goals and objectives that define what is appropriate. Thus, there are no inherently appropriate technologies, but only those that most expeditiously achieve certain results.

As used here, technology includes not only energy sources and tools, but also knowledge and skills, and social organizations that focus knowledge and power on particular tasks. Social elements are particularly important in traditional technology which consists more of methods' than equipment. Although the present focus is fragile lands in general, traditional managers usually deal with rural rather than urban or industrial lands, and most of the examples presented here will be of traditional farm or forest technology.

Traditional technology has been variously named (e.g., indigenous, preindustrial) and defined. I use power, tools, scale, and information to distinguish between types of technology, and to contrast modern (industrial; large-scale) and traditional (low external-input; small-scale). The extremes are easy to characterize: power from fossil fuels versus human or animal power; complex mechanical devices for transforming power into work versus simple tools; scales of operation commensurate with power sources; and modern science and information delivery systems versus ethnoscience and traditional information pathways (Wilken 1987:3ff.).

But these are the polar ends of a continuum: between lie most of the world's land management systems that use combinations of traditional and modern technology. For example, powered equipment is found in many traditional systems, and simple hand tools are in daily use on modern farms (Denevan 1980:234; Hopfen 1969:4). In the final analysis there are simply more and less traditional forms of technology, and more and less traditional systems.

In the last few years much has been learned about ancient and contemporary traditional resource management, and proposals for transferring traditional technology have appeared with increasing frequency (e.g. Altieri 1983; Chambers 1983; Klee 1980; Marten 1986; Richards 1985; Stigter 1987; Wolf 1987). But such transfers would not be simple, and would require much more rigorous analyses and evaluations than are available from the case studies and descriptions of traditional technology now available. In this paper I shall review some of the qualities of traditional technology, and propose some procedures for transfers to other regions and cultures.

Goals of Traditional Resource Management

Even with a focus on fragile lands, there are many goals. Five of the most common are: production, conservation, employment, income, and security. Priorities differ depending on perspectives: income and security might be of greatest concern to individual land managers; regional administrators may consider conservation of first importance; at the national level production and employment may be paramount (Ashby 1984). Some of these goals are related and even complementary whereas others are conflicting. For example, increasing production may involve practices antithetical to conservation. Similarly, increased employment may come at a cost of reduced income.

Since goal achievement has been identified as the criteria for identifying the appropriateness of any technology, traditional methods must face the same test. Although the data on traditional technology is still fragmentary, a few observations are warranted.

Production

We first distinguish between production per unit of land, and production per unit of labor. With respect to the former, Berry and Cline (1979:131–134) conclude that:

> . . . the small-farm sector makes better use of its available land than does the large-farm sector, largely through applying higher levels of labor inputs (family labor) per unit of land. This conclusion is supported both with extensive cross-country data (on cultivation rates by farm size) and with statistical tests on intensive data sets for six major developing countries.

Data on other types of traditional technology, such as forest or water management, are less common. Although some evidence suggests that traditional technology generally has a good record for sustained yields, the picture is clouded by different population densities and demands. In its favor, traditional production often occurs in the same place where consumption needs are greatest, such as isolated or crowded rural regions with poor distribution systems. Thus there may be efficiencies in the whole system of traditional production, delivery, and consumption that are not reflected in strict output comparisons.

Income

With respect to production per unit of labor, the case is not clear. If small-scale farm sectors make good use of available land because of high labor inputs, we might assume that output per unit of labor, will be low (Gollás 1973). But does this mean that traditional farmers are necessarily condemned to a life of marginal returns? Quantity of labor alone is a poor index: like other forms of power, labor may be applied efficiently or inefficiently (Hatch 1976). The quality of labor has a marked effect on production, especially in systems that rely so heavily on human and animal power.

The type of crop also matters. Pachico (1984) notes that some crops respond to high labor inputs while others do not. If crops are not neutral in this respect, neither are the technologies associated with their cultivation, and it may be possible to derive decent incomes with traditional, labor-intensive methods. Some land management procedures, such as materials transport, deep plowing, and compacting, favor powered equipment. But others, such as fine grading, selective cultivation, and some types of excavating, are done efficiently by hand (e.g., Coukis 1983; van Loon et al. 1979).

Increasing production does not necessarily increase income. The harvests of fields and forests must be channeled through exchange systems and since producers often have no control over markets or prices, increasing output may not result in significant increases in income (Ortiz 1973). Even if markets are not manipulated increasing supplies of commodities can weaken prices. Thus the income question actually has two parts: can traditional managers drive their resources to higher levels of productivity? And if they do, will they realize rewards commensurate with their efforts? Although questions of production rightly belong in a discussion of technology, questions of rewards lie beyond the farmers' fields, and solutions are found outside the realm of technology.

Conservation

An enduring myth is that traditional land managers live in mystic harmony with nature, attuned to natural laws and flows, and are culturally conditioned to husband their scarce resources. The myth does not square with the record: traditional managers past and present have proven quite as capable of destroying their resource bases as modern commercial farmers (although lacking powerful equipment, they are perhaps less efficient at it).

Farmers everywhere often respond to factors outside local systems. For example, in many parts of the tropics population pressure has driven traditional cultivators to destroy upland forests with subsequent degradation of soil and water resources. Similarly modern mid-latitude farmers, under pressure from government programs or to preserve income levels, plow and plant until erosion accelerates to unacceptable levels (e.g., Brink et al. 1977; Brown 1981; 1987; Carter 1977). Both groups are aware of the consequences of their actions, but ignore long-term costs in response to external pressures.

Some traditional methods are ecologically sound not because of inherent conservation techniques but because of the small scale of ecosystem disruption. The traditional agroforestry system known as shifting (swidden; slash-and-burn) cultivation is a good example: as long as only a fraction of a forest is under cultivation and fallow periods are long enough to permit forest recovery the system remains stable. But expanded operations and shortened fallow cycles, often associated with population growth, result in reduced soil fertility and vegetation quality. Other systems, especially those involving labor-intensive practices, are capable of sustaining dense populations without resource degradation. Whether traditional technology can offer viable alternatives to modern conservation measures will ultimately depend on its effectiveness under conditions of increasing populations and income expectations.

Employment

The labor-absorbing characteristics of traditional technology have been recognized and analyzed (e.g., Bayliss-Smith 1982; Coukis 1983). Owen (1971) proposes dual agricultural sectors consisting of modern sectors that would concentrate on production, and traditional or small-scale sectors that would absorb excess labor.

Reliance on human and animal power units is to Western eyes one of the most onerous aspects of traditional technology. Certainly land management by hand is not easy. But is the total effort greater than for similar tasks anywhere? Industrialized farmers argue that labor-saving machinery has not reduced their overall work so much as it has made it possible to accomplish more with the same effort. And in any event, are labor-intensive land management tasks truly more distasteful or dehumanizing than the routine cycles of offices or factories? It is more often social or economic circumstance, not arduous farm work, that induces farmers to leave rural areas.

Finally, dependence on human and animal power, rather than fossil fuels appeals not only to the countries that must purchase fuels, but also to the land managers themselves. Fuels and maintenance for traditional tools and equipment are locally procured, usually at lower cost and with greater reliability, than those for externally supplied equipment. In societies with imperfect market or distribution systems the labor costs associated with local technology may be preferable to the money costs and uncertainties of exotic technology.

Security

Security is often cited as a major goal of small-scale resource managers and as a rationale for their avoidance of risk and change. The notion has been challenged by studies that show the traditional manager is an entrepreneur and risk-taker, but understandably at a commensurately small scale. Even purely subsistence farmers confront the normal range of hazards in a universally hazardous business, and develop coping strategies (Clark and Haswell 1970; Wilken 1982).

In most traditional farming operations part of the production is sold to generate funds for necessities and to meet goals other than subsistence. Market involvement places traditional producers in an uncertain world where supply, demand, and prices are outside their control or even understanding. Part of their attitude toward risk can be assigned to normal concern for the vagaries of weather and market. But the additional and often real fear that markets are manipulated may account for extra caution on the part of traditional producers.

Summary

As with any body of technology, traditional systems have strengths and weaknesses. Some techniques have excellent records for maintaining and even enhancing the quality of resources, others do not. Unfortunately, most methods have not been seriously tested for ecological soundness, much less for effectiveness in achieving individual and national goals. In addition, little is known about how traditional technology will respond to demands of growing populations and increased income.

Despite the always lamentable lack of data, it appears that the traditional world could offer alternative, or perhaps better said, complementary technology for fragile land management. There truly exists a vast array of traditional methods for managing resources, developed under a wide variety of environmental and social conditions, with a potential for being technically and socially appropriate to other regions and cultures. The question is, how might this other world of technology be inventoried and evaluated, and made available to small-scale farmers in other regions, and perhaps even to receptive portions of the developed world?

Transferring Traditional Technology

The idea that traditional technology is easily understood, mastered, and transferred, and inherently appropriate to other traditional systems is patronizing. Traditional tools can be deceptively simple: often only shovels and hoes, ox-drawn plows, and perhaps a water-lifting device (e.g., Hopfen 1969; Molenaar 1956). But traditional technology consists less of equipment and more of ways for managing resources. If this technology is to be successfully transferred, it is first necessary to understand not only the tools and their efficient operation, but also the social and economic environment in which the procedures developed and function.[1] I propose a series of steps to facilitate this process.

Step 1: Identify Goals. Rather than begin with a description of traditional technology, a more logical first step is to identify the goals that a particular technology is designed to achieve. These can be divided among the individual, regional, and national levels where land management decisions are made. Clearly the goals of managers at one level are not necessarily those of the others. The ability of a particular technology to best satisfy the goals of a specific group of resource managers will be the measure of its appropriateness. Conflicting goals are inevitable, and conflict resolution is an essential component of technology transfer (Harwood 1979:21ff; Tendler 1982; Wharton 1969).

Step 2: Identify Purposes of Practices. The purposes of most traditional practices are relative easy to identify since they relate directly to management of specific resources. For example, the wide-spread practice of inter-cropping or mixed-cropping achieves crop complementarity, reduces soil exposure, and lessens risk of disease (Innis 1980; Norman 1979).

But the agroecological advantages of this technique may be secondary to social and economic factors. For example, intercropping may represent an adjustment to tenure systems that create artificial land shortages and compel intensive methods, and would be unattractive in regions where land was more abundant or equitably distributed. In addition, the technique may also depend on family structure, or division of labor in a particular society.

The point is not to emphasize the complexity of traditional systems, but rather to reiterate that transfers of technology even between traditional societies require a high degree of social and economic as well as technical congruence between senders and receivers (Samli 1985:xv–xvi).

Step 3: Identify Technical Characteristics of Practices. This descriptive step is commonly covered in field reports of traditional activities. The better studies go beyond the physical appearance of technologies such as tools, terraces, canals, and mulches, and include details of operation (e.g., use of cultivation equipment, spacing of terraces, size of irrigation network, and quantities of mulch on seed beds). Less obvious characteristics, such as ergonomics of tool use, slope and runoff, composition of mulch, and canal capacity and water losses, may escape notice.

There is a great need for performance evaluation of traditional technology in the same detail now reserved for modern procedures. But even if data are not presently abundant, sufficient descriptions are available to justify a global inventory of traditional land management practices similar to that being conducted for agroforestry (Nair 1985).

Step 4: Identify Physical Processes Controlled. This seems like an easy step since the purposes of land management practices should be clear to anyone familiar with the basic elements and processes, such as downslope water and debris transport, soil nutrient and moisture cycling, and vegetation composition. Unfortunately few natural scientists have been interested in traditional practices, and few social scientists have had the technical background to understand the processes at work on the slopes and fields where traditional managers practice their craft. The result has been two separate bodies of literature that are difficult to reconcile.

To complicate the matter, traditional managers themselves often do not understand all the ramifications of their efforts. For example, the primary effects of shelter belts of trees are well known, as are the relations of effects to height and density of the stand. Less obvious to farmers and field workers alike are the impacts of shelter belts on soil moisture and nutrients, evaporation, and surface temperatures (Wilken 1972).

Nevertheless, as was true with specific practices, sufficient detail exists in the literature for a first attempt at evaluating the effectiveness of traditional land management. Furthermore, results could be tested and correlated with controlled studies in established research centers.

Step 5: Identify Information Pathways. Information transfers from one generation to the next are the essence of traditional systems. The process at once suggests great local knowledge and experience, but also a degree of inflexibility with respect to new elements, especially those originating outside a system. Information developed internally should encounter fewer obstacles to diffusion. In fact, on-farm experiments and trials, such as are common in farming systems projects, are efforts to convert externally developed research into local experience and thus reduce resistance to adoption. Identifying external information entry-ways and internal pathways in particular systems is a critical step in technology transfers.

Step 6: Define How Specific Technologies Are Imbedded in Cultural Traditions and Social Organizations. Earlier it was noted that traditional technology consists more of ways of doing things than of equipment. Lacking the fuels and large power units of modern systems, traditional operators must rely on skillful use of local resources, among which are various forms of social organization.

In traditional societies local decision-making and land management commonly takes place at the individual, family, and community levels. Decision levels are commensurate with the tasks: smaller and routine jobs may be done by individuals without conscious decisions other than scheduling. Larger tasks involve family discussion and assignments.

Cooperative and communal systems are evoked for tasks whose scope and labor requirements are beyond the purview of an individual family.

Systems for developing decisions and organizing labor are no less parts of traditional technology than the terraces or canals they create, or the hoes and shovels used to build them. In fact, technology transfers more often founder on incongruent social organizations than on lack of familiarity with the actual land management practices or tools.

Easiest to identify are labor arrangements: family divisions of labor, inter- and extra-family labor exchanges, and community systems of organizing labor for tasks that require a great deal of power in a short time. Earth moving projects associated with terracing or canal construction are good examples, as are tasks that must to be done quickly, such as planting or harvesting.

In addition to informal and formal organizations oriented specifically toward resource management there are less obvious but no less important relationships involving land tenure, village hierarchies and power centers, and inter-village and rural-urban political and economic relationships that are beyond the scope of this paper. As Tendler (1982) cautions, land management projects that fail to consider social relations are doomed to failure.

Step 7: Establish Incentives and Linkages. The importance of incentives cannot be over-emphasized. Like land managers everywhere, traditional farmers and foresters look for short-term as well as long-term returns on their investments of time and effort. Technology that does not acknowledge immediate needs risks rejection, and rightly so. This has been a major stumbling block in conservation programs, especially those that withdraw traditional rights, such as fuel gathering or pasturing to protect reforestation efforts. Fragile land defense needs are obvious to conservationists and local managers alike. But traditional managers may find the costs of foregone income unacceptable, and reject or even obstruct the introduction of a new technology no matter how technically appropriate if it is socially or economically inappropriate (Fortmann and Riddell 1985; Noronha and Lethem 1983).

The importance of markets has already been noted. Non-market situations, such as management of public lands, fall into the domain of common property resources which have distinct characteristics. Common property resources must be depletable and renewable, over-depletion must diminish their rejuvenation capacity, and most important, those who benefit from their use are not necessarily those who bear the costs of maintenance. Common grazing lands are the case type but the category includes forests, ground water, and several other areas of interest to land managers. Special incentive systems are needed for common property management (Hardin 1968; Panel on Common Property Resource Management 1986).

Step 8: Correlate Classification Systems. Characteristics and relationships of climate, soil and vegetation provide a basis for developing common languages for land management systems regardless of technical level. Resource classification offers some of the best opportunities: plant and soil classifications are most common but other resources with variable qualities also are classified.

Farmers everywhere recognize differences in soils, and develop vocabularies and classification systems to express these differences. Traditional classification systems tend to be utilitarian rather than taxonomic, and are organized around qualities related to production and management. For example, traditional soil classifications usually include not only inherent characteristics (e.g., texture, structure, organic content) but also managerial characteristics (e.g., moisture retention; workability; response to fertilizer).

The same qualities will likely form the basis for farmer evaluation irrespective of system. For example, a fertile, sandy loam will be identified as such and valued on a large North American machine-worked field and also in a tiny African hoe-cultivated plot. Thus soil classification systems could form the basis for a common language, often with opportunities for direct comparison and conversion between systems. Classification schemes related to other resources, such as vegetation and water, are also useful. If classification systems need to be standardized, the receiver's rather than the sender's system should take precedence since it will reflect local as well as general qualities and conditions.

Step 9: Reduce Risk and Uncertainty. Schultz (1964:33) set forth a basic premise with respect to risk and uncertainty in traditional agriculture:

The concept of traditional agriculture implies long-established routines with respect to all production activities. Introducing a new factor of production would mean not only breaking with the past but coping with a problem, because the production possibilities of the new factor will be subject to risks and uncertainties as yet unknown. It is therefore not sufficient merely to adopt the new factors and reap the larger return; learning from experience what new risks and uncertainties are inherent in these factors is also entailed. The hypothesis bearing on this matter . . . is that the rate at which farmers who have settled into a traditional agriculture accept a new factor of production depends upon its profit, with due allowance for risk and uncertainty, *and in this respect, the response is similar to that observed by farmers in modern agriculture.* (Emphasis added.)

The paragraph needs little elaboration: traditional farmers are no more or less risk-conscious than farmers anywhere. When considering new crops or tools they balance potential gains against risks and make decisions accordingly. The only missing factor is scale: traditional farms and farming operations and financial reserves usually are small and the amount that can be placed at risk is commensurately limited.

Risks can be reduced on the input side by lowering costs of adopting new technology. Governments encourage innovations by subsidies or reduced tariffs. Insurance programs (e.g., crop insurance) are less common but also less disruptive since they impact less directly on price structures. On the output side reducing market risks with price supports is widespread but politically vulnerable since it requires long-term policy and financial commitments.

Too often the benefits of risk-reduction have gone primarily to large-scale farmers. If risk-reduction programs were focused on the crops and technologies that favor small-scale systems traditional farmers would more likely enjoy the benefits.

Conclusions

Despite the paucity of documented results, there is evidence that traditional technology can achieve some of the common goals of sustainable land and resource management. If so, then traditional methods, developed under a wide range of environmental and social conditions, offer attractive alternatives to the energy- and capital-expensive technology usually advocated in technology transfers.

But traditional does not necessarily mean easily transferred. Although traditional tools are often simple, traditional methods may be complex in the ways they are applied and integrated into a society. Thus, transferring traditional technology involves not only identifying suitable technical and environmental practices, but also examining the role of technology in society.

Transfers of traditional technology resemble transfers of any technology in that communication can be a major obstacle. There are two methods for overcoming this. The first is to instruct the technology receiver in the methods and terminology of the sender. This approach is well-known since it lies at the heart of most development efforts. The second approach is to adopt the practices and language of the receiver. This is the approach advocated here. A nine-step procedure is proposed that examines practices and results of traditional methods, evaluates social factors, and establishes common languages based on plant-environment relationships and management.

The task is daunting, especially since it reverses the usual sender-receiver relationship and requires substantial training and preparation on the part of technology senders. But technology must be appropriate, including the technology of technology transfer. The goal of fragile lands management is to develop approaches for conservation and efficient use. The vast array of field-tested traditional technologies should not be excluded from this effort. The goal of technology transfer is to diffuse tools and methods between societies so that more alternatives are available for solving problems. If the procedure suggested here would help achieve that goal, it would be worth the effort.

Acknowledgments

I thank Ali Firouzi, Colorado State University, and John Browder, Virginia Polytechnic Institute and State University, for constructive comments on early drafts of this paper.

Notes

1. After reviewing unsuccessful efforts to transfer traditional *chinampa* technology from highland to lowland Mexico Chapin (1988) concludes: "Technicians overlooked the wider social, economic, and political context in which the farmers lived, and therefore had no notion of how their model might adapt within that context."

References

Altieri, M. A. 1983. Agroecology: The scientific basis of alternative agriculture. University of California, Division of Biological Control, Berkeley.

Ashby, J. A. 1984. Participation of small farmers in technology assessment. International Fertilizer Development Center, Muscle Shoals, Ala.

Bayliss-Smith, T. P. 1982. The ecology of agricultural systems. Cambridge University Press, Cambridge.

Berry, R. A., and W. R. Cline. 1979. Agrarian structure and productivity in developing countries. Johns Hopkins University Press, Baltimore.

Brink, R. A., J. W. Densmore, and G. A. Hill. 1977. Soil deterioration and the growing world demand for food. Science 197:625–630.

Brown, L. R. 1987. Sustaining world agriculture. In L. R. Brown (ed.), State of the world 1987. New York: W. W. Norton & Co.

———. 1981. World population growth, soil erosion, and food security. Science 214:995–1002.

Carter, L. J. 1977. Soil erosion: The problem persists despite billions spent on it. Science 196:409–411.

Chambers, R. 1983. Rural development: Putting the last first. Longman, London.

Chapin, M. 1988. The seduction of models: Chinampa agriculture in Mexico. Grassroots Development 12(1):8–17.

Clark, C., and M. Haswell. 1970. The economics of subsistence agriculture (4th ed.) Macmillan, London.

Coukis, B. (coord.). 1983. Labor-based construction programs: A practical guide for planning and management. Oxford University Press, New Delhi.

Denevan, W. M. 1980. Latin America, pp. 217–244. In G. A. Klee (ed.), World systems of traditional resource management. V. H. Winston & Sons, New York.

Fortmann, L., and J. Riddell. 1985. Trees and tenure: An annotated bibliography for agroforesters and others. University of Wisconsin, Land Tenure Center, Madison; International Council for Research in Agroforestry, Nairobi.

Gollás, M. 1973. Mano de obra excedente y eficiencia económica en el sector tradicional de una economía dual: El caso de Guatemala. El Trimestre Económico 40:569–585.

Hardin, G. 1968. The tragedy of the commons. Science 162:1243–1248.

Harwood, R. R. 1979. Small farm development: Understanding and improving farming systems in the humid tropics. Westview Press, Boulder.

Hatch, J. K. 1976. The corn farmers of Motupe: A study of traditional farming practices in northern coastal Peru. University of Wisconsin, Land Tenure Center, Monograph 1, Madison.

Hopfen, H. J. 1969. Farm implements for arid and tropical regions. Food and Agriculture Organization of the United Nations, Rome.

Innis, D. Q. 1980. The future of traditional agriculture. Focus (American Geographical Society) 30(3):1–8.

Klee, G. A. (ed.) 1980. World systems of traditional resource management. V. H. Winston & Sons, New York.

Marten, G. G. (ed.) 1986. Traditional agriculture in Southeast Asia. Westview Press, Boulder.

Molenaar, A. 1956. Water lifting devices for irrigation. Food and Agriculture Organization of the United Nations, FAO Development Paper No. 60, Rome.

Nair, P. K. R. 1985. Classification of agroforestry systems. Agroforestry Systems 3:97–128.

Norman, M. J. T. 1979. Annual cropping systems in the tropics. University Presses of Florida, Gainesville.

Noronha, R., and F. J. Lethem. 1983. Traditional land tenures and land use systems in the design of agricultural projects. World Bank Staff Working Papers No. 561, Washington, D.C.

Ortiz, S. R. 1973. Uncertainties in peasant farming. Athlone Press, New York.

Owen, W. F. 1971. Two rural sectors: Their characteristics and roles in the development process. Indiana University, International Development Research Center, Occasional Paper 1, Bloomington.

Pachico, D. 1984. Bean technology for small farmers: Biological, economic and policy issues. Agricultural Administration 15:71–86. Panel on Common Property Resource Management (CPR), Board on Science and Technology for International Development, Office of International Affairs, National Research Council. 1986. Proceedings of the conference on common property resource management. National Academy Press, Washington, D.C.

Richards, P. 1985. Indigenous agricultural revolution. Hutchinson, London.

Samli, A. C. 1985. Technology transfer: Geographic, economic, cultural, and technical dimensions. Quorum Books, Westport, Conn.

Schultz, T. W. 1964. Transforming traditional agriculture. Yale University Press, New Haven.

Shaikh, R. 1981. Commentary: Reflections on appropriate science in India. Science for the People 13(2):26–27.

Stigter, K. 1987. Tapping into traditional knowledge. Ceres (FAO Review) 20(3):29–32.

Tendler, J. 1982. Rural projects through urban eyes: An interpretation of the World Bank's new-style rural development projects. World Bank Staff Working Papers No. 532, Washington, D.C.

Van Loon, J. H., F. J. Staudt, and J. Zander (eds.) 1979. Ergonomics in tropical agriculture. Centre for Agricultural Publishing and Documentation, Wageningen.

Wharton, C. R., Jr. 1969. Research priorities on subsistence agriculture. In Wharton (ed.), Subsistence agriculture and economic development. Aldine, Chicago.

Wilken, G. C. 1987. Good farmers: Traditional agricultural resource management in Mexico and Central America. University of California Press, Berkeley.

_____. 1982. Agroclimatic hazard perception, prediction, and risk-avoidance strategies in Lesotho. Boulder: University of Colorado, Natural Hazard Research Working Paper #44.

_____. 1972. Microclimate management by traditional farmers. Geographical Review 62:544–560.

Wolf, E. C. 1987. Raising agricultural productivity. In L. R. Brown (ed.), State of the world 1987. New York: W. W. Norton.

PART TWO

Strategies for Tropical Rainforest Management

4

Economic Prospects from Tropical Rainforest Ethnobotany

Ghillean T. Prance

Introduction

A few years ago the interdisciplinary association of economics and ethnobotany would have been an unusual topic for a paper. However, recent advances in the field of ethnobotany as well as the pressures to avoid deforestation by making natural areas economically productive have changed the situation and made the topic highly relevant. The ecological crisis facing the world's tropical rainforests has helped to change the science of economic botany. If there is to be any hope for conserving tropical rainforests and their myriad of species it will be through a balance of conservation and utilization, through the development of sustainable systems of use. It is in this balance that economic botany and ethnobotany have much to offer.

The rainforest crisis of today cannot be stressed enough. In spite of the growing grass roots awareness of the crisis in some tropical rainforest countries such as Brazil and the creation of a large network of reserves in others such as Costa Rica, the acuteness of the problem is growing and species loss is certainly accelerating. At the 1988 Brazilian Botanical Congress, held in Belém in late January, I was heartened by the emphasis on environmental issues and the Amazon rainforest crisis, which was the subject of three major symposia and many other contributed papers. On the other hand, I was shattered by the amount of information that indicates how much the crisis is accelerating in spite of the failure of many major development projects. In the dry season of 1987 Amazonia was undergoing the greatest destruction in its history and the forest was literally disappearing in smoke and flames at an unprecedented rate. Information gathered by the meteorological satellite NOAA-9 showed that at 4 p.m. on August 24, 1987 eight thousand square kilometers of rainforest were on fire (Anonymous 1987). The satellite image showed at least 6,800 individual fires in a rather small area of Amazonia that included the state of Mato Grosso, the eastern part of Rondônia and the south of Pará. We know that much destruction is going on in other regions such as the Northeast and east of Pará state, in the states of Roraima and Amapá and in certain parts of the large state of Amazonas. We cannot emphasize enough the gravity of the situation, and whatever our discipline may be, we must use our science to search for alternatives to this wanton destruction. I will present here a few of the ways in which the Institute of Economic Botany (IEB) of the New York Botanical Garden is addressing these issues through the sciences of economic botany and ethnobotany.

Quantitative Ethnobotany

During the last four years the IEB has been carrying out a series of experiments in quantitative ethnobotany designed to show the extent to which indigenous peoples use the Amazon rainforest. It has often been claimed in the conservation literature (e.g. Myers 1982, Fearnside 1985), as an argument for conservation, that the Amazon Indians use a large percentage of the plants around them, yet nowhere were we able to find precise details of the extent of this use. Because of this lack of quantitative data, we decided to make such a study of rainforest tribes. We now have complete data from four tribes and the study of another two is almost completed. The experiment involved a forest inventory of one hectare of rainforest in Indian territory in which every tree was numbered, herbarium material gathered to establish accurate botanical identifications, and standard measurements of diameter, tree height etc. were made. The individual trees and specimens were shown to a number of different independent Indian informants and data on uses were gathered. Full details of this with tables of all the useful plants are given in Prance et al. (1988). Studies have been made of the Chácobo Indians of Bolivia (Boom 1985a, 1985b, 1987), of the Panare Indians of Venezuela (Boom in press, Prance et al. 1988), and the Ka'apor and Tembé Indians of eastern Amazonian Brazil (Balée 1986, 1987).

The use categories which we found were grouped into six major categories: edible, construction material, technology (glue, pottery temper, dye, soap, arrow points etc.), remedy, commerce (rubber, souvenirs etc), other (miscellaneous uses such as toys, dog-fatteners, fermentation aids and scents). The results showed that the tribes studied indeed use a high percentage of the forest tree species around them: the Chácobo

Table 1
Percentage of Useful Tree Species of 10 cm in Diameter or More in One Hectare Plots for Four Indigenous Groups Showing the Use Categories

Use Category	Tribe			
	Chácobo	Ka'apor	Panare	Tembe
Food	40.4	34.3	34.3	21.8
Construction	17.0	20.2	2.9	30.3
Technology	18.1	19.2	4.3	21.0
Remedy	35.1	21.2	7.1	10.9
Commerce	1.1	2.0	4.3	5.0
Other	1.1	8.1	0.0	4.2

Source: Adapted from Prance et al. (1988).

78.7% Ka'apor and the Tembé 61.36%. A summary in the different use categories is given in Table 1.

These data clearly show that the Indians of the Amazon rainforest use a large number of trees from the forest wherever they are located. The use categories in the different tribes studied were generally similar, but species useful for identical purposes vary among the different groups. This reflects the availability of material since not all species grow within the range of all the tribes. The Indians were able to find substitute plants for their necessities, regardless of the local species composition of the forest.

As we talk of extraction as a way of forest use it is important to gather more quantitative ethnobotanical data from indigenous peoples who can begin to teach us new uses and a more integral approach to extraction. It will be hard to make extraction viable based solely on rubber and Brazil nuts. However, that is not necessary because there are so many other useful plants in the forest. Of course not all of these are commercially exploitable and the challenge for the future is to determine which are, and to develop markets for them.

Valuation of a Tropical Forest in Peruvian Amazonia

Here I am reporting on recent work by ecologist Charles M. Peters, botanist Al Gentry and economist R. Mendelsohn (Peters, Gentry and Mendelsohn in press). These authors also made an inventory of one hectare of terra firme Amazonia rainforest at Mishana near to the city of Iquitos in Peru. They found 842 trees of ten or more centimeters in diameter representing 275 species. The forest was therefore consid-

Table 2
Comparison of Species Diversity on Five One-Hectare Inventory Plots for Trees 10 cm in Diameter

Plot	Chácobo	Ka'apor	Panare	Tembe	Mishana
Number of species	94	123	70	138	275
Individual trees	649	519	324	456	842

Table 3
Economic Data from One Hectare[a] of Forest at Mishana, Loreto Department, Peru

Forest Product	No. of Species	Value of Sales $ (1987)	Production and Marketing Costs	Net Profit (per cycle)	NPV ($)
Fruit	11	650	250	400 ⎱	8,400
Latex	2	50	28	22 ⎰	
Timber[b]	60			310	490
Total					8,890

[a] The hectare contained a total of 275 species and 350 individuals of which 72 species were used economically from 350 individual trees.
[b] 25-year cycle.

Source: Adapted from Peters et al. (in press).

erably more diverse than any of the forests studied in the quantitative ethnobotany study summarized above (Table 2).

Of the 275 species in Mishana inventory 72 species (26.2%) representing 350 individuals (41.6%) yielded products which have monetary values on the urban markets of Iquitos. These comprised edible fruit from 11 species, 2 species of *Hevea* that produce commercial rubber latex and 60 species that yield commercial timber. The detailed study of Peters et al. (in press) calculated production rates of all products such as rubber latex and fruits and merchantible volume of timber, and also data on retail prices of each product involved. It also took into consideration labor and transportation costs.

The results indicate an estimated net present value (NPV) per hectare of natural forest of $8,890 (Table 3). This contrasts to similar NPV calculations for a managed plantation of pulp wood species (*Gmelina arborea*) in Pará, Brazil of $3,184/ha (derived from Sedjo 1983) and of a typical Amazonian cattle pasture in Venezuela of $2,960/ha (derived from Buschbacher 1987).

The value of the standing forest is matched by very few alternative systems such as intensive cultivation of tropical floodplain forest and a few well designed agroforestry systems such as that of Tamshiyacu,

Peru (Padoch et al. 1985) and of Ilha das Onças, Pará, Brazil (Anderson this volume). The pioneer study of Peters et al. needs to be followed up with many more from all over the tropical forests of Amazonia in order to produce the only data to which the developers will listen, the hard facts in dollars and cents. The implication of these results for extraction forests is obvious. However, a danger is the conclusion that we can go into any rainforest and produce such results. The Amazon region is varied in species composition, diversity, local endemism, soil types and many other factors. The potential economic values of any area to be considered for extraction forest must be calculated first just as it should be for any other type of land use.

Natural Species Aggregations

Another focus of our research at the Institute of Economic Botany has been the study of species of economic value which occur naturally in large aggregations or pure stands. It turns out that there are a surprisingly large number of these "natural monocultures" scattered throughout the Amazon region. In these cases the natural ecology points to species which can either be harvested from the wild or can be grown in monospecific cultures. Examples of these species include the babassu palm (*Orbignya phalerata* Mart.), the aguaje or buriti palm (*Mauritia flexuosa* Mart.), the açai palm (*Euterpe oleracea* Mart.), the sacha-mangua (*Grias* spp.) and the camu camu (*Myrciaria dubia* [HBK] McVaugh). All of these species provide good examples of an unusually dense clustering of individuals of a particular species in adaptation to specific environments. For example, *Grias, Mauritia* and *Euterpe* are well adapted in certain floodplain forests where they can dominate, *Orbignya* to transition forests where fire resistance gives it an advantage, and *Myrciaria* to long periods of flooding in nutrient poor black water igapó forest. It is significant that all of these and several other Amazonian species that tend to cluster are some of the species with the greatest economic potential for extraction products.

For example, the camu camu is a plant of the lake margin that matures its cherry-sized fruit as the river level rises. It is, therefore, easy to harvest from a canoe. The fruit of camu camu is sold in the markets of Iquitos for the preparation of fruit drinks and ice creams. It is also the fruit with the highest known content of vitamin C (approximately thirty times that of *Citrus* and twice that of acerola (*Malpighia*) widely touted as the richest species. It is widespread throughout Amazonia. It is under study by Charles Peters at Jenaro Herrera in Amazonian Peru, but I have also seen large aggregations on the upper Rio Negro and on the Xingu in Brazil. The study of a

Table 4
A Summary of Brazilian Exports of Amazonian Products in 1985[a]

Product	1985 Export Value($)	Method of Production	Harvest Kills Plant (K)	Average US$ Value of US Imports[b]
Cacao	778,212,352	Mainly plantation	–	–
Wood	169,536,947	Extraction	K	–
Sôrva latex	28,749,587	Extraction	K (?)	3,068,000
Brazil nut	25,539,505	Extraction	–	17,679,000
Guaraná	3,735,239	Plantation	–	–
Rosewood oil	938,065	Extraction	K	980,000
Piassaba fiber	474,745	Extraction	–	–
Tonka beans	365,024	Extraction	–	139,000
Copaiba balsam	125,426	Extraction	–	45,000
Massaranduba latex	12,425	Extraction	K	–
Balata latex	10,151	Extraction	–	–
Total	1,014,106,546			

[a] The values represent export sales only and many of these products also enter the domestic market extensively.
[b] Data from Prescott-Allen & Prescott-Allen (1986).

population of camu camu in an oxbow lake in Peru by Peters and Vasquez (1987) showed considerable economic potential. Peters calculated that at present market prices of camu camu a single hectare of lake margin camu camu scrub forest can yield $6,000 worth of fruit (pers. comm.). There are few products that can compete with this in Amazonia. The study of camu camu has further shown that a large percentage of the natural production of the fruit can be harvested without harming the natural population.

Some Recent Economic Plant Data
from Amazonian Brazil

A strong argument for the conservation of the Amazon rainforest can be made purely by showing the worldwide use that is being made of species from the region. The economic data from these species should be enough for us to pause before converting diverse rainforests to other less valuable and less productive uses. The contribution of the Amazon forests to world economy is substantial. Table 4 is a summary of Brazilian exports in 1985 from the seven Amazonian states and territories. It presents the data for eleven native species that are produced or harvested in a variety of ways as described below. Four of these species alone brought Brazil over one billion dollars in exports, and this list does not include many other economically important Amazonian plants consumed domestically such as rubber and cassava.

Cacao *(*Theobroma cacao *L.)*

This is by far the most important crop from the region today, mainly because of the increased area cultivated in Rondônia. The cacao is grown in plantations and hence is a cause of deforestation. However, since it is a perennial crop and soon forms a thick canopy over the soil, it is a far less destructive land use than cattle ranching. Cacao can also be used in multi-cultural agroforestry systems. In a few places it occurs in great abundance in natural stands and could be extracted from the wild, but at present this is not done on any large scale.

Wood

Relatively few Amazonian woods reach the international market, consequently, the few species that are preferred tend to be badly over-harvested. The best examples of that are the virtual elimination of mahogany (*Swietenia macrophylla* King) and Brazilian cherry (*Amburana acreana* [Ducke] A. C. Smith) from the state of Rondônia. Amazonian wood is harvested by extraction rather than from timber plantations which are generally still experimental apart from a few specialized plantations, such as the Jari project that was founded by Daniel Ludwig to produce pulp wood. This project can hardly be deemed a success (see Fearnside and Rankin 1982, 1985). Wood could be a sustainable and viable product from the Amazon forest, but is generally mismanaged to overexploit the particular species that are marketable. For example, the number of sawmills in Rondônia rose from 4 in 1959, to 141 in 1978, to 387 in 1982, mainly to exploit mahogany and Brazilian cherry. According to published export records, Brazil's exports of mahogany rose from 19,401 cubic meters in 1971 to 61,281 in 1983 when it reached its peak (Browder 1986, p.79).

Sôrva latex *(*Couma *spp.)*

The latex of two species of the genus *Couma, C. rigida* Barb. Rodr., and *C. utilis* Muell. Arg. (Apocynaceae) furnishes the type of latex that is used for chewing gum. Table 4 shows that Brazil earned over 28 million dollars from *Couma* latex exports in 1985. Traditionally the extraction of this latex has been done by felling the trees. Gradually over the years as millions of tons of latex have been exported, *Couma* trees have become rarer and rarer and the sorveiros who extract the latex have had to go to progressively more remote parts of the forest to find trees. This valuable export product has been mined out of the forest rather than managed. Recently, however, because of the increased rarity of the trees, techniques have been devised to tap the trees rather than fell them. If the tapping methods are increased and felling eliminated, *sôrva* could continue to be an extremely valuable product of the Amazon forest. It is an ideal plant for agroforestry systems since it also yields a delicious fruit (Arkcoll, 1986). The genus *Couma* is still the major source of chicle type latex in Amazonia rather than members of the Sapotaceae that are used in Central America. It is essential to bring the *sôrva* into carefully managed systems, to encourage research on methods of tapping, to end the wanton destruction that still continues today.

Brazil Nut *(*Bertholletia excelsa *[Humb. & Bonpl.])*

Brazil nut is also an important 25 million dollar export crop that comes from Amazon forests by extraction. The entire harvest is from wild trees rather than plantations. So far plantations have not worked well because of difficulties with pollination and soil fertility. The Brazil nut is an excellent example of extraction from the forest without loss of trees or damage to the forest. However, although it is officially illegal to cut down Brazil nut trees, the production is now falling markedly because of the number of production areas that are being deforested for other uses. For example, large areas of Brazil nut trees have been destroyed around Marabá in southern Pará (Kitamura & Müller in press) and in the state of Rondônia. The Brazil nut is an ideal product for extraction from the forest.

Guaraná *(*Paullinia cupana *H.B.K. var* sorbilis *Spix in Mart. ex Ducke)*

Guaraná is the source of a caffeine-rich soda beverage that is extremely popular in Brazil. It is grown in plantations mainly in the region of Maués in Amazonas state. It grows well on the poor soils of the region. The export figures in Table 4 of $3,735,239 do not reflect the true importance of this plant since it is used to a much greater extent on the internal Brazilian market rather than as an export crop. Currently there is much active research underway to improve guaraná production and produce new varieties. This crop is ideal for various agroforestry projects and it also has a far greater potential on the international market. The main constraint has been the inability to produce enough fruit for the export market. For a review of the use of guaraná see Henman (1982).

Rosewood Oil *(*Aniba rosaeodora *Ducke)*

The wood of this species contains the essential oil linalol which is extracted by steam distillation of the wood. The export figure of almost one million dollars in 1986 is low because the supply of wood is almost exhausted. Since commercial exploitation began in Brazil in 1924, stills have been set up throughout the range of this species. Laborers are then sent to fell every tree within a fifty kilometer radius of the still. Once the supply is exhausted the still moves on to another part of the forest. This gradual process has, without any replanting, caused the rosewood tree to become very rare. Experiments at the National Institute of Amazon Research (INPA) have shown that it can be grown in plantations and that gradual harvest of the leaves and branches also yields a good amount of linalol (Alencar & Fernándes 1978). Another possible source of this product is a common shrub of secondary forest in the region, *Croton cajucara* (Euphorbiaceae).

Piassaba Fiber *(*Leopoldinia piassaba *Wallace)*

The piassaba palm trunk is surrounded by fibers derived from the old leaf sheaths. The fiber is a strong broom fiber that has been gathered and used in both the domestic and export markets for many years. The fiber can be removed without destroying the tree and so this is another crop that can be extracted. In practice, however, the gatherers often cut down the larger palms to facilitate the collection of the fiber. The Amazon piassaba is a palm of restricted natural distribution in the region of the upper Rio Negro. Another palm native to the forests of Bahia, Brazil, gives a similar fiber: *Attalea funifera* Mart.

Tonka Bean *(*Dipteryx odorata *[Aubl.] Willd.)*

The tonka bean has long been an important Amazon product because of its rich content of coumarins. The market has fluctuated depending on the demand, but it is still a small source of income for many Amazonian residents. The seeds of this tree are collected and then the coumarins are extracted through the process of crystallization by repeatedly soaking the seeds in alcohol and then shading them. Since this product is from the seeds of a common Amazon tree it is another good extraction product.

*Copaiba Balsam (*Copaifera *spp.)*

Several species of the genus *Copaifera,* for example *C. langsdorffii,* Desf. and *C. multijuga* Hayne, are the source of an oleoresin that has long been extracted on a small scale both for use in medicines and in the varnish industry. If a hole is drilled into a heart wood of the tree trunk and a plug inserted, the oleoresin collects. When the plug is removed, from two to twenty liters of the liquid flow out. Another interesting property of this fluid, which is a sesquiterpene, is that it is combustible and will run a diesel motor. As a result it was promoted as a future energy source by Nobel Prize winning chemist Melvin Calvin (1983), who envisaged energy producing plantations. While the future of *Copaifera* as an economic source of energy is questionable because of its low productivity per unit are (Alencar 1982), the balsam has other uses and is still a viable product from extraction forests. The tapping of the tree does not adversely affect it and can be done at least twice a year.

*Massaranduba (*Manilkara huberi *[Ducke] A. Chev.), Balatá (*Manilkara bidentata *(A.DC.) A. Chev.)*

The last two products in Table 4 were very minor on the market in 1985 and have been much more important in the past when there was more demand for the balata type latex used in insulators, golf balls and marine cables. These latexes are both products that can be extracted from the forest without destroying the trees, although the massaranduba latex was usually extracted by felling. They are components of the forest that could have renewed future potential as petroleum products become scarcer.

The above list is of eleven species or products of Amazon origin that are contributing significantly to the export market of Brazil. The demonstration of the economic value should convince policy makers of the importance of the natural forest and of its future potential both as a source of income, and as the gene bank that harbors the relatives of important crop species such as cacau. This list does not include many other species of commercial importance from the region that enter mainly into the domestic market of Brazil, the two most important being cassava (*Manihot esculenta* Crantz) a widely cultivated crop plant, and rubber (*Hevea brasiliensis* Muell. Arg.) the most important extraction plant in Amazonia. The cassava is the staple carbohydrate crop of the Amazon region and of many other parts of the tropics where it has been introduced. It grows well in the poor soils of the region and will continue to be an important regional food product, and probably also a source of energy (Cock 1982).

Rubber latex is still an important regional product from extraction from wild trees. Rubber has never been completely successful in plantations in its native neotropical region because of diseases such as the leaf rust fungus *Microcyclus ulei*. It is a most successful plantation crop in tropical Asia where it is removed from its natural pathogens. Many Amazonian residents, however, do make their living from the extraction of rubber latex from the wild trees that are scattered throughout the floodplain or várzea forests of the region. Also the importance of local rubber production to Brazil must be emphasized since Brazil is still a net importer of rubber.

Each of the species mentioned above is one member of a genus of plants that has other wild species in the Amazon forest, for example, the 22 species of *Theobroma* that are relatives of the cacao (Cuatrecasas 1964) or the nine species of *Hevea* that are relatives of rubber (Pires & Prance 1977). The future of some of these Amazonian products will depend upon the characteristics of some of their wild relatives such as disease resistance, greater ecological amplitude, or higher productivity. The genetic material represented by these wild species is essential for the long-term viability of each of the crop species. Basic information about the relatives of species, their evolutionary relationships, their distribution, their pollination and their ecology is necessary for the establishment of conservation policy. We do not yet make enough use of this type of information except for a few major crops such as corn. The wild relatives of all the economic plants mentioned here could be a major source of information for conservation policy makers. In addition these wild relatives of already useful crops are often also the species with the most unrealized future potential in extraction forests.

Conclusion

This brief review of a few of the most important products of economic plants of Amazonia shows that some are currently produced in plantations (e.g. cacao, cassava and guaraná), some are mined from the forest through destruction of the tree (e.g. wood, sôrva latex and rosewood) and others are produced by non-destructive extraction (e.g. Brazil nuts, copaiba balsam, rubber and tonka beans). There are undoubtedly many other products that could be extracted rather than mined from the forest. So many data from economic botany are pointing to the fact that one of the best ways of conserving areas of Amazonian forest would be to use them as commercially productive extraction areas, rather than to cut the forest for alternative uses of dubious economic sustainability. The concept of extraction forests has gained a new momentum recently by the political organization of a rubber tappers' union in the state of Acre, Brazil. These people, who make their living from extraction of rubber and Brazil nuts from the forest, are becoming bitter as more and more of their forest is being destroyed for cattle pasture, farms, and plantations (Schwartzman 1987, this volume).

Rubber and Brazil nuts can form the basis for extraction forests, but other products will also be necessary to make them economically viable. One of the challenges to economic botany today is to find these products that can be produced from extraction forests such as oils, resins, balsams, latex fruits, fibers, nuts and medicines. Extraction forests, together with agroforestry projects that are closer to the indigenous systems, are probably the only way to save the Amazon forest. This is the decade in which the science of economic botany has become vital to the conservation and utilization of natural ecosystems and the species of the world's most diverse rainforest. We must expand our efforts to work with such groups as the rubber tappers' unions of Brazil who could become one of our greatest allies in forest conservation (Shwartzman this volume). The challenge to economic botany is to find the additional products that will raise the standard of living of rubber tappers and other traditional forest users to a position of dignity in human society, as well as to pursue research and present data which demonstrate the real value of standing rainforest.

Acknowledgments

I am grateful to the various staff members of the New York Botanical Garden Institute of Economic Botany for permission to use the results of their work in this paper, especially to Charles M. Peters and Christine A. Padoch. I thank John Browder for a critical review of an earlier draft, and Rosemary Lawlor for word processing assistance. Field work in Amazonian Brazil was supported by the National Science Foundation Grant BSR. 8646992.

References

Alencar, J. da C. 1982. Estudos silviculturais de uma população natural de *Copaifera multijuga*. Hayne-Leguminosae, na Amazônia Central 2—Produção de óleo-resina. Acta Amazonica 12:75–89.

———. & N. P. Fernándes. 1978. Desenvolvimento de árvores nativas em ensaios de espécies - 1. Pau rosa (*Aniba duckei* Kostermans). Acta Amazonica 8:523–541.

Anonymous. 1987. Queimadas preocupam na região amazônica. Enfoque Amazônico 7:7.

Arkcoll, D. B. 1986. *Couma utilis,* food and fruit-bearing forest species. Romie 44:109–11. 1986.

Balée, W. 1986. Análise preliminar de inventário florestal e a etnobotânica Ka'apor (MA). Boletim Museu Paraense Emílio Goeldi, Série Botânica, Vol. 2. Part 2:141–167.

————. 1987. A etnobotaânica quantitativa dos Índios Tembe (Rio Gurupi, Pará). Boletim Museo Paraense Emílio Goeldi, Série Botânica 3(1):29–50.

Boom, B. M. 1985a. Amazon Indians and the forest environment. Nature 314:324.

————. 1985b. "Advocacy botany" for the Neotropics Garden 9(3):24–32.

————. 1987. Ethnobotany of the Chácobo Indians, Beni, Bolivia. Advances in Economic Botany 5. The New York Botanical Garden. 68 pages.

————. In Press. Useful plants of the Panare Indians of the Venezuelan Guayana. Advances in Economic Botany.

Browder, J. O. 1986. Logging in the rainforest: A political economy of timber extraction and unequal exchange in the Brazilian Amazon. Ph.D. Thesis. University of Pennsylvania.

Buschbaker, R. J. 1987. Cattle productivity and nutrient fluxes on an Amazonian pasture. Biotropica 19:200–207.

Calvin, M. 1983. New sources for fuel and materials. Science 219:24–26.

Cock, J. H. 1982. Cassava: A basic energy source in the tropics. Science 218:755–762.

Cuatrecasas, J. 1964. Cacao and its allies; a taxonomic revision of the genus *Theobroma.* Contributions from the U.S. National Herbarium 35(6):379–614.

Fearnside, P. M. 1985. Environmental change and deforestation in the Brazilian Amazon. Pages 70–89 *in* J. Hemming, editor. Change in the Amazon basin, vol. 1. Manchester University press, Manchester, U.K.

———— & J. M. Rankin. 1982. The new Jari: Risks and prospects of a major Amazonian development. Interciencia 7:329–339.

————. 1985. Jari revisited: Changes and the outlook for sustainability in Amazonia's largest silvicultural estate. Interciencia 10:121–129.

Henman, A. R. 1982. Guaraná (*Paullinia cupana* var. *sorbilis*): Ecological and social perspectives on an economic plant of the Central Amazon basin. Journal of Ethnopharmacology 6:311–338.

Kitmarua, P. C. & C. H. Müller. In press. A depredação dos Castanhais nativos: O caso de Marabá - PA. (manuscript)

Myers, N. 1982. Deforestation in the tropics: who wins, who loses. Pages 1–24 *in* V. H. Sutlive et al., editors. Where have all the flowers gone? Deforestation in the Third World. Studies in Third World Societies, no. 13. College of William and Mary, Williamsburg, Virginia, USA.

Padoch, C., Chota Inuma, J., de Jong, W., and Unruh, J. 1985. Amazonian Agroforestry: A market-oriented system for Peru. Agroforestry Systems 3:47–58.

Peters, C. M., A. H. Gentry and R. Mendelsohn. In Press. Valuation of a tropical forest in Peruvian Amazonia.

_____ and A. Vasquez. 1987. Estudios ecológicos de Camu-camu (*Myrciaria dubia*). I. Producción de frutos en poblaciones naturales. Acta Amazonica 16/17:161–173.

Pires, J. M. & G. T. Prance. 1977. The Amazon forest: A natural heritage to be preserved. Pp. 158–194. In G. T. Prance & T. S. Elias. Extinction is forever. N.Y. Botanical Garden.

Prance, G. T., W. Balée, B. M. Boom and R. L. Carneiro. 1988. Quantitative ethnobotany and the case for conservation in Amazonia. Conservation Biology 1:269–310.

Prescott-Allen, C and R. 1987. The first resource: Wild species in the North American Economy. Yale University Press, New Haven.

Schwartzman, S. 1987. Extractive production in the Amazon and the rubber tappers movement. Mimeo of papers presented to Forests, Habitats and Resources, A conference in World Environmental History, Duke University.

Sedjo, R. A. 1983. The comparative economics of plantation forestry. Washington, Resources for the Future Inc.

5

Agricultural Systems on the Floodplains of the Peruvian Amazon

Mário Hiraoka

Introduction

The "development" of Amazonia continues unabated. Governments sharing the basin are promoting the occupation of the region for reasons that range from land pressures occasioned by inequitable land tenure systems or population pressure, expansion of food and fiber production to meet domestic needs or foreign exchange earnings, to exploitation of natural resources. Development models, however, have been based on those extraneous to the region. As exemplified by the monocultural forestry projects at Jarí, and by large scale cattle ranching projects in Brazilian and Colombian Amazonia, the new ventures have proved to be ill-suited to the region's environment and its inhabitants (Goodland and Irwin, 1975; Fearnside, 1982; Moran, 1981, 1983; Pires and Prance, 1977; Smith 1982). In response to this dilemma, some have proposed ways to delay or reduce the pace of resource exploitation, while others have suggested ecologically and economically viable alternatives.

A possible avenue of solution has been to incorporate the local inhabitants' knowledge in development planning (see Wilken, this volume). As the original stewards of the region, the natives and their mixed-blood offspring are believed to practice environmentally-compatible livelihood systems. This line of research has led some to the study of tribal Indians to gain knowledge of tropical rainforest resource perception, management techniques, and economic systems (Denevan and Padoch, 1988; Posey, 1983; Posey et al., 1984).

More recently, attention has focused on detribalized Indians and their mestizo descendants as sources of information and understanding of tropical ecosystem management (Hiraoka, 1985a, 1985b, 1986; Moran, 1974; Padoch, et al., 1985; Padoch, 1986; Parker, 1981; Ross, 1978).

These inhabitants comprise the majority of the population in contemporary riparian Amazonia. Since they participate in the local and regional economies, their livelihood patterns include a number of adaptations that enable the residents to interact with markets. As active participants in external systems, and as inheritors of native subsistence strategies based on extended utilization of local ecosystems, the inhabitants' cumulative knowledge is believed to offer alternate solutions to regional agricultural development planning. Realizing the potential contributions that mestizos and detribalized Indians could make, researchers have begun to study their resource use techniques. However, a meaningful generalization for the basin is still difficult, reflecting its diverse biophysical characteristics (e.g., hydrochemistry, landforms, and vegetation), as well as the sociocultural differences, and complex historical contexts.

The intent of this paper is to present information on the agricultural systems found among the floodplain inhabitants of the Northeastern Peruvian Amazon, and to learn the feasibility of adopting local techniques for the agricultural development of the regional riparian zone. The discussion is restricted to the explanation of the structure of floodplain farming and to the presentation of preliminary findings on the energetics of local agricultural systems. The findings, in turn, demonstrate the efficiency of traditional subsistence systems.

The study is based on a floodplain community of the Amazon, 45 km to the south and upriver from Iquitos, Peru where I have collected data continuously since 1982. The inhabitants of this village called San Jorge as well as those in the rest of riverine Amazonia of Peru are collectively called *ribereños*. Their livelihood is derived from a combination of crop cultivation, fishing, collecting of forest products, limited hunting, and occasional wage labor. Although long connected with external economies, the ribereños' current pace of integration is occurring at an ever increasing tempo.

The Floodplain Environment

The floodplain of the Amazon and its tributaries have traditionally supported a large human population. The heavy suspended load, resulting from the rapid erosion of Andean slopes under a heavy precipitation regime, the rich inorganic content of these sediments, the large volume of water, and the gradient of the river averaging less than 0.04 m/km through much of its length in the lowlands, formed a moderately fertile floodplain. Although Amazon floodplains occupy less than two percent of the basin's area, the combination of good cropland, rich aquatic fauna, and ease of transportation and communication, served to concentrate people on these strips of land.

Floodplain Biotopes and Climate

In my study area, the floodplain varies between 15 and 25 km in width, and is bounded by a geologically older and slightly higher terrain. These interfluves, rising between 5 and 40 meters above the mean river level, are locally called *altura*. In the Iquitos area, the altura's surface material consists of weathered sands and clays of the late Tertiary period. These Miocene-Pliocene sediments, referred to as the *Pebas* or Iquitos beds, are in most places heavily eroded and incised by small streams.

Bajo is the term that refers to the low-lying floodplain. Practically all the landforms on the bajo are the result of Quaternary ponding and sedimentation (Putzer, 1984). The floodplain is characterized by several biotopes. The highest relief is attained on the natural levees. These landforms are differentiated between a *restinga alta* and a *restinga baja*. The former is rarely flooded, while the latter are subjected to short annual inundations. Thus, nutrient-rich silts and mud are deposited seasonally on the restinga baja, but not on the restinga alta. The yearly sedimentation rates vary in inverse proportion with the distance from the river. Most of the deposits occur on a belt within 300 m from the river's edge. Flooding is not a problem on the restinga alta, but the absence of periodic silting does not allow the continuous cropping of annuals.

Several other biotopes occur on the floodplain. Sand bars (*playa*) and mud bars (*barreales*) appear regularly after the water subsides. Some of these bars, with appropriate current, accretion, and anchorage by vegetation may evolve into semi-permanent islands that are highly productive. The palm swamp (*aguajal*), back-swamp (*tahuampa*), lake (*cocha*), and side channels (*caños*) comprise the rest of the biotopes. These are managed for non-agricultural activities, such as, collecting of forest products, fishing, and hunting (Hiraoka, 1985a).

The Iquitos area is characterized by a high average temperature and precipitation. The mean annual temperature is 26 degrees C. During the period of reduced precipitation, July through September, daytime temperatures reach 34 to 35 degrees in the shade, but most of the year the daily high averages 30 degrees C, while the lows often dip into the high teens. Rainfall in the area averages 2,800 mm per year. Despite the large total, precipitation shows some seasonality. The short dry season is not as pronounced as in the central Amazon around Manáus. Even the driest month receives a mean of over 160 mm. But this reduction is sufficient to induce phenological changes in the plants. Litter fall of deciduous species is keyed with the dry season, and flowering of many plants, including economically valuable ones like *zapote* (*Quararibea cordata*) and *guaba* (*Inga edulis*), occurs toward the end of this period. The combination of reduced rains and decline of river water level leads ribereños to conduct activities such as *aguaje palm* (*Mauritia flexuosa*) fruit extractions and deforestation of restingas bajas. The dry forest floors enable easy transport of fruits, and the cloudless skies hasten the desiccation of felled flora.

Floral Associations

The inhabitants recognize three broad floral associations within the floodplain: The flood forest, the aguajal, and the *chicozal-gramalotal.* The flood forests covering the restingas are collectively called *monte.* This vegetation association is currently undergoing the greatest transformation. Inundated between three to five months, the interior of the flood forest can be easily reached by small canoes during the high water season. Easy access, and the existence of many palms, trees, and vines supplying food, fiber, timber, and medicinal substances have meant a long association and dependence of the ribereños on the flood forest. In addition, as Goulding (1980, 1981) notes, many trees serve as important sources of feed for fish. This vegetation association, especially along the river, is being removed to give way to farmland.

Aguajales are covered with almost pure stands of Mauritia flexuosa palms. Located away from the river and blocked by the restingas, the poorly drained terrain is almost permanently underwater. Without the infusion of nutrient-rich Amazon water, the standing water in the aguajal is acidic, and the soils gley. The Mauritia fruit attract a large number of floodplain fauna during the dry season. Animals like *tapir* (*Tapirus terrestris*), *motelo* (*Testudo tabulata*), and deer (*Mazama* spp.) were hunted in the past. As such, the aguajal, along with the flood forest, has been one of the most important hunting grounds for the villagers.

The floral association found on the islands and mud banks is known as the *chicozal-gramalotal.* It is represented by successional flora ranging from *Gramineae,* like *gramalote* (*Paspalum repens*) on the newly-formed sand and mud banks, to bushes and trees like *pájaro bobo* (*Tessaria integrifolia,*) and *cetico* (*Cecropia* spp.) on the higher and more stabilized portions of the bars. Excepting for the *caña brava* (*Gynerium sagitatum* spp.) used as fencing material, the chicozal-gramalotal flora are of minor economic value to the ribereños.

River Dynamics

The seasonal fluctuation of river level is one of the most significant annual events for the ribereños. The flood season is linked with the rainy season of the southern hemisphere. The heaviest precipitation in the central Andean headwaters come in January and February, while the corresponding counterpart in northeast Peru occurs in February-March. Reflecting these regimes, the river level at the study site begins to rise a few centimeters per day beginning in January and crests between April and mid-May. Once the maximum is reached, the floodwater begins to subside. The minimum is reached in mid-September. The mean annual range of water level is 8.5 meters, but variations of as much as 4.0 m above and below the mean are common. This dynamic of the river affects practically all biotic organisms and abiotic elements on the bajo. The deposition and removal of landforms, germination of flora, and life cycles of fauna are also adjusted to the river's behavior. The agricultural cycle on the restinga baja, barreal, and playa commences with the exposure of the silt-laden surfaces in May or June, and ends in January or February, with the rising water level. Hunting is done during the flood season, when animals are concentrated on the diminishing dry ground (Bergman, 1980). Fish runs usually occur in April-May, just about the time the river crests. Almost every activity is influenced by the water level changes, so that successful management of the bajo depends on the minute familiarity with the behavior of the water, and the multiple components of the biophysical world molded by the ebb and flow of the river.

The Ribereños of San Jorge

Most of the rural inhabitants of the Peruvian Amazon live in villages or *caseríos*. With a population varying between 100 and 300, these settlements are strung along the rivers. Little is known of their genesis and metamorphosis. Records of missionaries, government officials, and naturalists enable the reconstruction of the history of large settlements in the region, such as, Iquitos, Nauta, and Tamshiyacu, but recounting the events of any caserío is difficult because of limited information and the ephemeral nature of these settlements. Padoch (1986) retraces the evolution of a caserío along the lower Ucayali and demonstrates the constant flux of population, location and economic activities of riparian settlements.

A review of events that led to the development of present-day San Jorge and its inhabitants shows some parallels to Padoch's findings. Naturalists and travellers who visited the region in the nineteenth century do not mention the existence of rural settlements between Nauta and Iquitos, except for Omaguas (Herndon, 1952; Raimondi, 1907; and Smyth and Lowe 1836). If villages did exist, they would have been noticed by keen observers like Raimondi. It appears that, as elsewhere in the basin, the riparian population had been greatly reduced by repeated outbreaks of diseases and slaving raids.

Resettlement of the floodplain began in the latter part of the nineteenth century, following the beginning of the rubber boom in the 1880s. The existence of small *Hevea* stands led to the establishment of *fundos gomeros,* or latex collecting estates. San Jorge, as told by its last operator, was established in 1905 by his father, who controlled another fundo named Santa Ana, across the river on the altura. The estate was set up on a restinga alta along the left margin of the Amazon, at the point the Amazon forms a single channel and drains northward. As such, the location of San Jorge gave easy access to an extensive floodplain and its resources. Hevea trees in the area, however, were not numerous since the flood forests containing the resin-yielding trees form a ribbon of only 3–4 km wide along the river. Latex collecting was the main activity, but farming for staples, some hunting, fishing, and collecting for other forest products were also performed concurrently. The fundo operator was a mestizo from San Martin, and labor was provided by detribalized natives recruited from the upper basin, including the margins of the Huallaga, Marañon, and Ucayali rivers (San Román, 1975; Stocks, 1981). Analogous events seem to have occurred in much of the region. It appears that no more than 20–30 families were working at the fundo at any given time. At the turn of the century, fundos of similar size and economic function were also found on other floodplain sites, both up and downriver from San Jorge.

Following the collapse of the Amazon latex exports in the early 1920s, emphasis shifted to tagua nuts, the seed of the *yarina* palm (*Phytelephas macrocarpa*). As synthetics replaced it within a few years, the market for this vegetable ivory also disappeared by 1935. A series of short exploitive cycles based on forest or aquatic products, like *cumala* seeds (*Virola* spp.) for oil, animal skins, timber, and ornamental fish followed. A combination of overexploitation, substitution, or alternate opportunities in urban centers like Iquitos, led to the demise of most fundos. Control of San Jorge by its *fundero* ceased in 1968, when he and his family left for Iquitos to operate a bakery in the outskirts of the city. As this brief review of fundo development and demise reveals, the exploitation of floodplain resources served as the main source of income for both estate operator and laborers, but revenues from these activities were always so unpredictable that farming had to be carried out concurrently to produce the needed staples.

In 1984, the caserío of San Jorge had a population of 249, representing 36 households. As is true for much of the region, the inhabitants are very mobile (Hiraoka, 1985b; Padoch and de Jong in press). Some families can trace their origins to the beginning of the fundo, but others have arrived only within the last few years. The absence of private tenure of land in the bajo and the relative abundance of unused space undoubtedly contribute to the impermanence of people in a single location. The short distance to, easy access to and the wage earning opportunities in Iquitos are increasingly drawing individual members from the caseríos. Families, especially those with school-age children, often maintain dual residences: one in the caserío and another in either Iquitos or Tamshiyacu, where upper level educational institutions are found.

Agricultural Systems

The ribereño economy traditionally has been based on farming and exploitation of the floodplain biotopes. Cash producing activities were based on the exploitation of forest products. Today, some forest products are still extracted for sale, but the primary emphasis is again on agriculture. Crop cultivation provides the bulk of the staple and income needs.

At San Jorge, two agricultural systems are practiced concurrently: Short fallow swidden agroforesty and flood-zone seasonal farming. The former is practiced on the restinga alta, while the latter is found on the sand and mud bars, and the restinga baja. The above strategy should not be viewed as universal on the floodplains, but one of the many variations.

Short Fallow Swidden Agroforestry

The restinga alta swidden agroforestry at San Jorge is similar to those found elsewhere in the Peruvian Amazon (Denevan et al., 1984; Denevan and Padoch, 1988; Hiraoka, 1986). A high forest or regrowth is cleared and a combination of manioc and plantains/bananas are planted. Other crops, many of them fruit trees, are interplanted among the manioc-plantains over a period of several months. The actual mix of cultigens varies with the farmers' preferences and availability of planting stocks. Harvesting begins approximately 80–90 days after sowing, when short-cycled crops like maize and beans are ready for picking, and continues for approximately 10 years. Weed and insect control are attempted through the second or third year. As silting through flooding does not occur, and artificial manuring is not attempted, yields decline and rank growth control becomes increasingly time-consuming. At such a point, *chacras* or fields are left for the natural succession to proceed. However, as Denevan, et al. (1984), Hiraoka (1986), and Padoch, et al. (1985) point out, chacras are not abandoned, since they continue to produce a variety of items. This agroforest stage is called a *purma* by the ribereños. *Caimito* (*Chrysophyllum caimito*), guaba, peach palm (*Bactris gasipaes*), plantains, and others are produced. Labor inputs are limited, but are necessary for a number of tasks. For example, the base of fruit trees are weeded, and the plantains are propped to avoid falling to the ground. The agroforest, rich in seeds, fruit, and tubers, is covered by a dense vegetation; this provides an excellent feeding and protecting ground for animals known as *purmeros*. These semi-domesticated fauna are systematically harvested by the ribereños.

Purma hunting is important during the flood season, when fish, the main animal protein source of the ribereños, become dispersed on the floodforests and catches are small. Many of the purma's flora are also used for a variety of purposes. Plants produce fruit, medicine, fibers, and construction timber (Appendix A).

Reflecting the shortage of easily accessible chacra sites, the purmas are cleared in cycles that range between 5 and 10 years. According to the elders, most chacras in the vicinity of the caserío have been put into cultivation at least five times over the last 35–40 years. In the absence of time series data it is hard to substantiate, but some believe that the continuous reconversion of the purmas through the swidden is leading to a progressive deterioration of the yields with each cycle.

At San Jorge, the restinga alta chacras are viewed as one of the main sites for the production of their staples: manioc and plantains. In order to supply the household, each family clears and plants a new chacra every year or two. At the time of the survey, an average family held 5.4 fields on the restinga alta (Table 1). Of these, one was always in production, and the rest in various stages of growth ranging from newly opened chacras to agroforests. Chacras range in size between 0.2–1.5 ha, but the average field is about 0.4 ha in extent. Whenever possible, these gardens are located contiguously along the narrow levee, so that several plots can be visited in a single trip. The primary purpose of the chacras is to guarantee staple production, but increasingly, surpluses are being diverted for income generation. As different products are available during the year, they are sent to the market, often at the expense of household needs. For example, manioc and plantains from the chacras, yarina fronds, guabas, and caimitos from the purmas are sold. An adaptation to the market economy can be seen from the incorporation of cash crops like maize, or increased plantings of fruit like papaya in the swidden phase. Large scale fruit

Table 1
Number of Ribereño Plots by Ecological Zone, San Jorge

	Manioc, Maize, Plantains	Manioc, Plantains	Plantains	Purma	Rice	Vegetables, Melons Maize, Peanuts	Cow Pea
Restinga alta	16	31	12	109	–	–	–
Restinga baja	18	–	1	26	6	3	–
Barreal	–	–	–	–	3	–	–
Playa	–	–	–	–	–	–	4
Total number of farms	34	31	13	135	9	3	4

Notes: Average number of plots in crops/household = 3.03; average number of plots held/household = 7.38; average number of plots held/household on Restinga Alta = 5.40.

cultivation for the market, as in the altura agroforests has not developed yet in the bajo's swidden agroforests, but the inhabitants are experimenting with a number of items like pineapple, umarí, and guabas.

Restinga alta serves another major function for the San Jorginos, i.e., in the uniform distribution of labor during the year. Since activities on the dry levees are not seasonally dictated, ribereños spend the otherwise idle days of the flood season performing various tasks on the chacras. Other flood season activities exist, e.g., wage labor in the altura, logging in the flood forest, hunting, and aguaje fruit collecting, but none offers continuous employment for the entire family.

Seasonal Flood Zone Farming

One of the main components of floodplain subsistence is the cultivation of lands subjected to flooding. At San Jorge, each household manages an average of 2.0 plots in the flood zone, each between 0.3–1.2 ha in area. Yearly, floodwaters may deposit as much as 1.5 m of sediments along the riparian lands adjoining the river. The quantity and nature of the sediments vary with the hydrodynamics and location within the plain. Soils are usually basic in reaction, and they are relatively rich in plant macronutrients, except phosphorus (Appendix B). These edaphic resources occur on the restingas bajas, and barreales and playas.

In spite of the adequate nutrient levels in the soils, a major drawback of the area is the short growing season. The flood zone biotopes are dry for a maximum of nine months. This precludes the cultivation of perennial crops, except those that are flood-tolerant. According to the residents and the fluvial data at Iquitos, the unusually high and long-lasting floods of the last decade have destroyed crops like plantains, *taperiba* (*Spondias mombin*), and *mamey* (*Syzygium malaccensis*), that once lined the riverfront restingas bajas. These plants are adapted to the brief and shallow inundations of approximately two months duration.

The anomalous hydrological behavior and economics have led ribereños to increasingly concentrate on short-cycled crops, especially cereals like rice, maize, beans, and vegetables like tomato, cucumber, and melons. The recent focus on cash crops, especially rice and vegetables, is due in large measure to subsidized credit offered by the government or market stimuli by an increasingly urbanized population (Chibnik, 1986).

Activities on the bottomlands are largely determined by the seasonal rhythm of the Amazon. Restingas bajas emerge in early June. If the chacra was deforested in the previous year, planting begins immediately.

In the past, the chacras were intercropped with manioc, maize, plantains, beans, peanuts, and some vegetables. With increasing commercialization, monocultures are becoming the dominant form of land use. Weed control is a time-consuming task on the restinga baja. When water begins to subside, water-borne seeds and vegetatively propagating plants are left on the restingas. As they compete vigorously with the cultivars, one to two weedings are required prior to the onset of the next flood. The final activity on the bajo is called *despejo,* the slashing of unwanted species prior to the floods. The purpose is to assure that the sediments will bury the weed remains and that a clear garden will emerge in the following season.

The events on the barreales and playas are similar to those on the restingas bajas, except for the shorter growing season. The mud and sand bars are dry for only five months. These biotopes are also unstable and the proportion of sand and mud changes every year in response to water dynamics. In spite of the drawbacks, competition for the ephemeral terrains is intense, especially on the barreales. Attempts to control barreal lands often lead to inter-caserío conflicts. It is the desirability of the barreales for the cultivation of rice that leads to such discords. Rice is the only crop in the region with a fixed price. In addition, subsidized loans exist for the production of this cereal. Such a credit-marketing structure, and the fact that barreales require very limited vegetation clearing labor, have led to the intense race to acquire the barreales. On the barreal fronting San Jorge, as elsewhere in the Peruvian Amazon, rice is grown monoculturally. The playas, on the other hand, are less sought after since their sandy soils are less productive, and despite their proximity to water table, capillary activities are not well developed and droughts do occur. This biotope is usually planted with peanuts, cow peas, and occasionally melons and maize, and its products are primarily intended for home consumption.

Ribereño Energetics

San Jorginos produce a variety of crops, but their main emphasis is the cultivation of manioc and plantains that provides about 80 percent of the calory needs. Rice is the major cash crop, and only a small fraction of it is consumed in the caserío. Other items like maize, taro, beans, and fruit provide the rest of the dietary variety, along with forest and aquatic products. All activities related to agriculture, including deforestation with axes and machetes, burning of felled vegetation, planting with digging sticks, weeding with machete, harvesting with knives and machetes, and transporting with foot or canoe, are still done manually.

Energy expenditure estimates for the chacras on the restinga alta, restinga baja, and barreal are presented in Table 2. It can be observed

Table 2
Ribereño Agricultural Activities and Energy Expenditures, San Jorge[a]

| | Restinga Baja | | | | Barreal | | Restinga Alta | | | |
| | Rice | | Manioc, Maize | | Rice | | Manioc, Plantain (Monte) | | Manioc, Plantain (Purma) | |
Activities	hrs work	kcal eq	hrs work	kcal eq	hrs work	kcal eq	hrs work	kcal eq	hrs work	kcal eq
Undergrowth cutting	70	35,700	70	35,700	–	–	110	56,100	60	30,600
Tree cutting	160	71,400	160	71,400	–	–	109	55,590	90	45,900
Firing	4	1,200	4	1,200	–	–	4	1,200	4	1,200
Secondary burn	210	88,200	210	88,200	–	–	160	67,200	95	39,900
Planting	70	29,400	70	29,400	9	3,780	280	117,600	280	117,600
Bird scaring	180	46,440	–	–	180	46,440	–	–	–	–
Weed removal	210	75,600	210	75,600	140	50,400	225	81,000	335	120,600
Plantain care	–	–	–	–	–	–	70	29,400	70	29,400
Weed slashing	140	58,800	140	58,800	70	29,400	–	–	–	–
Harvesting	280	117,600	240	100,800	325	136,500	3,450	1,449,000	3,450	1,449,000
Storage building construction	42	17,640	–	–	42	17,640	–	–	–	–
Travel to field and crop transport	360	92,880	360	92,880	360	129,600	900	378,000	720	302,400
Total	1,706	634,860	1,464	553,980	1,126	413,760	5,308	2,613,090	5,104	2,136,600

[a] Energy expenditure calculations are based on the following figures: undergrowth and tree cutting = 510 kcal/hr; secondary burn, planting, weed slashing, plantain care, harvesting, and storage building construction = 420 kcal/hr; bird scaring, travel and crop transport = 258 kcal/hr; weeding = 360 kcal/hr.

that the highest labor inputs occur on the flood-free natural levees of the restinga alta where swidden-agroforestry is practiced. Table 3 summarizes the input-output data and presents information on labor productivity in each of the main agricultural biotopes. It is seen that the greatest returns on labor are attained on the periodically inundated levees and mud bars where manioc and rice are cultivated.

Assuming that a ribereño adult expends 2,600 kcal and a child 2,000 kcal per day, an average household with 6.9 members at San Jorge requires about 15,000 kcal of food. If 80 percent of the intake derives from manioc and plantains, 12,000 kcal are needed. This caloric requirement can be satisfied by 3.0 hrs of labor by an adult in a restinga alta chacra, or roughly 1.4 hrs/day on the restinga baja. On the other hand, if rice was diverted for subsistence purposes, an adult would need approximately 4.8 hrs of his efforts in the restinga baja or 1.8 hrs on the barreal. These figures suggest that the time required for subsistence production on the baja is relatively small, except for rice cultivation on the restinga baja. In terms of hours of effort for raising manioc and plantains, they are comparable to the findings of Bergman (1980:130), and Clark and Uhl (1987:9). The choice of manioc and plantains for staples enables the ribereños to efficiently secure their basic energy needs. This allows ribereños the time necessary for fishing (the main animal protein-getting activity), collecting of forest products, and leisure.

The management of chacras on both the flooded and non-flooded biotopes, whose combined area rarely exceed 1.5 ha, usually produce beyond the household requirements. Since surpluses occur in pulses, and not continuously during the year, the excesses are either exchanged with other villagers to guarantee a steady supply of food, or traded with altura inhabitants. For example, ribereños of the altura who produce fruits like umarí, cashew, Brazil nut (*Bertolletia excelsa*), and pineapples exchange them for plantains, cowpeas, and maize that are difficult to cultivate on the oxisols and ultisols. More recently, the surpluses are being diverted to the markets of Iquitos.

Nutritionally, the cultivation of crops on the inundation zone adds to the seasonal variation of crops, and to the dietary value of food intake among the residents. The high soil fertility level supports nutrient rich cereals like beans, rice, and maize on a continuous base. The increasing change in land use from varied food items to rice and vegetables for sale are creating two unwanted consequences. The impoverishment of the diet is the first. Practically all the rice is raised for sale. Secondly, the specialization of rice seasonally divert all the available labor to care for this crop, and thus, subsistence cultivation suffers. As the basic energy sources falter, food energy is imported from

Table 3
Ribereño Labor Productivity by Land Type and Crop

Location and Products	Output		Input		Labor Productivity	
	kg/ha	kcal	hrs/ha	kcal	kcal/ha	kcal/hr
Restinga Alta						
Manioc	14,647/24 mos[a]	15,379,350[b]	5,308	2,613,090	21,406,143	4,033
Plantains	14,187/30 mos	8,639,883[b]				
Restinga Baja						
Manioc	12,470/12 mos[a]	13,093,500[b]	1,464	553,980	12,539,520	8,565
Restinga Baja						
Rice	2,000/12 mos[c]	4,900,000[d]	1,706	634,860	4,265,140	2,500
Barreal						
Rice	3,200/12 mos	7,840,000	1,126	413,760	7,426,240	6,595

[a] Wet weight.
[b] Wet weight reduced by 30 percent to account for the skin portion. Manioc contains 150 kcal/100g, while plantains contain 87 kcal/100g.
[c] Husked weight.
[d] Milled rice equivalent is calculated at 70 percent of husked grain. Energy yield is calculated at 350 kcal/100g.

Table 4
Restinga Baja Rice Production Cost-Benefit Accounting (I$/ha)

Expenses	
Lodging and subsistence in Iquitos to secure loan and deliver rice	810.00
Production costs	
Deforestation	900.00
Firing	30.00
Secondary firing	900.00
Planting	300.00
Weed removal	1,500.00
Seed stock	301.50
Food for workers	2,107.50
Harvest	2,000.00
Storage shed construction	180.00
Transportation	1,265.00
Discount at the mill for grain breakage and humidity	1,040.00
Credit cost (3 months)	255.55
Total production cost	11,589.55
Income	
Sale of grain (2,000 kg, I$6.70/kg)	13,400.00
Less production-related cost	(11,589.55)
Net income per hectare	1,810.45

the urban markets. Within the last five years, the number of *chinganas* or small stores has increased from one to five in San Jorge, and each now stocks a variety of processed food items.

The transformation of former chacras and flood forests into cash cropping sites is not very rewarding economically either. A one hectare rice field on the restinga baja, cleared from tall forest is used for illustration (Table 4). The production cost, including site preparation, planting, harvesting, transporting, and financing, totals I$ 11,589.55.[1] The yield, estimated at 2 tons/ha (in husk) and purchased at the official price of I$ 6.70/kg, produces a gross income of I$ 13,400.00. The net income is thus I$ 1,810.00/ha (US $50.28/ha). Despite the limited net returns (15.6%) the excitement of receiving a lump sum at the time of rice delivery at the mill is sufficient inducement for many ribereños to concentrate increasingly on cash crop production. The progressive involvement with the market economy and the lure of purchasing manufactured goods are undoubtedly strong motivating factors.

Floodplain Farming and Environmental Stability

An attempt is made to evaluate the sustainability of present ribereño farming systems. Sustained-yield agriculture, would by extension imply resource management techniques without ecological disruptions. For the current inhabitants, environmental stability is of major significance since they still depend economically to a large extent on the resources from the forest and aquatic environments. The sustainability of farming is based on a review of production levels, farmland availability, and environmental changes.

Agricultural Output of the Ribereños

Floodplain agricultural output is relatively high, even when compared to world averages. The high returns have traditionally supported a large population on the floodplain zone. Actual population is hard to ascertain, but settlements over a league (about 6 km) in extent were found along the floodplain as late as 1639, almost a century after Orellana's trip, when the native population was already declining (Acuña, 1641:80). Based on historical and archeological evidences, Denevan (1976:218) proposes that the floodplains of large rivers supported as many as 28 persons per square kilometer at the time of European contact. Such a density would have been about six times as large as the present population of the floodplains around San Jorge. As seen above, the fortuitous combination of resource management techniques like multiple biotope integration and swidden agroforestry, annual deposition of fertile silts on the flood zone, and limited pressures on flood forests and aquatic resources enabled the food production on a sustained basis.

The production level of the main staples and cash crop are briefly illustrated. Estimates of manioc output from the chacras were made by weighing the tubers from 12 sample sites from the restinga alta, and five from the restinga baja. The number and weight of tubers for each plant within 10×10 m sample plots were determined. Once the average weight and number of plants in each grid were determined, they were used to extrapolate the figures for one hectare. The fields studied on the restinga alta were those converted from purmas, the most common method of establishing a chacra. The normal first manioc yield in a 9-month old chacra is 9.45 metric tons wet weight/hectare (t/ha), and the *cutipa* or second harvest produces 5.20 t/ha. Clark and Uhl (1987) present the figure of 4.7 t/ha from their study site in Venezuela. According to Cock (1982), the world average is 8.2 t/ha. The high output on the restinga alta is attributable to the nature of floodplain soils. Although partially leached of their nutrients, the high levee soils of recent geological deposition are superior in both structure and nutrient content to the oxisols and ultisols where most manioc is grown. On the restinga baja, the comparable figures are 12.47 tons/ha for a 7-month old chacra; an output approximately 50 percent higher than the world average.

Table 5
Farmland at San Jorge

Landform	Area (ha)	Percentage of Total Area
Restinga alta	600	11.4
Restinga baja	1,080	20.6
Along the river	180	3.4
Inland	900	17.2
Barreal and playa	20	0.4
In-floodplain water bodies and		
poorly drained terrain	3,540	67.5
Total caserío area	5,240	99.9

Plantain output from chacras on the restinga alta, conducted in similar 10 × 10 m plots by weighing the fruit in each stem, were extrapolated for one hectare plots. The nine fields studied indicated a yield of 14.19 t/ha during three harvests, over a period of 30 months. Bergman (1980) provides a figure of 5.88 t/ha from his study of Panaillo on the Ucayali River, but his findings refer to a single harvest. A figure comparable to that of San Jorge may have resulted, if outputs had been measured over three harvests. Surveys of rice yields on the restinga baja and barreal were made on site at the time of harvests. Information was also obtained from interviews. As previously indicated, the average output from the restinga baja is 2.0 t/ha, while that from the barreal is 3.2 t/ha. If one considers that the above figures are obtained without external energy subsidies, it is possible to state that they are remarkable even by world standards.

Cropland Available at San Jorge

As seen above, the floodplain at San Jorge consists of heterogeneous, low-lying terrains. Roughly 8 percent of caserío area consists of in-floodplain water bodies like lakes and ravines. Another 60 percent is taken up by poorly drained aguajal, tahuampas and swampy terrain around the margin of lakes (Table 5). The remaining 32 percent of a total of 52 km² floodplain resource zone, composed of the restingas, is available for crop cultivation under the present farming systems. Of the remaining 16.6 km² or 1,660 ha, only a thin strip of restinga baja, i.e., 180 ha, can be considered as the richest land (*restinga baja de orilla*). Mud and sand banks available to San Jorginos amount to 20 ha. The remaining 1,500 ha are composed of restingas altas occupying an estimated 600 ha, and inland restingas bajas taking up another 900 ha. Although not as productive as the riparian restingas, those on the interior can be put seasonally into crops if short fallows of approximately five years are included after three years of cultivation.

Comparative studies of cropland availability on the floodplains were made on nearby caseríos, and they indicate that cropping areas along the recently deposited alluvial areas are uniformly restricted. Exceptions occur where the altura adjoins the bajo. The above figures indicate that 461.25 ha are available annually to the residents, if fallowing terrain is discounted. Of these, 311.25 ha occur on the flood zone, but only 32.5 ha are currently in use. This suggests a considerable amount of land for future expansion, if farming is the sole concern.

Fallowed Land

Sustained-yield agriculture at San Jorge is based on the systematic fallowing of restingas alta plots, and on the annual siltation of restinga bajas, barreales, and playas. Thus, flood zone biotopes can be cultivated yearly, with relatively stable returns, while chacras on the restinga alta are converted to agroforests or fallowed in natural regrowth to restitute nutrients to the soils.

Ribereños are fully aware of the role of fallowing; however, opinions vary on a standard fallow period. Many believe that a minimum of five years is necessary prior to reconversion into a chacra. This rest period is said to be sufficient for an adequate production of manioc and plantains. In reality, many chacras are opened from 5–6 year old purmas. Others are of the opinion that 10–15 years are minimally needed for satisfactory yields. Findings on the subject are not uniform either. Based on Saldarriaga's study (1985) of Upper Rio Negro's plant biomass production in abandoned plots, Clark and Uhl (1987) adopt the view that 50 years should be the minimum fallow necessary for swidden plots on their research area. The Boras of Northeast Peru fallows a minimum of 10 years (Denevan and Treacy, 1988:8). Vasey (1979) is of the opinion that shifting cultivators in Asia and Africa rest their fields between 5–15 years. Although further studies are needed, it is possible that the nature of floodplain soils, the inclusion of Leguminosae like *Inga edulis,* and the practice of coppicing the desirable plants may contribute to the rapid nutrient recovery in the restinga alta forests. For this study, the figure of 10 years is taken to be the minimum fallow period (the respondents' average age of agroforest to field reconversion). With a 10-year agroforest or natural regrowth cycle, following a 30-month swidden, 150 ha are made available every year to the inhabitants for cropping, out of a total of 600 ha of restinga alta land. Overall, about 530 ha are made available for farming each year in the four major ecological zones (Table 6). Current uses amount

Table 6
Annual Available Farmland at San Jorge

	Area (ha)
Restinga alta swidden agroforest cycle	
Swidden use: 30 months	
Agroforest use: 120 months	
(600 ha)(30 mo)/120 mo =	150
Restinga baja (inland levees)	
Swidden use: 12 months	
Fallow: 60 months	
(900 ha)(12 mo)/60 mo =	180
Restinga baja (along the river)	180
Barreal and playa	20
Total	530

to approximately 27.4 ha. per year. This allows the bulk of the restingas altas to be left in monte or fallows.

Environmental Changes

In addition to farming, ribereño livelihood has traditionally been based on the exploitation of a variety of floodforest products. As agriculture was performed on a small scale, and floral exploitation cycles for exports were ephemeral, disturbance of the flood forest was selective but minor. In contrast, the current activities may bring about long-lasting changes on the floodplain biota.

With the rapid urban migration of ribereños, especially to Iquitos, rural traditions and culinary tastes have been transferred to the city. In order to supply these low-income consumers with "homeland" cuisine, ribereños devote an increasing proportion of their time to collect forest products that range from fruits, nuts, vines, and barks, to thatching and construction materials. Timber extraction, under contract to Iquitos and Pucallpa saw mills and plywood plants, is also on the rise as new technologies and machines enable the use of ever greater number of species. Desirable trees like mahogany (*Swietenia macrophylla*) and tropical cedar (*Cedrella spp.*) for cabinetry and canoe-making can no longer be found within a 2–3 km zone from the river, and along other water bodies that allow access to the main stream.

The removal of flora and fauna is also greatly facilitated by the breakdown of culturally-encoded resource conservation practices. Belief in forest and aquatic super natural beings like *yacu maman, shapshico,* and *sacha runa,* or spirits that once served to moderate the use of floodplain resources are no longer taken seriously by the younger villagers or outsiders without such environmental ethics and beliefs.

Expansion of agricultural activities on the bajo, especially rice, poses a major threat to the flood forest and the fauna dependent on it. Overhunting and habitat destruction, especially along the easily accessible riverine zone, have virtually eliminated many large animals, including the *capybara* (*Hydrochoerus hidrochaeris*), tapir, peccary (*Tayassu* spp.), and *cayman* (*Melanososochus niger*). River turtles (*Podocnemis* spp.) have largely disappeared from the region, just as manatees were overharvested by the early 1950s. Fish is still plentiful at San Jorge, but prized ones like *paiche* (*Arapaima gigas*), *gamitana* (*Colossoma macropomum*), and *paco* (*Colossoma bidens*) are now caught only on rare occasions. Aside from increased pressure on fisheries, the removal of floral cover from the floodplains is certain to affect many fish populations. As the cultivation of rice on the barreales and restingas bajas illustrates, the conversion of flood forests and chicozal-gramalotal for agricultural use is likely to accelerate. The same flood forests adjoining the trunk stream, however, are important seasonal feeding grounds for many Characins and catfishes, the two groups accounting for approximately 80 percent of the described species. Nuts, seeds, and fruit-bearing trees, keyed to ripen during the high-water season, serve as feed sources. The same environment is also significant for detritivorous and insectivorous species during the flood season. In addition, fish along with the flood water are the main dispersal agents of seeds in the inundated forest. The catfish, unable to crush the seeds they consume, serve to disseminate some of the flood forest flora (Goulding, 1980, 1985). Cattle and water buffaloes, kept in a small scale in dispersed locations of the bajo and altura, are likely to increase in number due to governmental encouragement and subsidies intended to decrease regional beef shortages. Combined with commercial fisheries and agriculture, these activities will invariably modify the floodplain ecosystem and bring changes in the ichthyofauna, the main source of animal proteins for the ribereños.

Conclusions and Recommendations

Farming at San Jorge indicates that the ribereños developed agricultural systems to utilize the diverse floodplains on a sustained basis. Swidden agroforestry is practiced on the dry levees. Aside from supplying the major staples, these chacras also contribute a variety of fruits, animal proteins, medicinal plants, and construction materials during the agroforest stage. The flood-prone restingas bajas, barreales, and playas have a growing season of less than nine months per year, but plant nutrients are renewed through floods. Most long-cycled crops cannot be cultivated, but yields of short-cycled plants are relatively high. In addition, the ability of the biotopes to produce nutrient-rich cereals serves to complement the restingas altas, where soils are able to support mostly carbohydrate-rich crops. Thus, the integrated management of multiple biotopes, the cultivation of items suited to each biotope, and the systematic harvests of flora and fauna from the agroforests, have supplied the ribereños with abundant and high quality food, fiber, and other needs on a sustained basis.

The floodplain farming, as practiced by the ribereños of San Jorge, illustrates the possibilities and limitations of adopting traditional agricultural systems to devise sustained-yield techniques compatible with contemporary needs and realities. The adoption of a farming system through inroads of an existing one, especially one where market adaptations have been made, is probably the most cost effective and ecologically sound.

The ribereño experience offers the following valuable guidelines:

1. The farming operations are best applied to small-scale agriculture. Central decision-making is difficult, as the numerous activities in gardens located in diverse biotopes require flexibility in operations. The existing systems realize fully the different abilities of individual members within a household.

2. As the floodplain is segmented into diverse biotopes, resource allocation plans have to take into account this geographical reality, and attempt to divide the resource base so that every family would have access to a number of biotopes. Emphasis should be placed in utilizing the varied terrain in an integrated manner, a strategy common among many peasant groups, including those of the Peruvian Andes (Brush, 1976, 1977).

3. The natural advantages of each biotope have to be realized in production planning. In a region where external sources of chemicals and energy subsidies are still uneconomical and difficult to acquire, attempts should be directed to maximize the potentials of each biotope. For example, microterrains on the flood-zone should be destined for protein-rich cereals and high value vegetables and fruit, while nutrient-deficient high levees be planned for carbohydrate production.

4. The possibilities to increase protein production on land are still unrealized. Barnyard fowl and hogs as scavengers can increase the output of animal proteins without much investments in time and effort, if kept on a small scale. Ribereños already keep fowl and occasionally some hogs, but without sustained technical advice from extension agents the animal population varies and are subject to frequent pest outbreaks. Improved management potentials of the agroforests for faunal produc-

tion, especially caviomorphs, exist. Increased supply of feed through protection of native species and variety in planted species, so as to offer continuous supply of food, would enable the systematic harvest of agroforest purmeros. Another source of amino acids is the flood zone. Heavier emphasis on leguminous cereals, e.g., soy beans, a variety of beans, and maize, could contribute to increase protein production. This is an important factor, since ribereños do not have an aversion to the consumption of beans. Such measures could possibly lessen the pressures on fisheries and augment total protein output from land biotopes.

5. Protection and conservation of flood forests and aquatic environments are important considerations for sustained-yield farming and subsistence on the floodplains. As our knowledge of Amazonian floodplain ecology is still limited, measures have to be taken to limit uncontrolled developments. The expansion of ranching operations, the recent introduction of water buffaloes in the region, the increased planting of rice on the restingas bajas, the logging operations, and the continuous destruction of aguajales, are diminishing the habitats for the floodplain flora and fauna, many of which have served as important resources for the ribereños. Present pressures are greatest on the biotopes adjoining the river, the habitats undergoing the most changes. Changes in marketing structure to give incentives to other crops, dispersal of cropping areas into inland restingas bajas, and greater intensification maybe some of the solutions.

Although the Amazonian floodplains offer potentials for increased agricultural production and possibilities for accomodating a large population, their development should proceed with caution. Although an increasing body of knowledge is accumulating, our current understanding of floodplain man-environment relations is far from adequate. This is especially so, because of the diverse nature of the floodplains. To avoid the costly environmental damages analogous to those of interfluves, the large scale conversion of the bajo should await further findings.

Acknowledgments

Financial support for field data collection was provided by the Millersville University Grants Committee and the National Geographic Society. I am grateful for both entities. Centro Amazonico de Antropología y Aplicación Práctica (CAAAP) gave me institutional support while in Iquitos. I am indebted to the ribereños of San Jorge and Tamshiyacu for introducing and teaching me about the fascinating world of the ribereños and the floodplain. Gratitude is owed to Margaret

Meszaros for typing the manuscript, and to Eiji Matsumoto and Teiji Watanabe for the soil analyses.

Notes

1. The exchange rate of the U.S. Dollar to the Peruvian Inti in August 1987 was at US$ 1.00 = I$ 36.00.

References

Acuña, C. 1641, Nuevo descubrimiento del gran río del Amazonas, en el año 1639. Pages 29–102 *in* Informes de jesuitas en el Amazonas 1660–1684, Monumenta Amazonica, B1, IIAP-CETA, Iquitos.

Bergman, R. 1980. Amazon economics: The simplicity of Shipibo indian wealth, Dellplain Latin American Studies no.6, University Microfilms, Ann Arbor.

Brush, S. 1976. Man's use of an Andean ecosystem. Human Ecology 4: 147–166.

――――― . 1977. Mountain, field, and family: The economy and human ecology of an Andean valley. University of Pennsylvania Press, Philadelphia.

Chibnik, M. 1986. New sources of credit in Peruvian Amazonian communities. Paper presented at the meeting of the American Anthropological Association, Philadelphia, December 7.

Clark, K. and C. Uhl. 1987. Farming, fishing, and fire in the history of the Upper Río Negro region of Venezuela. Human Ecology 15: 1–26.

Cock, J.H. 1982. Cassava: A basic energy source in the tropics. Science 218: 755–762.

Denevan, W.M. 1976. The aboriginal population of Amazonia. Pages 205-234 *in* W.M. Denevan (ed.), The native population of the Americas in 1492. University of Wisconsin Press, Madison.

Denevan, W.M., J.M. Treacy, J.B. Alcorn, C. Padoch, J. Denslow, and S. Flores-Paitán. 1984. Indigenous agroforestry in the Peruvian Amazon: Bora indian management of swidden fallow. Interciencia 9: 346–357.

―――――and C. Padoch (eds.). 1988. Swidden-fallow agroforestry in the Peruvian Amazon. Advances in Economic Botany vol. 5, New York Botanical Garden, New York.

―――――and J. Treacy. 1988. Young managed fallows at Brillo Nuevo. Pages 8–46 *in* W.M. Denevan and C. Padoch (eds.), Swidden-fallow agroforestry in the Peruvian Amazon. Advances in Economic Botany vol. 5, New York Botanical Garden, New York.

Fearnside, P. 1982. Deforestation in the Brazilian Amazon: how fast is it occurring? Interciencia 7: 82–88.

Goodland, R. and H. Irwin. 1975. Amazon jungle: green hell to red desert, Elsevier, New York.

Goulding, M. 1980. The fishes and the forest: Explorations in Amazonian natural history, University of California Press, Berkeley.

———. 1981. Man and fisheries on an Amazonian frontier. Developments in Hydrobiology 4, Dr. W. Junk, Pub., The Hague.

———. 1985. Forest fishes of the Amazon. Pages 267–276 in G.T. Prance and T.E. Lovejoy (eds.), Key Environments, Amazonia. Pergamon Press, Oxford.

Herndon, W.L. 1952, Exploration of the valley of the Amazon. McGraw-Hill, New York.

Hiraoka, Mário. 1985a. Floodplain farming in the Peruvian Amazon. Geographical Review of Japan (Series B) 58: 1–23.

———. 1985b. Changing floodplain livelihood patterns in the Peruvian Amazon. Tsukuba Studies in Human Geography 9: 243–275.

———. 1986. Zonation of mestizo farming systems in Northeast Peru. National Geographic Research 2: 354–371.

Moran, E. F. 1974. The adaptive system of the Amazonian caboclo. Pages 136–159 in C. Wagley (ed.), Man in the Amazon. University of Florida Press, Gainesville.

———. 1981. Developing the Amazon. Indiana University Press, Bloomington.

———. 1983. The dilemma of Amazonian development. Westview Press, Boulder.

Padoch, C., J. Chota-Inuma, W. De Jong, J. Unruh. 1985. Amazonian agroforestry: A market-oriented system in Peru. Agroforestry Systems 3: 47–58.

Padoch, C. 1986. The campesinos of Santa Rosa: History and ethnicity in an Amazonian community. Paper presented at the meeting of the American Anthropological Association, Philadelphia, December 7.

———. In press, Caboclos and ribereños: the forgotten Amazonians.

———. and W. De Jong. In press. Santa Rosa: The impact of forest product trade on an Amazonian village.

Parker, E.P. 1981. Cultural ecology and change: A caboclo várzea community in the Brazilian Amazon. Ph.D. dissertation, University of Colorado, Boulder.

Pires, J.M. and G.T. Prance. 1977. The Amazon forest: A natural heritage to be preserved. Pages 158–194 in Extinction is forever symposium. New York Botanical Garden, New York.

Posey, D. 1983. The indigenous ecological knowledge and development of the Amazon. Pages 225–258 in E.F. Moran (ed.), The dilemma of Amazonian development, Westview Press, Boulder.

———. J. Frechione, J. Eddins, L.F. Silva. 1984. Ethnoecology as applied anthropology in Amazonian development. Human Organization 43: 95–107.

Putzer, H. 1984. The geological evolution of the Amazon basin and its mineral resources. Pages 15–46 in H. Sioli (ed.), The Amazon limnology and landscape ecology of a mighty tropical river and its basin. Dr. W. Junk, Pub., Dordrecht.

Raimondi, A. 1907. Estudio de la provincia litoral de Loreto por Dr. Antonio Raimondi. Pages 119–278 in C. Larraburre i Correa (comp.), Vol. 7. Cóleccion de leyes, decretos, resoluciones i otros documentos oficiales referentes al departamento de Loreto. La Opinión Nacional, Lima.

Ross, E.B. 1978. The evolution of the Amazonian peasantry. Journal of Latin American Studies 10: 193–218.

Saldarriaga, J. 1985. Forest succession in the Upper Rio Negro of Colombia and Venezuela. Ph.D. dissertation, University of Tennessee, Knoxville.

San Román, J. 1975. Perfiles históricos de la amazonía peruana. Paulinas-CETA.

Stocks, A. 1981. Los nativos invisibles. CAAAP, Lima.

Smith, N.J.H. 1982. Rainforest corridors: The transamazon colonization scheme. University of California Press, Berkeley.

Smyth, W. and F. Lowe. 1836. Narrative of a journey from Lima to Pará across the Andes and down the Amazon. Milford House, Boston.

Vasey, D.E. 1979. Population and agricultural intensity in the humid tropics. Human Ecology 7: 269–283.

Appendix A
Flora and Fauna of Major Economic Value to Ribereños from the Purma

Common Name	Scientific Name	Uses
Flora		
Atadijo	*Croton* sp.	Construction
Bijau de purma	*Heliconia* sp.	Food wrapping, edible root
Bolaina	*Luehea tessmanii*	Beverage flavoring
Capinurí	*Rudgea cephalanta*	Medicinal, fuel
Capirona	*Calycophyllum* sp.	Medicinal
Cotochupan	*Inga plumifera*	Food
Cumala huasca	*Ipomoea phillomega*	Fiber
Espintana	*Anaxagorea* sp.	Construction
Huaira caspi	*Cedrelinga catenaeformis*	Medicinal
Mullaca	*Clidemia hirta*	Food
Ojé	*Ficus glabrata*	Medicinal
Pashaco	*Schizolobium excelsum*	Fuel, charcoal
Pichana	*Sida* sp.	Broom
Pichirina	*Vismia* sp.	Construction, fuel, charcoal
Shimbillo	*Inga* sp.	Food, fuel, charcoal
Sucova	?	Medicinal
Topa	*Ochroma* sp.	Fiber, raft
Ubos	*Spondias* sp.	Food
Yarina	*Phytelephas macrocarpa*	Food, thatch
Fauna		
Abeja	*Meliponida* sp.	Food
Añuje	*Dasyprocta amazonensis*	Food
Carachupa	*Dasypus novemcinctus*	Food
Majás	*Cuniculus paca*	Food
Motelo	*Testudo tabulata*	Food
Paloma de monte	?	Food
Punchana	*Myoprocta bratti*	Food
Sacha cuy	?	Food
Siqui sapa	*Atta cephalotes*	Food

Appendix B
Soil Test Data, Selected Samples, San Jorge

Site	Depth (cm)	pH	Al	Ca	Fe	K	Mg	Mn	Na	P	Si	mg/500 mg	
							mg/L					C	N
New chacra from 5-year fallow, restinga alta	5	5.12	0.7	3.6	0.5	0.0	1.3	0.2	2.2	0.0	14.1	–	–
	20	4.42	1.3	0.0	0.9	0.0	0.3	0.0	2.8	0.0	28.1	–	–
	40	4.30	0.7	0.3	0.4	0.0	0.1	0.0	2.2	0.0	32.0	–	–
Platanal, 2-year-old, restinga alta	5	5.41	1.8	8.7	1.2	1.6	2.1	0.0	2.1	0.2	9.2	2.85	0.24
	20	5.33	6.3	0.3	3.8	1.6	0.5	0.1	1.4	0.2	14.2	0.47	0.05
Fallowed chacra, 10-year-old, restinga alta	5	6.01	0.1	4.4	0.0	0.0	2.5	0.3	1.9	0.0	17.0	–	–
	20	5.50	0.5	0.3	0.3	0.0	0.3	0.0	1.9	0.0	26.9	–	–
	40	5.40	1.1	0.1	0.5	2.3	0.0	0.0	2.0	0.0	31.9	–	–
Fallowed chacra, 6-year-old, restinga alta	5	5.51	1.1	13.1	4.5	3.6	5.6	1.5	2.1	0.4	6.7	4.19	0.36
	20	5.10	0.6	0.2	0.3	1.0	0.1	0.0	1.6	0.0	6.5	0.65	0.07
Restinga baja, along river	12	8.02	0.0	62.3	0.0	2.2	4.9	0.0	2.5	0.1	3.0	0.96	0.05
Restinga baja, along river	12	8.00	0.0	31.2	0.0	0.8	2.4	1.3	1.7	0.1	4.3	0.26	0.01
Barreal	20	7.32	1.2	17.5	0.8	0.9	1.7	0.0	2.5	0.1	20.5	0.19	0.02
Playa	20	7.50	0.5	19.3	0.2	1.3	1.5	0.0	1.7	0.4	16.8	0.23	0.00

6

Production and Profit in Agroforestry: An Example from the Peruvian Amazon

Christine Padoch and Wil de Jong

Introduction

It is becoming increasingly commonplace to suggest that indigenous Amazonian forms of resource use may offer sound models for use of tropical forest lands by non-indigenous peoples. Researchers have succeeded in convincingly demonstrating that tribal peoples have profound and detailed knowledge of agricultural soils, useful plants and animals, and productive agricultural and forestry techniques, that allows them a varied and good diet and abundant subsistence supplies (Boom, 1987; Prance, 1984; Posey, 1982, 1984, 1985; Vickers and Plowman, 1984; Denevan and Padoch, 1988; and many others). However, quantitative data showing traditional practices to be economically attractive alternatives for non-indigenous people are still scant. The production and income figures, as well as data on labor requirements, that would convincingly argue that these resource use patterns can also yield an acceptable living for peoples who need and want market goods are more difficult to find.

Data detailing the commercial value of traditional Amazonian production are often missing because many researchers have chosen to study the few remaining remote groups whose market participation is minimal. The urgency of studying such fast-changing groups is undeniable. However, the life style of many tribal peoples is very distant from the dreams and realities of non-tribal Amazonians, and their resource use patterns need to be substantially modified if they are to be acceptable to immigrants and others.

The difficulty of collecting reliable production statistics on traditional cultivation systems, particularly on agricultural or agroforestry practices that include a diversity of species and that yield a large variety of products, accounts for the scarcity of such important data. The quantification of necessary labor inputs is extraordinarily difficult in complex systems. A lack of studies on prices, markets, and marketing in the Amazon Basin contributes as well to the difficulty of realistically assessing the commercial value of resource production by tribal methods.

The recent increased interest in studying the resource use patterns of indigenous or long-resident, non-tribal communities of Amazonia, such as Peru's ribereños (Hiraoka, 1985a, 1985b, 1986; Padoch and de Jong, 1987; Padoch et al., 1985; de Jong, 1987) or the caboclos of Brazil (Anderson et al., 1986; Parker, 1985) may help fill this significant gap in the discussion of development alternatives for the region. These populations are usually more closely tied with local and even export markets than are tribal groups, and often have needs and expectations that more closely reflect national norms. There still exists little quantitative information on the subsistence and commercial production of these heretofore poorly studied Amazonians. This article is an effort to add to this small but increasing body of knowledge.

Resource Use Among Peru's Ribereños

The ribereños of Peru have been called the "forgotten Amazonians." Considering their demographic predominance in the lowland Peruvian Amazon, and the importance of their environmental knowledge of a greatly varied area, the paucity of studies of these non-tribal peoples is surprising. When they have been noticed, ribereños have often been mistaken for recent immigrants and have been erroneously labelled colonists. Most ribereños are the descendants of detribalized natives and of immigrants who arrived in the Amazonian lowlands of Peru in generations past, many during the great rubber boom of the turn of the century. Many ribereño communities are located within the floodplain of the Amazon River or its major tributaries and their agricultural activities include the farming of seasonally inundated lands. A great many ribereño villages also make use of *terra firme* areas, that is, lands that stand above the river's flood.

A great variety of resource management activities tends to characterize most ribereño households (Hiraoka, 1986; Padoch, 1988). These often include the cropping of rice, beans, and cowpeas on annually flooded mudflats and beaches, the growing of a variety of grains, root crops, fruits and other plants on the relatively fertile natural levees, and the tending of diverse swiddens above the floodplain. However, several recent research projects on both *varzea* (seasonally inundated) and *terra firme* resource use by ribereños (Padoch and de Jong, 1987;

Padoch et al., 1985) and Brazilian caboclos (Anderson et al., 1986) have focused not on these more familiar agricultural activities, but specifically on agroforestry systems employed by these populations.

Amazonian agroforestry systems include a diversity of production patterns, ranging from the most subtle manipulation of largely natural forests to increase their economic yields, to the creation and maintenance of near monocultural commercial orchards (Hecht, 1982; Padoch and de Jong, 1987). Many of these systems are cyclic and are based on an alternation of intensively cultivated swiddens and less intensively managed fallows. Such swidden-fallow agroforestry techniques are based on indigenous practices. Tribal forms of swidden-fallow use have been studied in several parts of the Amazon basin including areas in Peru (Denevan and Padoch, 1988), Ecuador (Irvine, 1985), and Brazil (Posey, 1982).

Studies we conducted between 1984 and 1987 in the region of Iquitos, Peru, as part of a cooperative program of research between the Instituto de Investigaciones de la Amazonia Peruana and the New York Botanical Garden's Institute of Economic Botany, found that a large number of variants of swidden-fallow agroforestry are employed by ribereño farmers (Padoch and de Jong, 1987). In this paper we report on agroforestry production in only one village, Santa Rosa.

Agroforestry in Santa Rosa

The village of Santa Rosa is located on the true right bank of the lower Ucayali River, about 150 kilometers upstream from Iquitos. In 1986 it had a population of slightly over 300 persons. The community is a very complex mix of descendants of several tribal groups (now acculturated), and of families of some European ancestry but with a long history in the region. Few, except the very youngest Santa Rosinos have lived in the community all their lives; the life histories of many include several long migrations and changes of residence (Padoch and de Jong, in press).

The village is quite new. Many of its older residents once worked on a large plantation just a kilometer or two upriver. That enterprise folded about thirty years ago and the community of Santa Rosa was founded a few years later. The location of the village itself has moved several times in the last few decades. The present village site is on *terra firme,* although Santa Rosa villagers also farm many lower floodplain areas, including mud-flats and beaches that flood annually, and natural levees that flood periodically. Requena, a town of approximately 10,000 inhabitants is only 20 kilometers up the Ucayali. The town offers a convenient, if rather limited, market for Santa Rosa's produce.

Most Santa Rosa farmers spend less than half their working time cultivating the *terra firme* swidden plots that we shall describe here. However, at any time, almost everyone has at least one producing swidden on a *terra firme* site, and many maintain agroforestry plots.

All Santa Rosa agroforestry fields are established in largely the same way: swiddens are cut and cleared. The practice of transforming some cut vegetation into charcoal, rather than burning it all in the field (Padoch et al., 1985), is not unknown, but is rare. The assemblage of annuals and semi-perennials first planted into a swidden is a combination of subsistence necessities with some crops destined for the market. Manioc and plantains are most frequently found in such fields, but other annual crops such as rice are often planted, and quickly growing fruits, such as pineapples and cocona (*Solanum sessiliflorum*), are very common first-year crops.

In some Santa Rosa swiddens planting and maintenance cease after two or three years of intensive annual crop production. These fields are then fallowed, often for a brief period of five to six years, and are then cleared again. However, most farmers in the village choose to turn at least one or two to their swidden fields into agroforestry plots. When such a decision is made, planting of fruit trees (often a large number of species), usually begins in the first year of swidden production, with more trees planted as the field ages.

In the years following first clearing and planting, both the species produced in the swidden and the management given the field change. Manioc production usually fades quickly after a second annual harvest, and plantains will not produce for long on poor *terra firme* soils. The intensive weeding that is given these crops in the first two years usually begins to slack off, becoming less frequent and more cursory in the third year or so. The plants that gradually take over a swidden from the third year onward neither demand nor receive the intensive management that annuals are given. This change in management and production has been interpreted by many previous researchers as "abandonment" of the field. Although some Santa Rosa fields may indeed be abandoned at this point, many others continue to be managed and to produce economically valuable products.

Some of the early fruiting trees that are interplanted with annual crops may be harvestable in the second or third year after original clearing; other fruits take much longer to produce. By about the fifth or sixth year many swiddens in Santa Rosa have become orchards. For many years thereafter, tree seedlings and even shade-tolerant herbaceous crops may continue to be planted into orchards. To an untrained eye the diversity of species present at this stage is visually confusing and such fields may easily be mistaken for unmanaged forest.

Production in Santa Rosa Agroforestry Fields

It is difficult to make any but the broadest generalizations about Santa Rosa orchards; both species composition and production are highly variable from one plot to another. Age of the field is an obvious factor in determining what and how much an orchard produces. There are, however, many other important determinants, including the amount and type of management a farmer chooses to employ in the field and his or her own particular choice of species to plant.

In order to determine the production of useful (mostly edible) products in Santa Rosa fields, we both regularly measured the production of useful products in a sample of orchards and asked farmers to keep diaries of their orchards' production. The difficulty of measuring production on highly diverse plots and persuading Santa Rosa residents to maintain accurate diaries over a years' time, allow us to reliably describe only a few of Santa Rosa's many agroforestry plots.

The data presented in Appendix A summarize one year's per hectare production of items with current commercial value in four agroforestry plots in Santa Rosa. These four plots obviously differ very greatly in the species they include and in the level of production that their owners obtain. While none can be said to be typical of Santa Rosa's agroforestry fields, each represents a stage or type of plot that is repeatedly found— with some variation—in the village and in surrounding communities.

Plot 1 is a managed fallow that was originally cleared and planted many years ago. The precise date of the plot's original establishment is not known to us, but twenty-five years ago is a reasonable estimate. The plot was first cleared by the present owner's father. Many of the larger trees now in the field were planted within the first few years after clearing and several of them are impressively large with diameters of 50 to 75 cm.

Plot 2 is a much younger swidden-fallow. It is only four years old, and intensive management of annuals ceased only about two years ago.

Plot 3 is a somewhat older fallow plot, approximately 6 years since initial felling and contains a slightly different array of plants than the previous example.

Plot 4 is approximately the same age as Plot 3, but the former has been subjected to much less maintenance in the last four years than the latter.

Diversity of Production in Agroforestry Fields

Differences in diversity and level of production among swidden-fallow agroforestry fields in Santa Rosa are quite dramatic. It must be emphasized that the data presented in Appendix A summarize only the per hectare 1986 production of items with some commercial value in the four plots sampled. Plants that actually yielded products with a significant market value are but a small fraction of all those found in any one of the fields studied. The total number of plant species as well as of all species that yielded useful, but not necessarily commercially important items, in any field is much higher.

Plot 1, an old, actively managed orchard, produced commercially valuable products of 23 different species. Most of these were fruits, but one tuber species and several construction timbers were also included. It should also be noted that many of the species included in this plot produced items that are not noted in Appendix A because there is little market demand for them in the region at present. For instance, *leche caspi* produces commercially valuable timber, bears an edible fruit, has a latex that is used as a medicine and as a gum for a variety of household needs, and was once an important industrial export of the Peruvian Amazon (Villarejo, 1979; Denevan and Padoch, 1988).

Plot 2, the youngest, was second in diversity of production with commercial materials from 15 species. Plot 3 produced items from 14 different species, and the unmanaged fallow, Plot 4, produced only five different kinds of products.

The differences in diversity among the fields studied can be attributed to many factors. Among the most important factors are the age of field, the selective clearing and weeding patterns followed by the farmer, and the amount and type of maintenance work subsequently put into the field. Without a precise history of each plot, it is often difficult to decide exactly which factor weighs most heavily in explaining the specific composition of any field.

Plot 1 with its long history of planting and other management is a very diverse orchard. Most of its production comes from tree species, and it contains very few herbaceous plants when compared with the other plots. However, there are a few non-tree crops in the old field. The owner, although he also maintains some younger swiddens, continues to propagate a few plants such as the tuber *daledale*, in this old orchard. Plot 2, on the other land, is a young field rich in pineapples, sugar cane, peppers, cocona, and other herbaceous crops.

With age, one can expect that Plot 2 will begin to increasingly resemble Plot 1. However, this will only be the case if maintenance practices, including subsequent planting and selective weeding, of the two plots are similar. Plot 1 is given a slash weeding once or twice a year. The only new plants that are spared in such cleanings are volunteers that grow from seeds of already established cultigens. Several tropical cedars and some of the individual fruit trees in Plot 1 are not strictly planted, as they result from such natural seeding. However, little or no forest regrowth is allowed to survive the weedings of Plot 1. Plot 4, in contrast, is a field where weeding almost stopped after the second year. Except for a little protection of plaintains, maintenance work has ceased. Forest regrowth has eliminated several less competitive plants, although some fruit trees, such as the *anonas* and *Ingas* continue to produce in quantity.

The variety of producing species in the highly diverse Plot 1 is also the result of the owner's long history of planting desirable species in the orchard. The owner is a man who likes plants and likes to see variety in his garden. The presence of some palms, such as the *huicungo* and *pona* is rather unusual and reflects his pride in this garden's diversity. No two Santa Rosa gardens are likely to incorporate exactly the same species.

Few studies of traditional Amazonian agroforestry have discussed in any but very general terms, the actual or potential commercial output of the systems studied. From those that have (Anderson et al. 1986; Padoch et al., 1985; Hiraoka, 1986) it is obvious that actual and/or potential commercial production in agroforestry plots can be substantial. The agroforestry systems that have been shown to produce commercial products in quantity differ greatly in diversity and mangement.

The market-oriented agroforestry plots we described in the village of Tamshiyacu along the Amazon River (Padoch et al., 1985), produce substantial quantities of fruit for the market in Iquitos. Most of the fields, however, are very low in diversity; some are near monocultures of umari (*Poraqueiba sericea*). The greater species diversity in the orchards of Santa Rosa may be attributable to the difference in marketing opportunties available to producers in the two communities. The city of Iquitos with its quarter-million inhabitants is quite easily reached from Tamshiyacu. Transport of fruit from Santa Rosa to Iquitos, on the other hand, is difficult, since cargo and passenger boats travel only twice a week and fares and cargo charges are high for local residents. Requena is the usual market for Santa Rosinos. Given the small population of Requena, production of a small quantity of many fruits, rather than specialization in one, is economically advantageous.

Maintenance and Labor Costs

Most discussions of agroforestry systems suggest that low labor expenditure is one of their particularly attractive aspects. However, little exact data on the labor costs of traditional agroforestry patterns is available, largely because of the difficulty of accurately measuring the work done on such diverse systems. Not only is it nearly impossible to assess the time put into the harvesting of a myriad of fruit species, but much of the maintenance of agroforestry fields is done in very short time segments and is often done casually.

Cleaning agroforestry plots, particularly older ones, often takes the form of only slash weeding around a few valuable trees. This operation can be done in a few minutes and may be quickly forgotten by the farmer. Much harvesting also takes place casually. Picking a few fruits is not perceived nor reported as work.

We attempted to estimate the amount of time farmers spend on their agroforestry plots by enlisting their help in noting their agricultural activities in diaries. The owners of Plots 1 and 2 were among the farmers who participated consistently in the labor survey.

The owner of Plot 1 reported that in 1986 he spent only a total of two and a half days working on this particular agroforestry field (1.75 days were spent in harvesting). The owner of plot 2 reported a more substantial 21 days spent working. Three days were devoted to planting, 13.5 to weeding, and five to harvesting.

We assume that the datum cited for Plot 1 is a low estimate. Since the plot is located adjacent to the farmer's house, we believe that much of the work done on the field is carried out in a sporadic, casual fashion. It is interesting to note, however, that the farmer does not perceive the maintenance of the field as a labor-consuming task. The substantially longer time the owner of Plot 2 spends in his field is predictable, as the plot is younger and the larger number of herbaceous crops in the field demand more thorough weeding and closer attention. The labor required is, however, still relatively low when compared with other forms of traditional agriculture in the humid tropics.

The Market Value of Agroforestry Products

The two examples of low labor requirements we cited appear especially impressive when the data presented in Appendix A are translated into the monetary value of production from the two plots. In estimating the commercial value in dollars we used average mid-1987 Iquitos market prices of the items produced in the Santa Rosa plots; in some cases we had to estimate average fruit, tuber, or leaf production per plant. The prices were then converted to U.S. dollars, using the mid-1987 exchange rate of I/.35 = US$1.

Using this method, we found that if all the items produced in Plot 1 had been marketed at the average prices in Iquitos, the owner of the plot would have realized a gross income of $653 per hectare. The owner of Plot 2 would have obtained gross earnings of $635 per hectare.

These estimates should be treated with great caution; they are presented merely to illustrate our point that agroforestry production can have considerable commercial value in the Peruvian Amazon. In a previous article (Padoch et al., 1985) we described the very substantial market production that is realized from the large orchards in the town of Tamshiyacu. That town, however, may be considered somewhat unusual since it is situated in a favorable location in relation to the major market of Iquitos. Santa Rosa, more typical of Amazonian villages, has no major market within easy reach. The town of Requena offers only limited marketing opportunities.

Commercialization of agroforestry produce, especially fruits, is fraught with difficulty for small Amazonian farmers (Denevan and Padoch, 1988; Padoch and de Jong, 1987): transport facilities are poor and costs high; markets are small and extremely volatile; storage facilities are few and poor, and processing facilities are usually non-existent. Farmers also have notoriously poor knowledge of what is happening in markets since communication facilities are poorly developed.

The difficulty of marketing perishable produce is largely responsible for the fact that only $16/per ha was actually realized by the owner of Plot 1 and $22/ha by the Plot 2 owner; 2.4% and 3.5% of the potential respectively. A good deal of the production was consumed by the household and some went to other residents of the community. The farmers may also have underreported their earnings which include income from the sale of rice and other cash crops and some fish.

Summary and Conclusions

We have presented a small sample of data concerning production of materials with commercial value in some agroforestry fields located in the Amazonian village of Santa Rosa. The fields are different, diverse, and productive. The production, we have suggested, is achieved with a small amount of labor. The potential commercial returns are substantial, but the actual market returns are small.

We believe that the data presented here and elsewhere (Denevan and Padoch, 1988; Padoch and de Jong, 1987; Padoch et al., 1985) have shown that Amazonian agroforesters can produce substantial quantities of commmercial crops, but are constrained by inadequacies of transport, marketing, and export facilities. Much enthusiasm has been expressed for the extension of agroforestry practices and the promotion of the planting of tree crops, including fruits. Those who wish to promote agroforestry, however, should take a broad approach to research and extension, and include in their work a realistic assessment of the problems of marketing in areas such as the Peruvian Amazon.

Acknowledgments

The research upon which this paper is based was undertaken as part of an agreement between the Institute of Economic Botany of the New York Botanical Garden and the Instituto de Investigaciones de la Amazonía Peruana (IIAP). We would like to acknowledge the assistance of many of our colleagues from IIAP, especially Jose López Parodi, Marcio Torres, Ruperto de Aguila and Humberto Pacaya. Our deepest thanks go to the residents of Santa Rosa who patiently tolerated our constant inquiries.

References

Anderson, A.B., Gely, J. Strudwick, G.L. Sobel and M.G. C. Pinto. 1986. Um sistema agroflorestal na várzea do estuário amazônico (Ilha das Onças, Municipio de Barcarena, Estado do Pará) *Acta Amazonica.*

Boom, B. 1987. Ethnobotany of the Chacobo Indians, Beni, Bolivia. *Advances in Economic Botany* 4.

De Jong, W. 1987. Organización del trabajo en la Amazonía Peruana: El caso de las sociedades agrícolas de Tamshiyacu. *Amazonía Indígena* 7(13):11–17.

Denevan, W.M. and C. Padoch, eds. 1988. Swidden-fallow agroforestry in the Peruvian Amazon. *Advances in Economic Botany* 5: New York.

Hecht, S.B. 1982. Agroforestry in the Amazon Basin: Practice, theory and limits of a promising land use. Pages 331–371 in S.B. Hecht, ed., *Amazonia: Agriculture and land use research.* Centro Internacional de Agricultura Tropical (CIAT): Cali, Colombia.

Hiraoka, M. 1985a. Mestizo subsistence in riparian amazonia. *National Geographic Research* 1:236–246.

———. 1985b. Changing floodplain livelihood patterns in the Peruvian Amazon, *Tsukuba Studies in Human Geography* 3:354–371.

———. 1986. Zonation of mestizo riverine farming systems in northeast Peru. *National Geographic Research* 2:354–371.

Irvine, D. 1985. Succession management and resource distribution in an Amazonian rainforest. Paper presented at meeting of the American Anthropological Association. Washington, D.C.

Padoch, C. 1988. People of the floodplain and forest. *In* J.S. Denslow and C. Padoch eds., *People of the tropical rain forest.* University of California Press: Berkeley and Los Angeles.

Padoch, C. and W. de Jong. 1987. Traditional agroforestry practices of native and ribereño farmers in the lowland Peruvian Amazon. *In* H. L. Gholz, ed., *Agroforestry: Realities, possibilities, and potentials.* Martinus Nijhoff: Dordrecht.

———. in press. Santa Rosa: The impact of the minor forest products trade on an amazonian village. *Advances in Economic Botany* 7.

Padoch, C., J. Chota Inuma, W. de Jong, and J. Uhruh. 1985. Amazonian agroforestry: A market-oriented system in Peru. *Agroforestry Systems* 3:47–58.

Parker, E.P., ed. 1985. *The Amazon caboclo: Historical and contemporary perspectives.* Studies in Third World Societies 32.

Posey, D.A. 1982. Keepers of the forest. *Garden* 6(1):18–24

————. 1984. A preliminary report on diversified management of tropical forest by the Kayapo Indians of the Brazilian Amazon. *in* G.T. Prance and J. Kallunki, eds., *Ethnobotany in the Neotropics, Advances in Economic Botany* 1.

————. 1985. Indigenous management of tropical forest ecosystems: The case of the Kayapo Indians of the Brazilian Amazon. *Agroforestry Systems* 3:139–158.

Prance, G.T. 1984. The use of edible fungi by Amazonian Indians. *In* G.T. Prance and J. Kallunki, eds., *Ethnobotany in the Neotropics, Advances in Economic Botany* 1.

Vickers, W.T. and T. Plowman. 1984. Useful plants of the Siona and Secoya Indians of eastern Ecuador. *Fieldiana*: Bot., N.S. 15:1–63.

Villarejo, A. 1979. *Así es la selva.* Centro de Tecnología Agronómica (CETA): Iquitos.

Appendix A
Santa Rosa Agroforestry Fields, 1986: Production/Hectare[a]

Product	Unit	1	2	3	4
Anona (*Annona* sp.)	Fruits	37	300	0	121
Barbasco (*Lonchocarpus* sp.)	Trunks	0	38	0	0
Bijao (*Heliconia* sp.)	Plants	0	8	93	0
Breadfruit (*Artocarpus altilis*)	Fruits	67	0	0	0
Caimito (*Pouteria caimito*)	Fruits	1,517	0	337	333
Coffee (*Coffea arabica*)	Kgs.	9.6	0	0	0
Cocona (*Solanum sessiliflorum*)	Plants	0	25	0	0
Coconilla (*Solanum* sp.)	Plants	0	171	0	0
Daledale (*Calathea allouia*)	Plants	22	0	0	0
Guaba (*Inga edulis*)	Fruits	0	3,163	6,607	2,048
Guaba pelusa (*Inga* sp.)	Fruits	15	0	0	0
Guava (*Psidium guajava*)	Fruits	0	525	100	0
Huasai (*Euterpe precatoria*)	Trunks	15	0	0	0
Huicungo (*Astrocaryum huicungo*)	Trunks	0	0	3	0
Jute seeds (*Urena lobata*)	Kgs.	0	0	3	0
Leche caspi (*Couma macrocarpa*)	Trunks	7	0	0	0
Lemon (*Citrus aurantifolia*)	Fruits	285	0	0	0
Limon dulce (*Citrus* sp.)	Fruits	437	0	0	0
Macambo (*Theobroma bicolor*)	Fruits	56	0	17	0
Mamey (*Syzygium malaccensis*)	Fruits	922	0	0	0
Orange (*Citrus sinenesis*)	Fruits	999	0	0	0
Papaya (*Carica papaya*)	Fruits	0	204	27	0
Peach palm (*Bactris gasipaes*)	Racemes	373	64	80	0
Peppers (*Capsicum* sp.)	Fruits	0	208	0	0
Pineapple (*Ananas comosus*)	Fruits	4	871	3	0
Plantain (*Musa paradisiaca*)	Racemes	19	260	137	52
Pona (*Socratea* sp.)	Trunks	11	0	0	0
Sachamangua (*Grias peruviana*)	Fruits	15	0	0	0
Sachapapa (*Dioscorea trifida*)	Plants	0	8	23	6
Sugarcane (*Saccharum officinarum*)	Stalks	0	188	3	0
Huitina (*Xanthosoma* sp.)	Plants	0	4	0	0
Tropical cedar (*Cedrela odorata*)	Trunks	7	0	0	0
Umari (*Poraqueiba sericea*)	Fruits	3,478	0	0	0
Uvilla (*Pourouma cecropiifolia*)	Racemes	444	279	396	0
Yarina (*Phytelephas macrocarpa*)	Trunks	4	0	0	0
Zapote (*Quararibea cordata*)	Fruits	2,109	0	0	0

[a] The table lists all resources that were available for marketing in 1986. Timber trees, including palms used for construction (e.g., *huicungo* and *pona*), are included in the summary of production, although their value does not represent annual production.

Source: Authors' field research, 1986.

7

Costs and Benefits of Floodplain Forest Management by Rural Inhabitants in the Amazon Estuary: A Case Study of Açai Palm Production

Anthony B. Anderson
and Mário Augusto G. Jardim

Introduction

This chapter is a case study of an economically productive and ecologically sustainable land use that has evolved among traditional inhabitants in the floodplain of the Amazon estuary. These river dwellers ("ribeirinhos"), typically mestizo in ethnicity, constitute a living bridge between indigenous Amerindian knowledge of the natural diversity and inherent productivity of the Amazon's floodplain resources and the modern world with its more limited view of the economic potential of natural ecosystems. The river dwellers of the Amazon estuary participate in the market economy, and are often mistakenly included in the economically marginal, rural population of lesser-developed countries that recent multi-lateral development programs have sought to advance. What prevailing development programs have failed to consider is how the river dwellers' knowledge of their environment can contribute to a better use of fragile lands in the floodplain.

The present case study does not aspire to propose a comprehensive sustainable land-use strategy for the Amazon's floodplain ("varzea"). Rather, it focuses on the economic potential of one important natural resource element in the regional economy, the "açai" palm (*Euterpe oleracea* Mart.). We report the findings of a field experiment designed to measure the effects of different management practices utilized by river dwellers on fruit yields in natural stands of açai. Although measurements of the effects of these practices on other floodplain forest species were not included in this experiment, our findings are important since açai is the foremost commercial floodplain forest resource for rural inhabitants over extensive areas of the estuary.

The case study described in this chapter is particularly interesting because rural inhabitants of the Amazon estuary implement an extensive form of land use (extraction of native forest products) in a biotope generally considered to have the greatest potential for intensive agriculture in Amazonia: the varzea or floodplain of sediment-rich rivers (Hiraoka, 1985; Lima, 1956; Roosevelt, 1980). Forest resources are the most fragile component of the floodplain, which has served as the principal location for agriculture in Amazonia since aboriginal times. The açai palm is an especially fragile resource, as it has been subjected to intensive exploitation in the form of palm heart extraction since the 1960s. In contrast to other floodplain areas (Hiraoka, 1985; Sternberg, 1975), however, river dwellers in the estuary we studied have largely maintained the native forest cover and have developed management practices that assure the sustained utilization of forest resources such as açai.

The general adoption of a less intensive form of land use in a biotope of high agricultural potential is frequently viewed as a sign of the inhabitants' lack of industry, "collecting mentality," Indian blood, and "primitive" land-use practices (Ross, 1978). However, this option is in fact a rational one from ecological, cultural, and economic perspectives. Elsewhere, the ecological and cultural bases for this option have been examined in detail (Anderson et al., 1985; Anderson in press). Here we shall examine this option from an economic perspective by conducting a cost-benefit analysis of various management practices carried out by local inhabitants in naturally occurring stands of the açai palm.

The Forest Resource

Floodplain forests cover approximately 25,000 km² in the Amazon estuary (less than 1% of the Amazon Basin). In contrast to the far more extensive upland or terra firme forests of Amazonia, biotic diversity is relatively low in the floodplain (Figure 1). Concomitant with comparatively low diversity is a frequently high dominance by one or a few tree species, which in many cases form nearly pure stands. Such forests are especially common on excessively moist sites. Dicotyledonous tree species of economic value often abound in floodplain forests of the Amazon estuary: examples include rubber or "seringueira" (*Hevea brasiliensis* ((Willd. ex A. Juss)) M. Arg.); "andiroba" (*Carapa guianensis* Aubl.), an important medicinal plant as well as a source of

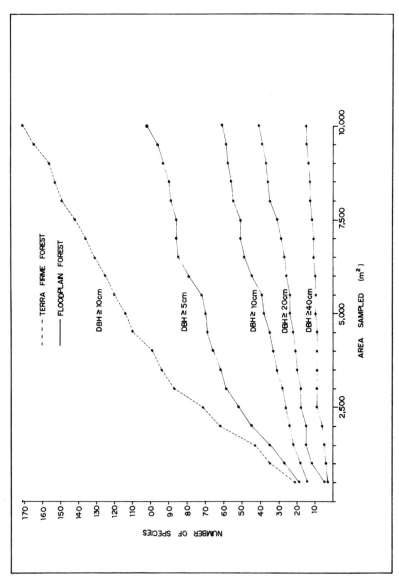

Figure 1 Number of species per hectare by diameter at breast height (DBH) in estuarine floodplain, Ilha das Oncas, Para, and on terra firme, central Rondonia (Salomão and Lisboa, in press).

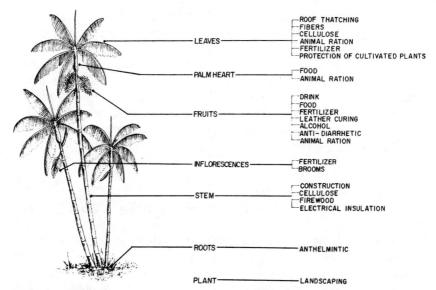

Figure 2   Uses of açai palm (*Euterpe oleracea* Mart.).

high-quality timber; "virola" or "ucuúba" (*Virola surinamensis* [Rol.] Warb. and other species of this genus), likewise used medicinally and as timber and plywood veneer; and cocoa or "cacau" (*Theobroma cacao* L.), originally introduced in the floodplain during colonial times (Ducke, 1953) but now a self-regenerating element that often dominates the forest understory. Although these species are abundant, floodplain forests in the Amazon estuary are frequently dominated by economically important species of palms that appear to thrive under excessively moist conditions: examples include "buriti" or "miriti" (*Mauritia flexuosa* L.f.) an important source of edible fruits and fiber; "ubuçu" or "buçu" (*Manicaria saccifera* Gaertn.), which provides fiber and thatch; "murumuru" (*Astrocaryum murumuru* Mart.), the fruits of which are used for animal feed and as game attractants; and "açai" (*Euterpe oleracea* Mart.), which is especially important as a source of edible fruits and palm heart, in addition to a host of other uses (Figure 2).

The açai palm is widely distributed on bottomland sites in northern South America, but attains its greatest concentrations in the Amazon estuary, where it is estimated to dominate approximately 10,000 km^2 (40%) of floodplain forest (Calzavara, 1972). In general, the palm is most abundant on topographially low to intermediate floodplain sites, which are subjected to periodic tidal-driven inundations: such sites are referred to locally as "varzea baixa." An inventory from one such site (0.25 ha) reveals the ecological and economic importance of açai (Appendix A). This palm is not only the most abundant, frequent and dominant species in the floodplain forest surveyed, but it is also the most important economic resource.

Açai produces a wide variety of market and subsistence products (Figure 2). The foremost of these, in both market and subsistence economies of the Amazon estuary, is a beverage obtained from the pulp of the fruits. This beverage is consumed on an almost daily basis throughout the region, especially among poorer segments of the population. Contrary to popular opinion, it is not particularly nutritious: protein content ranges from 1.25–4.34%; fatty acids range from 7.6–11.0%; Ca, P, and Fe average 0.050%, 0.033% and 0.0009%, respectively; and traces of vitamins B_1 and A occur (Altman, 1956; Campos, 1951; Mota, 1946). Yet the beverage is extremely filling, especially when mixed with manioc flour.

Local inhabitants harvest açai fruits by climbing the palm: an experienced collector can obtain up to 180 kg of fruits per day during the main fruiting season (August to November in the Amazon estuary). Men are more actively engaged in harvesting fruits, although women and children frequently assist in this task. Most of a family's production is destined for commercialization, which is generally carried out at specific locales such as the so-called Açai Market ("Feira do Açai") in Belém, the principal port on the Amazon River. Because the fruits spoil when stored at ambient temperatures for longer than 48 hours, commercialization of açai fruits is limited to areas in close proximity to regional market centers. Although most fruits are usually sold, a variable portion of a family's production is inevitably reserved for domestic consumption, where it represents a staple food. The fruits of açai thus play important roles in both regional market and subsistence economies.

The açai palm is also the major source of palm heart in Brazil. Because regional consumption is minimal, practically all production is destined for non-local markets, either elsewhere in Brazil or abroad. Derived from several species in Brazil, palm heart is extracted by cutting the stem. In species with solitary stems, this procedure kills the individual palm, which accounts for the virtual extinction of native populations of *Euterpe edulis* Mart. in the South and Southeast of Brazil. In contrast, açai possesses basal ramification of various stems per individual (Hallé et al., 1978). This characteristic permits rapid regeneration of native populations of açai after palm heart extraction and could serve as the basis for the sustainable exploitation of these populations.

Despite their obvious potential for rational management, açai stands were initially subjected to widespread clearcutting when palm heart extraction began in the Amazon estuary. Uncontrolled extraction continues in certain areas of the Amazon estuary today, with negative consequences for large segments of the rural population that depend on the harvest of açai fruits for subsistence and sale (Anonymous, 1985).

Alternative land-use practices that permit both fruit harvest and palm heart extraction appear to be increasingly implemented by rural inhabitants in the Amazon estuary. For example, inhabitants commonly introduce seeds or seedlings of açai onto shifting cultivation plots, thus promoting establishment of high-density stands that can be utilized during subsequent fallow periods (Anderson, in press). In already existing stands (established either spontaneously or through human intervention), commonly utilized management practices consist of selective pruning of açai stems combined with selective thinning of forest competitors. An individual açai palm may be comprised of over a dozen stems, and local inhabitants report that selective pruning not only provides palm heart but enhances fruit production in the remaining stems. In a floodplain forest adjacent to Belem, Anderson et al. (1985) found that the mean number of stems per açai clump declined from 9.5 in unmanaged forest to 6.5 on a managed site. When pruning, local inhabitants tend to eliminate young juvenile and old adult stems, thus favoring life stages in which current or imminent fruit production is greatest.

Likewise, selective thinning of forest competitors preserves a wide variety of forest resources. Selective thinning tends to concentrate on vines and trees that are used primarily for timber of firewood. Trees that branch at a height of 10–15 m and consequently interfere directly with the crowns of mature açai stems are especially prone to thinning.

Preliminary data from three islands in the Amazon estuary indicate that this and other forms of floodplain forest management are practiced over far greater areas than more intensive land uses such as shifting or semi-permanent cultivation (Anderson, unpublished data). Although exceptions to this pattern occur in localized areas such as near the towns of Abaetetuba and Igarapé-Miri (Figure 3), our field observations indicate that it appears to hold over most of the floodplain of the Amazon estuary. Many inhabitants report that shifting cultivation results in a long-term (generally greater than 10 years) elimination of crucial forest resources, which is not compensated by the short-term returns from agriculture. In contrast, management of floodplain forests appears to require minimal costs and provide substantial benefits. Quantifying these costs and benefits should provide insight concerning the rationale behind local inhabitants' land-use decisions in the Amazon estuary.

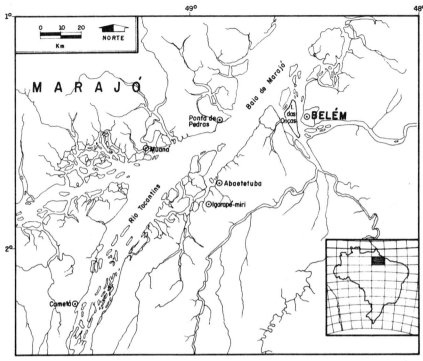

Figure 3   Location of study site (Ilha das Oncas, Para).

Methods and Materials

Study Site. To quantify the costs and benefits of managing native populations of açai, we established a field experiment on Ilha das Onças ("Jaguar Island") adjacent to the port city of Belem (Figure 3). The climate is the Af type in the Kóppen system. Mean annual rain fall is 2,739 mm, with relatively high amounts during the first semester and low amounts during the second. Tides represent the most striking environmental factor, provoking inundations over most of the island, especially during the equinoxes. The soil is a slightly humic gley ("glei pouco húmico," according to Viera et al., 1971), characterized by high clay content. The vegetation is comprised of floodplain forest with continuous cover and high occurrence of economically important tree species (Anderson et al., 1985).

Field Procedures. To determine the effects of local management practices on production of açai, 16 permanent plots, measuring 32 × 32 m each, were demarcated in an area of mature floodplain forest exhibiting minimal signs of disturbance. In each plot an area of 20 ×

20 m was utilized for experimental evaluation. The two treatments utilized in this experiment were:

(a) Selective pruning of açai. Under natural conditions, individuals (genets) of açai can form clumps comprised of over a dozen stems (ramets). This treatment eliminated stems that were excessively tall (height > 15 m) and/or excessively thin (diameter < 10 cm) and/or insufficiently straight; according to local inhabitants, such stems produce few fruits. After applying this treatment, usually only one to three mature stems remain per clump. Inhabitants utilize the cut stems for subsistence consumption as well as sale of palm heart.

(b) Selective thinning of forest competitors. This treatment consisted of cutting or ringing trees and vines considered by local inhabitants to be of no or minimal value, as well as trees with low branches that interfere directly with the crowns of açai. Inhabitants generally utilize felled trees as a source of firewood.

The two treatments were applied in four combinations over the entire area (32 × 32 m) of each plot: (1) control (no treatment), (2) pruning of açai clumps, (3) thinning of forest competitors, and (4) pruning and thinning. Each treatment was replicated on four plots, giving a total of 16 plots arranged in a completely randomized experimental design. In each plot all woody plants with diameters at breast height (DBH) > 5 cm were mapped, labelled, measured and identified.

Experimental Evaluation. To determine the influence of the various treatment combinations on açai fruit production, phenological observations were initiated in February of 1986. The observations were carried out bi-weekly except during the period of maximum fruiting (August-November), when they were made weekly to minimize loss of mature fruits. In a 20 × 20 m area of each plot (excluding the 6 m wide borders), observations of flowering and fruiting were carried out on all mature stems occurring in a 300 m² area (excluding a 10 × 10 m subplot located in the center of the plot, which was reserved for studies of regeneration). Mature fruit bunches were harvested and weighed with and without fruits.

The field data were used to calculate the means and standard deviations of the fresh weights of fruits produced per stem, clump, and area (plot). Data on fruit weights were compared statistically using analysis of variance (Ayres & Ayres Junior, 1987). The values of fruit production were calculated using the monthly production of each treatment combination during 1986, converted to local currency using the mean monthly price in the Açai Market of Belém, and finally converted to U.S. Dollars using the mean monthly official rate of exchange. The values of palm heart extraction carried out by pruning in the experimental plots were estimated using the mean price for medium quality palm hearts (Cz\$ 2.00, or U.S.\$ 0.14 each) during February-March 1986, which was the peak extraction period for that year among producers on Ilha das Onças.

Results

The experimental evaluation was carried out by comparing fruit productivity (kg/year) per stem, clump, and area in the four treatment combinations.

Analyzing the productivity per area (Appendix B.1) and per vegetative clump (Appendix B.2), no significant differences were detected between the four treatment combinations.

A comparison of productivity per stem among the four treatment combinations (Appendix B.3) reveals significant differences between the control and thinning, and between the control and the combined treatments of pruning and thinning. There were no significant differences among the other treatment combinations.

Appendix B.4 shows the analysis of variance of fruit productivity per stem between the two main treatments (pruning and thinning) and their interaction. This analysis, which determines the effects of isolated application of the treatments, reveals a significant effect due to thinning, whereas the effect of pruning alone was not significant; no interaction occurred between the two treatments.

The experimental responses indicate that pruning of açaí stems does not produce significant effects on fruit productivity. This result shows that rational extraction of palm hearts—equivalent to the pruning treatment utilized in the experiment—can be carried out in populations of açaí without reducing the fruit harvest. In fact, this practice actually seems to increase the harvest, as indicated by the slightly (although not significant) increased productivity in plots subjected to pruning compared to untreated (control) plots.

Our results also show that selective thinning of forest competitors produces a significant increase in fruit productively per açaí stem. In conjunction with pruning, this treatment serves to concentrate production in a smaller number of stems, thus facilitating the task of fruit collecting. Thinning also serves to increase access within the floodplain forest, thus facilitating the gathering of other forest products upon which riverine populations depend, such as wood, fibers, latex, edible fruits, medicinal plants, etc. (Anderson et al., 1985).

Discussion

Although we do not have sufficient data to conduct a complete analysis of the costs and benefits of floodplain forest management as carried out by local inhabitants in the Amazon estuary, we can make a number of general affirmations. The principal benefit, according to the actual practitioners of this management, is due to increased productivity of açai fruits. The data summarized in Table 1 show that the increase in the value of açai fruit yield between untreated plots (control) and plots subjected to both treatments (pruning and thinning) was U.S. $136.33. For present purposes we shall assume that this value represents the gross increment in revenue per hectare of floodplain forest subjected to management.

The labor allocated to site preparation represents the principal cost associated with the forest management practices described in this chapter. The labor necessary to implement site preparation (i.e., pruning and thinning) is highly variable, depending on the initial condition of the forest. In an exceptionally dense floodplain forest, local inhabitants estimate that the labor for site preparation would be equivalent to 10 man-days per hectare. Utilizing the mean minimum wage (the local standard) during 1986, this labor represents a cost of U.S. $26.50.

This analysis reveals that the economic benefits of managing native populations of açai (U.S. $136.33) outweigh the costs (U.S. $26.50) by U.S. $109.83 per hectare, which represents an increase of 46.7% in the value of annual production of açai fruits over unmanaged floodplain forest.

In relation to benefits, this analysis fails to take into account the value of other forest products extracted during site preparation, especially high-value items such as palm heart and timber. For example, selective harvesting from the experimental plots would have yielded an average of 337 palm hearts per hectare. At the in situ price of U.S. $0.14 per medium grade (10–19 cm in diameter) palm heart prevalent during 1986, this would represent an additional (although not annual) income of U.S. $47.18 per hectare. Data from one family (Figure 4) indicate that sale of fruits and palm hearts obtained from açai constitute the largest share of total household income. The income increments generated by management—although small on a per-area basis—make a substantial contribution to household survival under the extensive land-use systems that prevail in the Amazon estuary. Furthermore, we have not considered the greater facility of obtaining economic products from açai and other forest resources in managed as compared to unmanaged areas, a fact that is frequently alluded to by local inhabitants. In relation to costs, most of the operations associated with site preparation need not be repeated annually, thus reducing costs in subsequent years.

Conclusions

Under the management system utilized by river dwellers in açai stands of the Amazon estuary, we predict that the economic benefits

Table 1
Productivity and Value of Acai Fruits in Four Experimental Treatments[a]

Treatment Combination	Productivity (kg/ha/year)	Value (US$/ha/year)
Control (no treatment)	1,158.8	235.25
Pruning only	1,491.8	282.51
Thinning only	2,437.6	504.60
Pruning and thinning	1,854.8	371.58

[a] Each number represents the mean value of four plots.

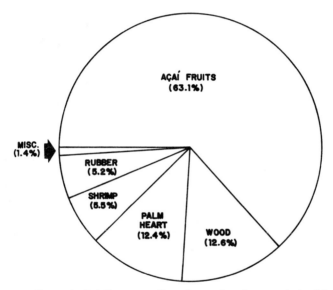

Figure 4   Relative proportion of monetary income derived from natural products obtained by a single family on Ilha das Oncas during 1986.

derived from açaí fruit production will remain more or less constant, whereas the costs are likely to decline over time. The costs associated with this management involve minimal cash outlays which are usually paid in kind. Although net income returns may vary from year to year, an average of U.S. $110.00 (1986) per hectare apppears to be a reasonable minimum estimate.

In contrast, more intensive forms of land use such as cultivation of annual crops typically involve considerably greater investment per unit of land. Although higher economic returns from annual cropping are possible, the corresponding risks are also greater. Of primary concern among local inhabitants is the fact that more intensive land uses result in a long-term transformation of the native forest, and consequently a prolonged loss of forest resources.

Although the extensive form of forest management described in this chapter provides relatively low economic returns per unit area, it appears to be economically rational due to its low cost requirements, minimal risk, and apparent sustainability. This management permits the multiple use of the açai palm—resolving the conflict between fruit collection and palm heart extraction—as well as of other forest resources, thus enabling the use of a wide range of products that are important in both local market and subsistence economies. Finally, this form of management illustrates one way in which tropical floodplain forests, instead of being destroyed, are simultaneously used and conserved by rural populations.

Acknowledgments

The establishment and maintenance of the field experiment on Ilha das Onças were supported by grants from the Conselho Nacional de Desenvolvimento Científico e Tecnológico (CNPq) and by the Ford Foundation. The World Wildlife Fund—U.S. provided a fellowship to Mario Jardim to execute the fieldwork, and a travel grant to Anthony Anderson to present this paper at the Fragile Lands Symposium at Tulane University. The authors would like to thank dona Alice Damulakis and her son, Diogenes, who graciously permitted the execution of the field experiment on their land; and to other inhabitants in the Amazon estuary who have patiently explained the various forms of floodplain forest management described here. We thank Dr. William Overal for his statistical advice, Sandoval Martins for drawing the figures, and Lylianne Theodoro for typing the manuscript. A preliminary version of this manuscript, in Portuguese, was submitted to the Boletím de Pesquisa Florestál of the Centro Nacional de Pesquisa Florestál (CNPF-EMBRAPA) in Curitiba, Brazil.

References

Altman, R.F.A. 1956. O caroço de açai (*Euterpe oleracea* Mart.). Boletim Técnico do Instituto Agronômico do Norte 31:109–111.

Anderson, A.B. In press. Extractivism and forest management by rural inhabitants in the Amazon estuary. *In*: A.B. Anderson (editor), Alternatives to deforestation: Steps toward sustainable use of the Amazon rainforest. Columbia University Press.

————, A. Gely, J. Strudwick, G.L. Sobel & M.G.C. Pinto. 1985. Um sistema agroflorestal na várzea do estuário amazônico (Ilha das Onças, Municipio de Barcarena, Estado do Pará). Acta Amazônica, Suplemento 15(1–2):195-224.

Anonymous, 1985. Açai some de Vigia devido à extração descontrolada. "O Liberal," 29 Nov. Page 5.

Ayres, M.& M. A. Ayres Junior. 1987. Aplicações estatísticas em basic. Editora McGraw-Hill Ltda., São Paulo.310 p.

Calzavara, B.B.G. 1972. As possibilidades do açaizeiro no estuário amazônico. Boletim da Fundaçâo de Ciéncias Agrárias do Pará (FCAP), no.5,103 p.

Campos, F.A.M. 1951. Valor nutritivo de frutos brasileiros. Instituto de Nutrição, Trabalhos e Pesquisas 6:72–75.

Ducke, A. 1953. As espécies brasileiras do gênero *Theobroma* L. Boletim Técnico do Instituto Agronômico do Norte 28:3–20.

Hallé, F., R.A.A. Oldeman & P.B. Tomlinson. 1978. Tropical trees and forests: An architectural analysis. Springer-Verlag, New York.v 441 p.

Hiraoka, M. 1985. Mestizo subsistence in riparian Amazonia. National Geographic Research 1:236–246.

Lima, R.R. 1956. A agricultura nas várzeas do estuário do Amazonas. Boletim Técnico do Instituto Agronômico do Norte 33:1–164.

Mota, S. 1946. Pesquisas sobre o valor alimentar do assaí. Anais da Associação Química do Brasil 5(2):35–38.

Roosevelt, A. C. 1980. Parmana: Prehistoric maize and manioc subsistence along the Amazon and Orinoco. Academic Press, New York.

Ross, E.B. 1978. The evolution of the Amazon peasantry. Journal of Latin American Studies 10(2):193–218.

Solomão R. de P. & L.B. Lisboa. In press. Análise ecológica da vegetação de uma floresta pluvial tropicál de terra firme, BR-364 entre os municípios de Ji-Paraná e Presidente Médici, Rondônia. Boletim do Museu Paraense Emilio Goeldi, Série Botânica.

Sternberg, H.O.R. 1975. The Amazon River of Brazil. Franz Steiner Verlag GMBH, Wiesbaden.

Vieira, L.C., N.V. Carvalho e Oliveira & T.X. Bastos. 1971. Os solos do estado do Pará. Cadernos Paraenses do IDESP: 1–137

Appendix A

Species with DBH ≥ 5 cm, Collected in a 0.25-ha Area of Unmanaged Floodplain Forest on Ilha das Onças with Scientific and Vernacular Names and Data on Ecology and Uses[a]

| N | Scientific Name | FAM | Vernacular Name | Abundance | | Frequency | | Dominance | | Importance | Uses |
				n	%	n	%	cm^2	%	%	
—	Euterpe oleracea Mart.	PAL	açaí	100	38.3	10	7.9	13,814	13.8	20.0	F, M, W, G, U, X
1405	Pterocarpus officinalis Jacq.	LEG	mututi	6	2.3	5	4.0	21,408	21.5	9.3	E, G, U
1437	Spondias mombin Urb.	ANA	taperebá	4	1.5	3	2.4	16,770	16.8	6.9	F, E, G
1402	Pithecellobium latifolium (L.) Benth.	LEG	jarandeua	23	8.8	9	7.1	1,587	1.6	5.8	E
—	Carapa guianensis Aubl.	MEL	andiroba	8	3.1	6	4.8	6,357	6.4	4.8	M, W, G
—	Astrocaryum murumuru Mart.	PAL	murumuru	12	4.6	7	5.6	2,223	2.2	4.1	F, G, U
1417	Hevea brasiliensis (Willd. ex A. Juss.) M. Arg.	EUP	seringueira	5	1.9	4	3.2	4,844	4.9	3.3	G, X
1424	Cynometra marginata Benth.	LEG	maraximbe	4	1.5	3	2.4	5,430	5.4	3.1	W, E
1416	Inga cf. alba Willd.	LEG	ingá branco	8	3.1	5	4.0	2,143	2.1	3.1	F, E, G, X
1413	Macrolobium angustifolium (Benth.) Cowan	LEG	ipê	4	1.5	4	3.2	4,343	4.4	3.0	W, E
1404	Matisia paraensis Huber	BOM	cupuaçurana	6	2.3	5	4.0	2,333	2.3	2.9	E
1408	Pentaclethra macroloba (Willd.) Kuntze	LEG	pracaxi	6	2.3	4	3.2	3,259	3.3	2.9	E
1412	Quararibea guianensis Aubl.	BOM	inajarana	6	2.3	4	3.2	1,155	1.2	2.2	M, W, E
1420	Dalbergia monetaria L. f.	LEG	verônica vermelha	7	2.7	4	3.2	235	0.2	2.0	M
1411	Protium cf. polybotrium (Turcz.) Engl.	BRS	breu branco	7	2.7	3	2.4	989	1.0	2.0	E, G
1414	Terminalia dichotoma G. Meyer	CMB	cuiarana	2	0.8	2	1.6	3,740	3.7	2.0	W, E, U
1427	Derris cf. negrensis Benth.	LEG	cumacaí	4	1.5	4	3.2	126	0.1	1.6	M, U
1432	Crudia sp.	LEG	—	2	0.8	2	1.6	1,955	2.0	1.5	E

(Continued)

Appendix A (Continued)

Species with DBH ≥ 5 cm, Collected in a 0.25-ha Area of Unmanaged Floodplain Forest on Ilha das Onças with Scientific and Vernacular Names and Data on Ecology and Uses[a]

N	Scientific Name	FAM	Vernacular Name	Abundance		Frequency		Dominance		Importance		Uses
				n	%	n	%	cm^2	%	%		
1410	*Mora paraensis* Ducke	LEG	paracuúba	1	0.4	1	0.8	2,463	2.5	1.2		M, W, G
1438	*Symphonia globulifera* L.	GUT	anani	3	1.1	2	1.6	186	0.2	1.0		M, W
—	Other species (33)			43	17.0	39	31.2	4,427	4.5	17.1		F, M, W, E, G, U, X
Total				261	100.5	126	100.6	99,787	100.1	99.8		

[a] Numbers (N) refer to collections of A. B. Anderson et al. F=food, M=medicine, W=wood for construction or furniture, E=energy in the form of firewood or charcoal, G=game attractant, U=utensils, X=other uses.

Appendix B

B.1
Acai Fruit Output (kg/year) per Plot (300m^2) in Four Treatment Combinations

Treatment Combination	Mean Output	Standard Deviation	Number of Plots
Control (no treatment)	34.8	25.3	4
Pruning only	44.8	18.0	4
Thinning only	73.2	46.8	4
Pruning and thinning	55.7	22.7	4

B.2
Acai Fruit Output (kg/year) per Vegetative Clump in Four Treatment Combinations

Treatment Combination	Mean Output	Standard Deviation	Number of Clumps
Control (no treatment)	6.6	6.0	21
Pruning only	6.9	5.3	26
Thinning only	9.4	6.6	32
Pruning and thinning	8.0	5.4	28

B.3
Acai Fruit Output (kg/year) per Stem in Four Treatment Combinations

Treatment Combination	Mean Output	Standard Deviation	Number of Stems
Control (no treatment)	4.4^a	3.2	32
Pruning only	6.6^{ab}	5.2	27
Thinning only	7.5^b	5.2	40
Pruning and thinning	7.4^b	5.6	30

a ≠ b, $p < .05$, test T.

B.4
Acai Fruit Output (kg/year) per Stem in the Two Experimental Treatments

Sources of Variation	DF	SQ	F-Value
Pruning	1	38.93	1.63
Thinning	1	122.60	5.14^a
Interaction	1	43.98	1.18
Error	125	2,982.37	

a $p < .05$, $F_{.05,1,125} = 3.92$.

8

Sustained Yield Management of Natural Forests: The Palcazú Production Forest

Gary S. Hartshorn

Introduction

Tropical deforestation often occurs on soils that cannot sustain intensive agriculture. The seemingly inexorable advance of the agricultural frontier on forest lands not only destroys vast quantities of wood, it also rapidly exhausts the natural productivity of the soil, usually leading to abandonment or conversion to extensive pasture. Wherever virgin lands are accessible (e.g. roads for oil exploration, logging, etc.), strong socio-economic and political pressures often promote spontaneous or directed colonization; invariably this means deforestation.

Peru's Pichis-Palcazú Special Project (PEPP), with the financial and technical support of the United States Agency for International Development (USAID), is addressing the problems of inappropriate land use and uncontrolled agricultural colonization through an innovative approach to rural development (JRB, Inc., 1981): The Central Selva Resources Management Project which is implementing sustained yield management of natural forests as the principal development activity in the Palcazú Valley, while protecting the traditional culture of the local Amuesha Indians. By integrating intensive forest exploitation, local processing of timber and natural regeneration of native trees, the forest management project is expected to maximize sustainable productivity of the forest resources and to increase the income and social well-being of the indigenous communities and farmers in the lower valley. In general terms, this practice is known as production forestry.

The Tropical Science Center (TSC) provides technical assistance to the forestry and land-use components of the Palcazú development project. TSC designed a vertically integrated system for local transformation and national marketing of wood products, with management of native forests based on natural regeneration and sustained yield (Tosi 1982). The Palcazú project promoted the formation of the Yanesha Forestry Cooperative, a local indigenous organization, and is developing a wood processing center for the Indian cooperative.

The Area

The small Palcazú Valley (140,000 hectares (ha)) is at the eastern base of the Peruvian Andes. The Palcazú watershed (189,200 ha) is formed by the rugged Yanachaga range (3,800 m above sea level) to the west and the lower San Matías range (1,200 m) to the east. The Palcazú river flows north, where it joins the Pozuzo river, both of which are tributaries of the Pachitea river. Base elevations vary from approximately 270 m at the northern end of the valley to 350 m in the southern foothills. Forestry development activities are limited to the lower end of the valley, generally below 500 m in elevation.

As part of the Central Selva Resources Management Project, USAID is assisting with the creation and consolidation of the Yanachaga-Chemillén National Park (122,000 ha) and the San Matías Protection Zone (33,000 ha). These conservation units (Aguilar 1986) include considerable areas of protection forests on the steep slopes of the upper Palcazú watershed.

The population of the Palcazú Valley is estimated to be 6,000 inhabitants, including 3,500 Amuesha (Yanesha) Indians. Most of the Amueshas live in 12 native communities, where they practice traditional shifting cultivation of manioc, maize, and upland rice on small holdings, alternating these short-term crops with longer periods of bush or forest fallow. As part of the Palcazú project, the 12 native communities have been officially recognized and granted property titles by the Peruvian government. The rest of the valley's population is made up of mestizo settlers, some Campa Indians, and a significant component of cattle ranchers descended from German, Swiss, and Austrian immigrants attracted to the region by the turn-of-the-century rubber boom.

Detailed mapping of life zones indicates that 85% of the lower valley is in the tropical wet forest life zone (Bolaños and Watson 1981). Average precipitation in the lower valley is about 6,300 mm/yr (about 250 inches). Such high rainfall and the lack of an effective dry season produce natural vegetation commonly called tropical rain forest.

Approximately 75% of the lower valley retains its coverage of primary forests. Most of the deforested areas are along the rivers and on the low hills close to these rivers. The Palcazú Valley appears to be especially rich in native plant species. R. Foster and A. Gentry of the Missouri Botanical Garden (pers. comm.) are discovering an impressive number of plant species with medicinal or pharmaceutical uses. I estimate that there are at least 1,000 native tree species in the Palcazú Valley.

The Palcazú Valley's soils, like most soils supporting tropical forests, are unsuited for conventional commercial farming. The red clay soils of the extensive rolling hills in the lower valley are highly acidic (pH 3.8–4.5), with an abundance of aluminum. Furthermore, these soils are highly leached and almost devoid of major nutrients, especially calcium, phosphorus, and potassium. Also present in the valley are old riverine terraces with white sandy-clay loam soils that are even less fertile than the red clay soils. The Amueshas do not use these old terraces for shifting cultivation, hence these poor soils generally have well-developed primary forests (Hartshorn 1981) with an abundance of valuable trees such as rubber (*Hevea brasiliensis,* Euphorbiaceae), and tornillo (*Cedrelinga catenaeformis,* Mimosaceae).

Because of the high rainfall and rolling-to-steep terrain, the red clay soils are highly erodible when cleared of their protective forests and used for agriculture or pasture. A survey of the land-use capability in the lower valley indicates the following distribution of maximum sustainable use: 7.6% suitable for annual or seasonal crops; 13.3% for pasture; 14.4% for perennial crops; 46.2% for production forestry; and 18.6% should be kept in undisturbed protection forests (Tosi 1981). In this classification system, less intensive uses are permissible, such as production forestry on lands suitable for agriculture or grazing. But the opposite (pasture on forestry land, for example) is not sustainable, and should be avoided. The project includes a program for mapping land-use capability of the lower valley, as well as actual land-use, with a view to adjusting current land-use practices to sustainable use of the natural resources. Thus, some 44,000 ha of remaining forests in the lower Palcazú Valley could be under permanent management for production forestry.

Background

Numerous efforts to manage heterogeneous tropical forests have failed due to difficulties such as: 1) the low volume of commercial woods per unit area, there being as many as 200 tree species in one hectare; 2) very high extraction costs associated with the practice of high-grading only the quality timber; 3) lack of understanding about the dynamic nature of most tropical forests; 4) a general lack of information about the regeneration requirements and silvics of canopy tree species; 5) government policies (e.g., short-term concessions for large volumes, minimum diameters for cutting) that discourage sustained yield forest management or make it economically unattractive; 6) national and international agencies that promote agricultural colonization on lands that cannot sustain agriculture or cattle ranching; and 7) agencies in charge of forestry that do not define and protect permanent forest lands for timber production.

This complex array of factors has given rise to a pervasive attitude among forestry professionals, development agencies, and the public in general that it is economically unjustifiable and ecologically impossible to manage tropical forests (Leslie 1977). Nonetheless, significant economic changes in the demand for tropical woods and recent advances in our understanding of tropical forest dynamics have reawakened interest in the potential for managing tropical forests for sustained production of wood, without resorting to plantation forestry.

Perhaps the most important change has been the dramatic opening of national markets to a much wider range of Amazon timber species. National markets traditionally accepted only the finest tropical woods, which often meant only 10 to 50 of the thousands of native tree species. However, in the past decade as high-grading depleted stocks of premium timber and deforestation destroyed substitute species, national markets are opening up to more timber species that were heretofore commercially unacceptable. Where timber is scarce, as in much of Central America and the Andean highlands, local markets now accept any log of adequate size and decent form. Generally, many tree species are marketed under a single generic name, for example "common oak" in Chanchamayo, Peru, or "mountain oak" in central Ecuador. Market acceptance of a large number of native species literally opens the door to intensive management of tropical forests as an alternative to the selective exploitation of a few species.

The incredible richness and diversity of tree species in tropical forests have long been formidable obstacles to economic management of these forests. Most previous attempts at forest management failed because they focused on one or a few quality timbers (e.g., cedar, ebony, mahogany), which are even scarce in undisturbed primary forest. Due to the great complexity of most tropical forests, the competition of one species against hundreds of others was doomed ecologically, or was prohibitively expensive to control.

Forest Dynamics

During the last decade, some researchers working independently in Southeast Asia and in tropical America discovered that tropical forests are very dynamic (Hartshorn 1978; Oldeman 1978; Whitmore 1978). This means that rapid renewal of the primary forest generally occurs with the fall of large trees, and their replacement with young, fast-growing trees. One of the key components of this natural renewal is a surprisingly high dependency of tree species on natural openings (gaps) in the canopy for successful regeneration (Hartshorn 1980). At the La Selva Biological Station in northeastern Costa Rica, 50% of the native tree species require gaps for regeneration. If we consider only the tree species that form the forest canopy, 63% are gap species. The shade intolerant species that colonize gaps are fast-growing trees that fill a gap within a few years and reach the forest canopy in 20-30 years. In the La Selva primary forest in Costa Rica, the median life-span of trees greater than 10 cm (diameter at breast height) is just 34 years (Lieberman et al. 1985). Forest renewal through gap-phase dynamics, the principle pattern of natural regeneration in most tropical forests, is the key to our management plan for natural forests in the Palcazú Valley.

Management Plan

TSC designed a forest management plan based on the above-mentioned ecological factors (Tosi 1982). Timber exploitation is limited to long, narrow clear-cuts interspersed in the natural forest. Considering topography, each new strip will be 30 to 40 m wide. Where feasible, strips 200-500 m in length will be oriented with the topography to minimize crossing ridges and streams. In effect, each strip is an elongated gap, bordered on each side by intact forest, which is the source of seeds for natural regeneration of trees in each clear-cut strip. In successive years, the new strips will be located at least 100m from recently cut strips. TSC is projecting a 30 to 40 year rotation between the successive harvests of a specific strip in this strip shelterbelt system.

Two demonstration strips were harvested in 1985, the first (20×75 m) in April-May and the second (50×100 m) in October-December. The natural regeneration of trees within a few months of harvest was striking. In addition to abundant regeneration from seed, many stumps displayed vigorous sprouts; even some of the very dense and beautiful hardwoods like *Tabebuia obscura* (Bignoniaceae), *Myrocarpus* sp. and *Vatairea* sp. (both Fabaceae) had abundant stump sprouts on the demonstration strips. In a complete inventory of regeneration of the first strip 15 months after harvest, we found approximately 1,500 individuals (>50 cm tall), representing 132 tree species. At 27 months, there were 155 tree species with saplings more than 1 m tall. This wealth of tree species regenerating is more than double the number of tree species harvested from the first demonstration strip (.15 ha). We think that the proximity of excellent seed sources and the absence of burning and cropping are critical factors in the diversity and abundance of natural regeneration of trees on the demonstration strips.

The management plan also includes the possibility of silvicultural treatments. Once the young trees have formed a closed canopy (at about 5 m), the competitive equilibrium can be adjusted to favor particularly desirable individuals, or to eliminate undesirable individuals. In year 2 or 3, the number of stump sprouts was reduced to 1 or 2, depending on the size of the stump. As the canopy closes, climbers are cut to prevent lianas from overtopping or damaging the young trees. Thinning of trees will not be initiated until the canopy is fully closed, in order to allow the natural suppression of weeds and vines.

Wood Uses

The harvesting and processing of timber are integral components of forest management. In order to promote natural regeneration of shade intolerant tree species, the canopy opening must be sufficient to allow sunlight to reach the forest floor. Thus the management plan requires clear-cutting and the use of almost all of the cut biomass. All trunks and large branches are extracted, leaving only the small branches and leaves on the ground to provide nutrients for the regenerating forest.

Draft animals (such as oxen or water buffalo) are used to extract the logs, poles, posts, and fuelwood. The few exceptionally large logs can be sawn lengthwise to facilitate the extraction. The logs are moved by draft animal to a road head for transport to a local processing center. The use of such simple technology to extract logs is feasible because extraction is concentrated in a small area and the distances are not great. Hence, extraction of logs is considerably cheaper with draft animals than with articulated tractors or skidders. In addition, the negative impact of extraction on the soil is much less with draft animals than with heavy machinery, and the investment is minimal.

Processing of the wood is done locally in the valley, at an integrated processing center organized cooperatively by the producers of the raw materials. This set-up will ensure that the added-value from processing remains in the hands of the owners of the forest. The Yanesha Forestry Cooperative consists of five native communities and 96 individual members. The cooperative has identified approximately 1,000 ha of production forests and is developing operational plans for each pro-duction block (Sanchoma et al. 1986). The Yanesha Forestry Cooper-ative is the first forestry cooperative ever organized among indigenous groups in the Amazon Basin. The Cooperative plans to involve all the native communities of the valley and bring their 25,000 hectares of natural production forests under sustained yield management.

Economic Aspects

Inventories of the lower valley forests carried out by the PEPP forestry unit indicate that there is an average of 150 m³/ha of timber in saw logs, plus 90 m³/ha of roundwood for poles and posts. The inventory data do not include branchwood, which can be sawn for specialty items or converted to charcoal. Much of the smaller dimension timber is marketable as utility poles and posts, which will be treated with a preservative to increase longevity and value. Much of the non-resistant sawnwood will also be treated with a preservative for use as form lumber in construction. The untreated hardwoods are sold in specialized markets based on their specific wood properties and workability, which are determined by laboratory tests and trial in a local carpentry shop. Timber that cannot be transformed into sawn products or preserved poles and posts will be converted to charcoal, for which there is a considerable demand wherever energy sources are scarce, such as the high Andes and the coastal deserts of Peru.

The first processing center located in Shiringamazú has a "Mighty-Mite" portable sawmill and a bank of 44 Pres-caps for preserving roundwood (Krones 1987). At this first stage, the cooperative can process 12 hectares of timber per year. For 1989, there are plans to diversify and expand the processing center's productive capacity by adding a band resaw, an automatic sharpener, 2 miter saws, 1 table saw, 1 molder, 2 driers, 3 duplicating lathes, 2 sanders, 50 Pres-caps, and a complete "slurry seal" system for preserving sawnwood.

Given the current unstable economic situation in Peru, any long-range projection of the financial performance of the Palcazú project would be unrealistic. Over the short term, TSC economic calculations indicate that the limited capability of the current processing center (portable sawmill, 44 Pres-caps, and a portable charcoal kiln) will produce net returns of about US $3,500 per hectare of forest harvested and processed locally. Under full development, the planned diversification and expansion of the local processing center at Shiringamazú should increase net returns to an estimated US $27,555 per hectare worked (Simeone et al. 1986). These values are the net return captured once during a proposed 30 to 40 year cycle. Assuming a 35-year rotation, annual net income at full development would be US $786 per hectare worked. At full development, about 20,000 ha would be exploited over a 35 year period (about 570 hectares per year). It is important to emphasize that these estimated profits to the Yanesha Forestry Cooperative are based on current market values and transport costs for wood products in Peru which are likely to change radically even over the short-term. Nevertheless, once local processing is available, this integrated forest management system will produce attractive profits beginning in the first year of operation, while guaranteeing the sustained production of timber from managed natural forests.

Conclusions

Several factors may affect the long-term success of the Palcazú project. First, the project still depends heavily on foreign financial assistance. If this initial start-up aid were cut-off or reduced before the project reaches full-development, then the Yanesha Forestry Cooperative, as a local development organization, would be seriously jeopardized.

The strength of the Cooperative is essential for two other reasons that may influence the project's viability. A strong cooperative reinforces the commitment of individual Amuesha to abide by the concept of collectively enforced sustained use. Without a strong cooperative, Amuesha may be tempted to sell off their land-rights to loggers or accelerate harvesting rates to unsustainable levels in order to get larger profits in the short-term. Increasing pressure from "outsiders" to do just this is putting the Cooperative to an early and critical test.

Finally, the Palcazú project, not to mention any strategy for sustainable development among the Amuesha, depends on continuing government recognition of Indian land rights. A strong and effective cooperative increases the chances of political support for such land rights.

Clearly, the most important aspect of the Palcazú project is the opportunity and potential for sustainable development of tropical forests. Instead of the typical pattern of temporary prosperity for a few years based on traditional high-grading of the forest followed by expansion of the agricultural frontier, sustained yield forest management will generate incomes adequate for local communities to realize their development priorities. If the Palcazú project is successful, the exploitation and integrated management of natural forests should become a powerful development model for tropical forests that are suitable only for production forestry. Sustained yield management of tropical forests would considerably diminish the growing pressures to convert forests to agricultural lands or pastures, at the same time reducing the rate of tropical deforestation.

References

Aguilar D., P.R. 1986. Yanachaga-Chemillén: Futuro Parque Nacional en la Selva Central del Perú. Boletín Lima 45:7–21.

Bolaños M., R. and V. Watson C. 1981. Report on the ecological map of the Palcazú valley. In JRB, Inc. 1981, Appendix C, 15 p.

Hartshorn, G.S. 1978. Tree falls and tropical forest dynamics. In Tomlinson, P.B. and M.H. Zimmerman, eds. Tropical Trees as Living Systems. Cambridge University Press, pp. 617–638.

————. 1980. Neotropical Forest Dynamics. Biotropica 12(suppl.):23–30.

————. 1981. Forestry potential in the Palcazú valley, Peru. In JRB, Inc. 1981, Appendix G, 16 p.

JRB, Inc. 1981. Central Selva Natural Resources Management Project. USAID/Peru, Project No. 527-0240, 2 vol.

Krones, M. 1987. Informe final sobre las actividades desarrolladas en la implementación y puesta en marcha del primer núcleo de transformación en la cooperativa forestal "Yanesha." TSC Report No. 114-C, 131 p.

Leslie, A.J. 1977. When theory and practice contradict. Unasylva 29(115):2–17.

Lieberman, D., M. Lieberman, R. Peralta and G. Hartshorn. 1985. Mortality patterns and stand turnover rates in wet tropical forest in Costa Rica. Journal of Ecology 73(3):915–924.

Oldeman, R. A. A. 1978. Architecture and energy exchange of dicotyledonous trees in the forest. In Tomlinson, P. B. and M. H. Zimmerman, eds. Tropical Trees as Living Systems. Cambridge University Press, pp. 535–560.

Sanchoma R., E., R. Simeone G., M. Velis, and H. Vílchez B. 1986. Plan de manejo forestal: Bosque de produción de la Comunidad Nativa Shiringamazú, 1987–1989. TSC Report No. 105-C, 37 p.

Simeone, R., W. Aspinall, M. Krones and H. Greub. 1986. Propuesta para la ampliación del centro de trasformación integral de productos forestales en el valle del Palcazú. TSC Report No. 083-C.

Tosi, J.A. 1981. Land use capability and recommended land use for the Palcazú valley. In JRB, Inc., 1981, Appendix N, 70 p.

————. 1982. Sustained yield management of natural forests: Forestry sub-project, Central Selva Resources Management Project, Palcazú Valley, Peru. Report to USAID/Peru, 68 p.

Whitmore, T. C. 1978. Gaps in the forest canopy. In Tomlinson, P.B. and M.H. Zimmerman, eds. Tropical Trees as Living Systems. Cambridge University Press, pp. 639–655.

9

Cuyabeno Wildlife Production Reserve

James D. Nations
and Flavio Coello Hinojosa

Introduction

From the elevated floor of his palm-thatched house, Froilan Paya-guaje watches the Terapuy River—stained tea-colored by forest tannins—as it rushes through the tropical rainforest of eastern Ecuador. Downstream, the river will flow into three others, each progressively larger, before merging with the world's largest river, the Amazon. For centuries, Payaguaje's Siona-Secoya ancestors have lived in this rainforest, enjoying a bounty of fish and turtles, hunting monkeys and agoutis, and harvesting manioc and corn from small garden clearings. Life has been much the same for hundreds of years.

But, today, Froilan Payaguaje's life is different—due not so much to changes among the Siona-Secoya themselves as to changes in the rainforest environment that surrounds them. In a scene that is mirrored throughout the earth's tropical belt, outsiders are clearing and burning the rainforest of eastern Ecuador to transform it into agricultural lands and cattle pastures. Of our planet's original 17 million km² of tropical rainforest, 9 million km² have now been eradicated, and 60,000 to 75,000 km² more of what remains are wiped out every year (Melillo et al. 1985:37–40). In Ecuador, where 121,876 km² of national territory is covered by Amazon rainforest, approximately 1,200 km² are destroyed each year (Landázuri 1987:20; CONADE/PNUMA 1987:32, 63).

As a result of this radical environmental change, the lives of the Siona-Secoya are in rapid flux. Not all the changes are negative, however. In the midst of forest destruction and acculturation, positive elements are taking shape. For Payaguaje, these changes take the form of activities as the head indigenous park guard for the Cuyabeno Wildlife Production Reserve, a conservation unit operated by Ecuador's Departamento de Áreas Naturales y Recursos Silvestres. The Cuyabeno Reserve incorporates part of the Siona-Secoya's traditional territory. As one of a half-dozen indigenous park guards who live inside the Cuyabeno reserve, Payaguaje is charged with seeing that the reserve continues to move toward its two primary goals: (1) to preserve the biological diversity of Ecuador's lowland tropical rainforest and, (2) to simultaneously provide economic benefits to the indigenous and colonist communities who live within the reserve and on its borders.

Within the Cuyabeno Reserve, Payaguaje oversees the controlled harvesting of edible wildlife by his Siona-Secoya relatives. On the reserve's borders, he and other indigenous guards have begun work with biologists from Ecuador's Departamento de Áreas Naturales y Recursos Silvestres and with local colonists to raise wildlife such as river turtles, capybaras, peccaries, agoutis, and pacas. When populations of these and other wildlife species reach suitable levels, the animals will begin to be harvested for meat and skins. In such a fashion, Cuyabeno's guards and researchers are seeking to increase the food supply and income of both the reserve's indigenous inhabitants and immigrant colonists. Their goal is to protect the survival of these wildlife species and their habitat by using them in a sustainable fashion.

Background

This paper focuses on the economic aspects of land-use and natural resource management within the Cuyabeno Wildlife Production Reserve. Here, we demonstrate that, in addition to protecting some of the most biologically important natural resources on earth, the 2,550 square kilometers of the Cuyabeno Reserve are also valuable in economic terms. We propose that the Cuyabeno Reserve can produce more income for local populations in the Ecuadorian Amazon and more income for Ecuador as a whole if it is left in forest as a wildlife production reserve than if it falls prey to the more common land-use patterns that characterize the Ecuadorian Amazon in the 1980s.

These more common and destructive land-use patterns center on logging the forest for commercial timber, then clearing and burning what remains to dedicate the thin tropical soils to the production of cattle, coffee, maize, rice, and African oil palm. Combined, these land-use patterns are rapidly eradicating the natural vegetation and wildlife habitat of the Ecuadorian Amazon. More than half of the forest cleared ends up as cattle pasture. The Ecuadorian Amazon presently has 750,000 hectares of man-made pasture—an amount seven times the territory dedicated to agriculture—despite the fact that 86 percent of Ecuador's Amazon region has fragile soils, low fertility, and high soil toxicity that make the region suitable only for forestry and other non-disruptive activities (CONADE/PNUMA 1987:32, 63).

The Cuyabeno Wildlife Production Reserve was created in 1979 in response to the region's rapid rate of forest destruction on these fragile soils. But like most national parks and wildlife reserves in the developing world, the Cuyabeno Reserve must go beyond the traditional conservation goals of protecting species and habitat. It must also balance the conservation of natural resources with the economic requirements of human communities located within it or on its borders, as well as with the broader economic interests of Ecuadorian society.

With these goals in mind, the Department of Natural Areas and Wildland Resources of Ecuador has determined that the Cuyabeno Reserve should focus on four specific objectives:

(1) protection of the reserve's flora and fauna,
(2) protection of the tribal territories and cultural traditions of the reserve's indigenous communities,
(3) management of scientific research and tourist activities, and,
(4) development of viable wildlife management programs in conjunction with local communities.

By definition, the Cuyabeno Wildlife Production Reserve was established to foment the economic use of wildlife, including photographic safaris, the harvesting of natural wildlife populations for skins, meat, and live specimens, and the breeding and control of managed wildlife populations (Putney 1979:40).

Because of its unique terrestrial and aquatic wildlife, the Cuyabeno region is an ideal place to attempt these programs. The Cuyabeno Reserve is located within one of the most biologically diverse areas on earth—the Solimóes-Amazonas rainforest of northwestern Amazonia (Wetterberg, Prance, and Lovejoy 1981). It lies along the western border of the Napo center of diversity, an area considered by many researchers to be a Pleistocene refugia (Prance 1973; Gentry 1977; Barrett 1980:225; Myers 1979:600; Myers 1980:141).

The reserve is drained by western tributaries of the Amazon river and is dotted with 14 interconnected tropical lakes. It protects animal species found in large numbers in no other region of Ecuador, among them the fresh-water dolphin, manatee, 10 species of primates, tapirs, caimans, the giant armadillo, and innumerable birds and amphibians (Ulloa 1988). An estimated 30 percent of the reserve's 2,550 square kilometers is characterized by rivers, lakes, swamps, or seasonally inundated forest, making the area a rare combination of rainforest and wetlands.

Human Populations

The Cuyabeno area is not devoid of human populations. The same factors that draw our interest to the reserve today have in the past drawn both indigenous people and colonist populations to settle there. The Cuyabeno Reserve forms part of the traditional territory of the Siona-Secoya Indians, and a dozen families of this group hold legal title to 744 hectares located precisely in the center of the reserve. The Siona-Secoya see the reserve as providing them with a buffer zone between their traditional territory and the outside world, and as an opportunity to control the impact of Western society on their cultural traditions. Another group of 400 Siona-Secoya live in a legal reserve that shares a border with the Cuyabeno Reserve (Vickers 1983).

The Siona-Secoya are not the only group attracted by Cuyabeno's resources. Cuyabeno also has a half-dozen producing oil wells of Texaco and CEPE, the Ecuadorian State Oil Corporation. During the early 1980s, before the reserve had a full-time manager and park guards, these oil companies bulldozed roads into the extreme western region of the reserve, and several hundred colonist families from other parts of Ecuador moved down these roads into the edge of the reserve (Coello Hinojosa 1985; Hiraoka and Yamamoto 1980; Rudel 1983). They promptly began clearing 50 hectare plots for coffee, maize, cacao, and plantain production. Today, more than 1,000 people strain at the edges of the Cuyabeno Reserve, peering across the newly-cut border at the abundant wildlife and forest resources inside. The reserve's most pressing problem is these families' competing desire for the land the reserve occupies.

In a move designed to flow with, rather than violently confront, this wave of colonization, the Departamento de Areas Naturales worked out a compromise. The colonizing families were given legal title to their plots on two conditions: First, that they help physically delineate the reserve's revised boundaries by cutting a 3-meter wide path (*brecha*) around it, and second, that they sign a contract which states that if new colonists come in behind them, they themselves lose their right to the land. Needless to say, the fiercest defenders of the reserve's borders are now the colonists who once threatened to over-run it.

To compensate for the land ceded to these colonists, the *Patrimônio Foresta*, the National Forestry Institute of Ecuador, gave the Cuyabeno Reserve an additional 60,000 hectares of unpopulated rainforest and wetlands on the reserve's eastern border. This act increased the size of the reserve beyond what it had been before the wave of colonization.

Tourism and Scientific Research

The three aspects of economic production within the Cuyabeno Reserve use the presence of the colonists and the Siona-Secoya as a springboard for action. The first of these activities is tourism and scientific research. The Cuyabeno Reserve already receives an average of 150 registered visitors per month, most of them European, Israeli, and North American adventure-travelers. They visit the reserve by making arrangements with tour companies in Quito or directly with Siona-Secoya Indian guides at the reserve's headquarters in the small town of Tarapoa. The visitors travel down the reserve's rivers to its lakes by motorized dugout canoe in groups of five or six. The visitors pay $25 per day if they make arrangement with tour companies, and slightly less if they deal directly with indigenous guides. The tour companies pay the Siona canoeists and guides $25 per day for their services, with the tour companies providing the gasoline and oil. Within the reserve, one of six indigenous guards unobtrusively monitors the visitors' activities.

Before entering the reserve, each foreign visitor pays a $10 visitor's fee to the department guard stationed at Tarapoa, or the tour company pays the fees in bulk to the Department headquarters in Quito. Ecuadorian nationals pay only $1.50 per visit. All of these funds—a total of $18,000 a year—go into a general account within the Departamento de Areas Naturales for use by Ecuador's entire system of parks and reserves.

Probably an equal number of unregistered visitors come into the Cuyabeno Reserve by canoeing from the town of Lago Agrio up the Río Aguarico and, then, up the Río Cuyabeno. The Departamento de Áreas Naturales calls these unregistered visitors *fantasmas*, or ghosts, because they enter without paying the $10 fee. But they do pay canoeists from Lago Agrio $30 a day for the trip, or a fixed fee of $156, without food. If the park guards spot these ghost visitors, they also charge them the $10 entrance fee.

Because of fees paid directly to canoeists and guides, tourism injects more than $30,000 per year into the Siona-Secoya community of the Cuyabeno Reserve. One of the problems with this set-up is that only a few families—those with canoes with outboard motors—directly benefit from these funds. In particular, one family has standing contracts with two tour companies in Quito, and this family takes the bulk of tourism income.

On the other hand, several other Siona families benefit because one of their members serves as a park guard, receiving $75 per month in salary. But most of the dozen Siona-Secoya families produce cash income be selling corn, beans, rice, plantains, and manioc to local colonists.

One other man, the traditional leader of the Siona-Secoyas, and his wife earn $76 a month as the permanent guide and cook, respectively, to the Quito-based Universidad Católica. The university operates a biological research station on the largest of Cuyabeno's 14 tropical lakes. This research station trains Ecuadorian students in biology and ecology, and some of these students later enter the Departamento de Áreas Naturales as park biologists or managers.

Combined, scientific research, tourism, and reserve guard salaries provide more than $54,000 per year to local populations and to the Departamento de Áreas Naturales, not counting the income earned by Quito-based tourism companies.

Scientific research and tourism also provide other benefits to the reserve, because researchers and tour company operators constantly remind local residents that protecting the reserve's wildlife populations is important to their own economic future, just as it is important to the biologists and tour company operators.

Wildlife Harvesting

The other two aspects of economic production in the Cuyabeno Reserve focus on the use of wildlife as a protein source. Again, the local people, the Siona-Secoya and the colonists, are the foundation for this production.

As centuries-long residents of the Ecuadorian Amazon, the Siona-Secoya know better than anyone how to feed themselves from the natural resources the Cuyabeno Reserve is designed to protect (Vickers and Plowman 1984; Myers 1986). Fishing and hunting provide about 25 percent of the total caloric intake of the reserve's indigenous families and of the individuals of the Siona-Secoya Reserve that borders on Cuyabeno (Vickers 1976; 1983:456; 1984).

All of these individuals are allowed to practice subsistence hunting and fishing within the reserve, using shotguns, blowguns, and fishing lines. They are prohibited by park guards from using rifles, dynamite, or fish poisons. Through talks with the park manager and tour company operators, the Siona-Secoya have also agreed not to hunt around the lakes or along the Río Cuyabeno, because these areas make up the primary zones of tourist visits. Also, on their own, they have decided not to hunt the reserve's rarer species—species such as the giant *paiche* fish, manatees, and fresh-water dolphins—in agreement with the goal of increasing the reserve's wildlife populations for tourism and management.

How much income the Siona-Secoya's fishing and hunting represents in economic terms is difficult to establish. Data gathered in the Brazilian Amazon by Alfred Gardner of the U.S. Fish and Wildlife Service and Angel Paucar of Ecuador's Departamento de Areas Naturales indicate that five of the reserve's six largest mammals—peccaries, deer, tapirs, agoutis, and pacas—can be harvested at the average rate of 240 kilograms of meat per square kilometer per year, with a value of almost $500 per square kilometer, without decreasing natural populations (Paucar and Gardner 1981:3). Paucar and Gardner estimate that if we include the other species of mammals, fish, birds, and turtles normally consumed by populations in the Cuyabeno region, the total value of bushmeat reaches more than $4,000 per square kilometer per year (Pacuar and Gardner 1981:3).

Paucar and Gardner also state that the caiman of eastern Ecuador can be harvested at the rate of two per year from each hectare of swamp and river. The skin of each caiman is worth $75 in local markets. They conclude that each square kilometer of swamp and river can produce $14,500 worth of caiman skins per year (Paucar and Gardner 1981:3). Considering that 30 percent of Cuyabeno is caiman habitat, the controlled harvesting—not production—of caiman could produce hundreds of thousands of dollars of income per year, not counting the value of the meat.

By Paucar and Gardner's calculations, the 2,550 square kilometers of the Cuyabeno Reserve could produce millions of dollars a year in fish, skins, and bushmeat without destroying what is a renewable resource. This total seems almost incredible, but by any calculation the resource is considered significant enough by the Siona-Secoya that they are the first to report illegal poaching within the reserve by colonist populations or the occasional safari hunter.

The key point in this analysis is that legal harvesting of the reserve's wildlife is restricted to the Siona-Secoya, and pending further research, is not yet permitted on a large scale. This is not to say, however, that commercial hunting is not already practiced in the reserve. Two other indigenous groups who do not have legal hunting rights sometimes secretly enter the reserve and take out canoe-loads of bushmeat. A dozen families of Shuar, or Jívaro, Indians from the southern Ecuadorian Amazon have settled along the reserve's southwestern border in response to a political dispute within the Shuar Federation in the Province of Morona Santiago. Although the Shuar live mainly from agriculture and fishing, they sometimes hunt illegally and take out bushmeat and timber.

Another group, the Cofán Indians, have a legal reserve a few kilometers southwest of Cuyabeno, where until recently they lived by subsistence hunting. More recently, they have turned to commercial hunting to sell bushmeat to colonists and skins and feathers to tourists in the nearby town of Lago Agrio, and they have severely depleted the wildlife inside their legal reserve.

Led by the son of a North American missionary couple, the Cofanes have begun to enter the more isolated reaches of the Cuyabeno Reserve, where they kill any animals they find to obtain meat, skins, and feathers to sell. The managers of the reserve have had some success in gaining the cooperation of the local military garrison in controlling this commercial hunting, but the problem is still in need of solution.

Wildlife Production in Semi-Captivity

The final aspect of Cuyabeno's economy is still in its initial stages. This is the production and management of wildlife populations in semi-captivity, and it is this program that promises to serve as the backbone of the reserve's wildlife production economy.

In 1988, the Department established experimental *zoocriaderos*, or wildlife production areas, with the financial assistance of the World Wildlife Fund–U.S. and a $50,000 grant from the U.S. Agency for International Development. These initial experiments are focusing on the production in semi-captivity of charapa river turtles *Podocnemis expansa*, two species of peccaries, capybaras, agoutis, and pacas.

The work is being carried out with the ethnozoological knowledge of the Siona-Secoya Indians and with the labor and interest of local colonists. The goal is full-scale production of bushmeat for food, so that colonists can produce meat protein for consumption and sale, rather than sneaking into the reserve to poach existing wildlife populations.

Data gathered in the Brazilian Amazon by Paucar and Gardner indicate that raising charapa river turtles can produce 22,000 kilograms of turtle meat per hectare per year in small ponds (Paucar and Gardner 1981:14). By contrast, beef cattle production in the Cuyabeno region produces only 50 kilograms of meat per hectare per year and requires the clearing and burning of the natural forest (Paucar and Gardner 1981:14).

In 1988, charapa turtle meat sold in the Cuyabeno region for 300 Sucres per kilogram—about 94 cents at the March, 1988 rate of exchange. By those calculations, turtle meat can produce more than $20,000 per hectare per year, as opposed to $47 dollars per hectare per year for beef cattle. And it does this without eradicating the tropical forest. Charapa turtle eggs are also actively sold in the Cuyabeno region—currently from unmanaged deposits laid on exposed beaches along the region's rivers. Each turtle lays 30 to 90 eggs per year, and each egg is worth about three cents.

Capybaras, the fastest reproducer of the animals that the Departamento is planning to raise, produce between four and six progeny per litter and between 1.2 and 1.8 litters per year under natural conditions (González-Jiménez 1977:26). Each mature capybara weighs between 30 and 60 kilograms (Fundación Natura 1987:256–257). That means that, accounting for bone and other inedible parts, each capybara should be worth about $28 for meat alone, not counting hides, which are exported by some South American countries to Europe. Capybara hides are prized in glove manufacturing, because they stretch in one direction, but not in the other (González-Jiménez 1977:28).

Cuyabeno Reserve staff members are now gathering data on the production requirements of other edible animals. During 1988, they are visiting animal production facilities in Peru, Colombia, and Venezuela, and with the information they gather, they will begin construction of production facilities inside the Cuyabeno Reserve.

Conclusions

The actual amount of income that Cuyabeno will eventually produce for local indigenous and colonist populations is still unknown. If we take Paucar and Gardner's calculations for the production of bushmeat and skins—produced both through controlled hunting and in semi-captivity—it seems clear that the reserve can generate a minimum of several hundreds of thousands of dollars per year.

By contrast, we can look at land-use practices outside the reserve, where the common practice is to log the area, raise several years of maize, rice, and plantains, then dedicate the area to beef cattle. Colonists who sign contracts with lumber companies receive up to $78 per hectare to see an average of 15 commercial trees per hectare pulled out (Dirección Nacional Forestal, MAG 1988, personal communication). If the colonists then dedicate the land to food crops, then to cattle production, as more than half of them do, they may hope to receive an income of a few hundred dollars per hectare per year over the decade or less that the thin, tropical soils will produce.

The colonists' alternative is to take part in the reserve's wildlife production systems, which promise—even at the lowest calculations— an income of $1,000 or more per hectare per year, in perpetuity. It is this temptation that the reserve's managers hope will draw in not just the populations living on the borders of the reserve, but also those who live in the buffer zones around it.

In providing this alternative economic system, the Cuyabeno Wildlife Production Reserve will gradually achieve its long-term goal of balancing the requirements of biological conservation with the economic needs of local populations. In doing so, it will provide another important alternative for the fragile lands of Latin America.

References

Barrett, Suzanne W. 1980. Conservation in Amazonia. *Biological Conservation* 18:209–235.

CLIRSEN. 1985. Levantamiento Forestal de la Región Amazonica Ecuatoriana (Sector Norte: Provinicia de Napo). Centro de Levantamientos Integrados de Recursos Naturales por Sensores Remotos. Dirección Nacional Forestal, Ministerio de Agricultura y Ganadería, Quito, Ecuador.

Coello Hinojosa, Flavio. 1985. *Censo y Diagnóstico de la Reserva Faunística Cuyabeno, Napo.* Departamento de Parques Nacionales y Vida Silvestre, Dirección General de Desarrollo Forestal, Quito.

CONADE/PNUMA. 1987. Proyecto Propuesta de Manejo de Recursos Naturales en la Región Amazónica Ecuatoriana. Consejo Nacional de Desarrollo, Programa Nacional de Unificación y Manejo, Secretaría General de Planificación, Quito, Ecuador.

Dirección Nacional Forestal. 1988. Personal communication. Ministerio de Agricultura y Ganadería, Quito, Ecuador.

Fundación Natura. 1987. Estudio para el Establacimiento de una Fundación para la Conservación de los Recursos Bióticos de la Amazonía. Informe Final, Quito, Ecuador.

Gentry, Alwyn H. 1977. Endangered Plant Species and Habitats of Ecuador and Amazonian Peru. Pp. 136–149, in: Ghillean T. Prance and Thomas S. Elias, editors, *Extinction Is Forever.* Bronx, New York: New York Botanical Garden.

González-Jiménez, E. 1977. the Capybara: An Indigenous Source of Meat in Tropical America. *World Animal Review.* Napoli, Italy: Food and Agriculture Organization.

Hiraoka, Mario and Shozo Yamamoto. 1980. Agricultural Development in the Upper Amazon of Ecuador. *Geographical Review* 70(4):423–445.

Landázuri, Helena. 1987. La Cuenca Amazónica: Argumentos en Favor de un Manejo Integrado. International Institute for Environment and Development, Ediciones Abya-Yala, Quito, Ecuador.

Melillo, J.M., C.A. Palm, R.A. Houghton, G.M. Woodwell, and Norman Myers. 1985. "Comparison of Two Recent Estimates of Disturbance in Tropical Forests," Environmental Conservation 12 (1).

Myers, Norman. 1979. Islands of Conservation. *New Scientist* 83(1169):600–602.

———. 1980. *Conversion of Tropical Moist Forests.* Washington, D.C.: National Academy of Sciences.

———. 1986. Forestland Farming in Western Amazonia: Stable and Sustainable. Forest Ecology and Management 15:81–93.

Paucar, Angel M. & Alfred L. Gardner. 1981. Establecimiento de una Estación de Investigaciones Científicas en el Parque Nacional Yasuní de la República de Ecuador. Reporte Preparado Bajo el Programa Nacional Forestal, Ministerio de Agricultura y Ganadería, Quito, Ecuador.

Prance, G.T. 1973. Phytogeographic Support for the Theory of Pleistocene Forest Refuges in the Amazon Basin, Based on Evidence from Distribution Patterns in Caryocaraceae, Chrysobalanceae, Dichapetalaceae and Lecythidaceae. *Acta Amazonica* 3(3):5–28.

Putney, Allen D. 1979. *Estrategia Preliminar para la Conservación de Áreas Silvestres Sobresalientes del Ecuador.* United Nations Development Program/ Food and Agriculture Organization-Ecuador/71/527, Documento de Trabajo No. 17. Quito: Departamento de Parques Nacionales y Vida Silvestre, Dirección General de Desarrollo Forestal. pp. 47.

Rudel, Thomas K. 1983. Roads, Speculators, and Colonization in the Ecuadorian Amazon. *Human Ecology* 11(4):385–403.

Ulloa, Roberto. 1988. Estudios Sinecologico de Primates en la Reserva de Producción Faunística Cuyabeno. Tesis de Licenciatura. Universidad Católica, Quito, Ecuador.

Vickers, William T. 1976. *Cultural Adaptation to Amazonian Habitats: The Siona-Secoya of Eastern Ecuador.* Ph.D. thesis, University of Florida, Gainesville. (University of Texas Benson Latin American Collection).

———. 1983. The Territorial Dimensions of Siona-Secoya and Encabellado Adaptation. Chapter 15, Raymond B. Hames and William T. Vickers, editors, *Adaptive Responses of Native Amazonians.* New York: Academic Press.

———. 1984. The Faunal Components of Lowland South American Hunting Kills. *INTERCIENCIA* 9(6):366–376.

Vickers, William T. and T. Plowman. 1984. Useful Plants of the Siona and Secoya Indians of Eastern Ecuador. Fieldiana Botany, New Series 15. Field Museum of Natural History, Chicago, Illinois.

Wetterberg, Gary B., Ghillean T. Prance, Thomas E. Lovejoy. 1981. Conservation Progress in Amazonia: A Structural Review. *Parks* 6(2):5–10.

10

Extractive Reserves: The Rubber Tappers' Strategy for Sustainable Use of the Amazon Rainforest

Stephan Schwartzman

Introduction

There are approximately 1.5 million people in the Brazilian Amazon who depend on the forest for their living. Of these, some 300,000 depend on sustainable harvesting of wild rubber (IBGE, 1980). In addition, it is believed that there are substantial numbers of agriculturalists and urban wage workers in the region who depend on forest product extraction for a crucial portion of household income. In spite of their numbers, little is known about the microeconomies of Amazon rubber tappers. In a recent conference on extraction in the Amazon, a Brazilian government official, discussing a survey of rubber tappers in the state of Rondonia, summed up the problem this way: "We know they live [in the forest], but we don't know how they live." Recent work, both historical and ethnographic, suggests that these populations are more diverse, resilient, and adaptive to both ecosystems and markets than was previously realized (Weinstein, 1983; Almeida, in press). The aim of this study is to discuss the resource management and income generation strategies of independent rubber tappers in the Acre River Valley of western Brazil with the hope that this information may improve development plans for the fragile Amazon rainforests.

The data presented here are based on a survey of 33 rubber collector households planned and executed by the Institute for Amazon Studies in collaboration with the National Council of Rubber Tappers (CSN), in October and November 1987, on Seringal Cachoeira, in the municipality of Xapuri, Acre, Brazil.

Extractive Reserves

Extractive reserves as defined by the Ministry of Agrarian Reform and Development (MIRAD) are forest areas inhabited by extractive populations granted long-term usufruct rights to forest resources which they collectively manage.

The concept of extractive reserves emerges as a local, Amazonian response to massive deforestation and environmentally and socially disastrous development schemes. According to recent studies, some 12% of the entire Amazon forest has been cleared to date, and this has occurred over only about the last 13 years (Setzer et al., 1987). This means that about 4.7 million hectares of Amazon rainforest are deforested each year. The dynamics of this destructive process are complex, but two factors are central. The leading cause of deforestation in the Amazon is conversion for cattle pasture (Hecht et al., in press). A related or triggering factor is road construction (Fearnside 1986; Malingreau and Tucker, 1988), which permits access to isolated areas and also plays a key role in the dynamics of land speculation, intimately linked to cattle ranching in the Amazon (Hecht et al., in press). Areas of rapid development are characterized not only by massive deforestation, but acute land conflicts and violence (Branford and Glock, 1985), high rates of colonist attrition from official and spontaneous colonization projects, varying between 50% and 80% (Hecht, 1987), and rapid, uncontrolled rural to urban migration (Wood and Wilson, 1984; Hecht et al., in press).

The conservationist response to this process has been to call for the creation of protected areas—parks—where flora and fauna of scientific and aesthetic importance may be preserved. The model for this sort of conservation is found in the United States and western Europe, and in key points this model is problematic for Brazil, and third world countries in general. The National Park system in the U.S. depends on the existence of large, middle class constituency that supports the creation and protection of parks, and uses them regularly for educational, leisure or aesthetic experience. The U.S. system is also founded on a long history of wildlife legislation and legal action, as well as federal and state institutions designed to safeguard natural resources including uninhabited natural areas. In the Amazon, there is little evidence that such an approach can succeed. There are no strong constituencies to defend parks. Environmental agencies are relatively powerless to prevent disregard for the areas they create, and in the Amazon such agencies, rarely have any effective presence. The Brazilian Institute for Forestry Development (IBDF) has 800 wardens to control the use and management of 28 National Parks and 15 Biological

Reserves nationally, including administrative personnel. In Rondonia, for example, where specific protected areas were funded by the World Bank, all have been invaded by loggers, miners, or colonists.

Extractive reserves are important precisely because they are not simply another U.S.-style conservation proposal, but an organized initiative directly undertaken by Amazonian grassroots groups and sympathetic national organizations, to change the course of official regional development policy for the benefit of local Amazonian communities. Because the concept of extractive reserves originates with local groups who depend on the standing, living forest for their livelihood, it addresses both economic and environmental considerations in an integrated fashion. Extractive reserves propose that much-discussed but rarely realized anodyne for development debacles, sustainable development.

It is particularly important to understand the conditions that enable rubber tappers to remain viable in the forest, and how their local economies are organized. Rubber tapper organizations have made unprecedented advances in influencing both national and international development policy since the first national meeting of rubber tappers in Brasilia in 1985 (Schwartzman and Allegretti, in press). The rubber tappers proposal for "extractive reserves," or collectively managed forest areas for extractive populations, has been endorsed by the World Bank and the Inter-American Development Bank (IDB) as ". . . the most promising alternative to land clearing and colonization schemes . . ." (World Bank, 1982). The World Bank is supporting the creation of five extractive reserves totalling 1 million ha in Rondonia, while the IDB will support the creation of four reserves, totaling some 500,000 hectares as part of the recently renegotiated Plan to Protect the Environment and Indigenous Communities (PMACI) associated with the IDB financed Porto Velho-Rio Branco road improvement project. The state governments of both Acre and Rondonia (in particular the former) have embraced the extractive reserves concept as a locally appropriate conservation/development proposal (*Jornal do Brasil,* 2/28/88). The Ministry of Agrarian Reform and Development has adopted a legal measure for the creation of the reserves (Portaria 627, July 30, 1987), created by the former Institute of Colonization and Agrarian Reform in collaboration with the CSN and the Institute for Amazon Studies. This legal mechanism, the "extractive settlement project," establishes the real possibility, if not obligation, for MIRAD to establish extractive reserves on government land or land expropriated for agrarian reform all over the Amazon. While institutional mechanisms and support for the creation of reserves exist, even minimal baseline data on petty extraction in areas where reserves are being created is weak or non-existent. Studies of these systems are urgently needed, particularly in light of current environmental trends in the Amazon.

Extraction and Autonomous Rubber Tappers:
Units of Production and Land Tenure

The basic unit of native rubber production in the Amazon since the rubber boom has been the *seringal,* translated by Weinstein (1983) in her study of the rubber boom as "rubber estate."[1] During the rubber boom, and up to the present in many regions of the western Amazon, the seringal was subdivided into a *barração,* or depot, the headquarters of the patron's operation where rubber was bought and merchandise sold, and a number of *colocações,* or holdings, the residences of rubber tapper families. In the seringais occupied by independent rubber tappers, the barração no longer exists, since the patrons have either abandoned the seringais or sold out to cattle ranchers from the south (Schwartzman and Allegretti, in press). In seringais with ongoing conflicts, the barração has typically become the ranch house or headquarters of the cattle ranch.

Seringal Cachoeira, located in the municipality of Xapuri some 15 kilometers south of the BR-317 highway on the Bolivian border, occupies 24,898 hectares and is inhabited by 67 rubber tapper families, or about 420 people. The average size per holding is about 372 ha.

Seringal Cachoeira, like the majority of the seringais in Xapuri, was sold to a cattle rancher in 1978 whose manager lives where the depot formerly stood. Unlike on the other seringais in the vicinity of the county seat and near the road, the rancher who claims Cachoeira has not deforested any of the land. In October 1987, the rubber tappers staged a successful demonstration against the opening of a road which the rancher had wanted to run through the seringal, and blocked its construction. Like most of the seringais in the area, Seringal Cachoeira is also claimed by the rubber tappers who live there (many of them for over thirty years). Legal title to clearly delimited areas of land was relatively unimportant during the rubber boom. Control over a labor force dispersed through the forest according to the location of unevenly distributed rubber trees was more important. Consequently, many of the titles sold during the land boom of the 1970s are imprecise or conflict with other claims. In addition, untitled occupants (*posseiros*), such as the rubber tappers who can show that they have been on the land for more than a year and have made improvements, have rights under Brazilian land legislation. Seringal Cachoeira was surveyed in

1978 by the National Institute of Colonization and Agrarian Reform (INCRA), and the presence of the rubber tappers as untitled occupants was registered. Final resolution of conflicts such as this one depends on a number of factors: actual occupation of the land, access to legal counsel, awareness of judicial procedures, productive use made of the land, and political influence. In this case, the Xapuri rubber tappers' union is actively pressing INCRA and the state government for the creation of a reserve on Cachoeira, and has made important advances in this effort.

Cachoeira, like every seringal, is divided into a number of holdings or areas of usufruct (*colocações*), and each coloçacão constitutes a production unit, its residents retaining rights to exploit the resources on it. Cash income is largely generated through sale of rubber and Brazil nuts, while household subsistence is guaranteed through small scale agriculture and livestock, hunting, fishing, and collecting. An average holding exploits about 1,100 rubber trees, distributed over six *estradas de seringa,* or rubber trails, has 2.16 hectares of land in agriculture and 5.9 hectares of pasture. Rubber trails vary in length and configuration according to the natural distribution of the rubber trees in the forest, and this is basic to understanding rubber tapper land use techniques. Rubber tappers, who extract other forest products as well (Appendix A), know precisely the limits of each holding (so much so that if a Brazil nut tree is on the boundary of a holding, the nuts that fall to one side belong to one household, and those on the other side to the other household). Rubber tappers also carefully calculate the size and location of their gardens and pasture areas on their holdings relative to the varied natural resources they extract. Consequently, in cases where INCRA has expropriated rubber estates in conflict and granted title to the rubber tappers according to a standard 50 or 100 hectare module, the effect is often that the rubber tapper communities can no longer make a living on the land, and leave the seringal. Some holdings lose part or all of their rubber or Brazil nut trees, thereby reducing income. In such cases households are forced to over-exploit the land for agriculture, then sell it, typically to cattle ranchers. The end result is the concentration of landholdings, forest conversion to cattle pasture, and out-migration. A number of families interviewed in Cachoeira left the neighboring Seringal Ecuador because it was divided into 50 to 100 ha lots, and some recent urban dwellers gave this as the cause of their migration to the city. Failure to recognize the spatial configuration of rubber tapper land use on the part of the government's land agencies contributes directly to land concentration, deforestation, and rural to urban migration.

Income Generation, Social Structure, and Surplus Accumulation on the Seringal

Two central points emerge from our survey. First, the population of the seringal has been able to maintain itself on this or other seringais in the region over a long period of time. Second the mixed economy of the rubber tappers produces a surplus on the seringal itself, not counting the surplus obtained from the commercialization of rubber latex, and does so without degrading the natural resource base.

The population of Seringal Cachoeira is predominantly Acrean— 85% percent of the families surveyed are from Acre, and 60% from the municipality of Xapuri. The average time of residence on the holding was 11 years, and some 30% of the residents have been on the same holding for more than 15 years. In comparative regional terms this is a very stable population (Wood and Wilson 1984). In terms of income, an average family produces 750 kg of rubber and 325 *latas* (or 4,500 kg) of Brazil nuts per year, with a combined gross cash value of about U.S. $960[2] and the upper 30% of the households surveyed had annual incomes from rubber and Brazil nut extraction of over U.S. $1,500. This calculation excludes housing material, fodder, fruit, and increase in small livestock herds, as well as income generated in the most prosperous households through commercial transactions. To put this in regional context, 50% of the economically active population in 1980 in the Brazilian Amazon (North) region earned slightly less than one minimum salary per month (IBGE 1984), whereas the population in our survey earned almost two minimum monthly salaries.

There is, however, an internal social stratification in the seringal; some of the oldest, largest and wealthiest holdings are occupied by rubber tappers who are also petty merchants, the first in the chain of middlemen who buy and sell rubber and Brazil nuts and exchange merchandise on credit. These middlemen, and other urban residents, advance goods and cash against future rubber production. Although the traditional company store system under which rubber tappers were tied to a single patron for all transactions has ended on Cachoeira, as on most estates in the region (rubber tappers are free to commercialize their products where they can), many rubber tappers are in debt to middlemen. This may be reflected by our observation that about 55% of our sample households had a cash deficit at the time of our survey of about $350 per family. However, 44% of the sample had a cash surplus of an average of $680. A key question is whether this difference in financial performance is significant, and if so, what factors explain the difference.

The seringal as a whole may be regarded as a micro-economy based on rubber production and cash. This is indeed the way that middlemen, both in the city of Xapuri and on the seringal itself regard it, advancing goods and cash against future production. The rubber tappers own both fixed and semi-fixed assets of considerable value. The coloçacão, or holding, has an average cash value of $322, and most families own livestock—chickens, ducks, pigs, sheep, cattle, horses, and donkeys. Counting only larger livestock (i.e. not chickens and ducks, the most common livestock), the survey-typical rubber tapper household owned about $532 worth of animals.[3] Livestock, like land holdings, are acquired with cash, or its equivalent, rubber. Looking only at cash income and expenditures, any actual accumulation of surplus on the seringal would be inexplicable, since household cash income and cash expenses tend to balance. Successful subsistence agricultural production permits some accumulation of surplus. The more successful a family is in producing beans, rice, corn, manioc, milk, game, etc., the less it must buy from middlemen in a given year, leaving cash profit to be invested for example, in livestock, or a motor to run a mechanized manioc grater. The diversity of the production system not only permits long-term occupation of the seringal and household reproduction, it also produces surplus in two paradoxical ways: middlemen accumulate a surplus from rubber tappers who are unsuccessful subsistence producers; and those rubber tapper families who are self-sufficient in food production in the seringal accumulate a surplus from extraction.

The production system of the seringal appears to be indefinitely sustainable. Many rainforest areas have been occupied by rubber tappers for over 60 years, and some families have been on the same holdings for 40 or 50 years, yet about 98% of each holding is in natural forest. This is perhaps permitted by a short fallow farming cycle: informants state that a new garden is planted with rice then cleared toward the end of the rainy season in April and planted with beans, which are harvested in June. The garden is then cleared again and manioc is planted, which is typically harvested within a year to eighteen months. There are then two alternatives: the area may be planted with grass for pasture, or it may be allowed to return to secondary forest. In the latter case, the agricultural cycle may be begun again after six to seven years. In either case, it is apparent that large parts of each holding which contain both rubber and Brazil nut trees permanently remain in primary forest.

Interestingly, while seringeiros are competent extractors, their performance as farmers is less impressive. Agricultural yields are low by regional standards and gardens are not always successful: This may be a major cause of cash deficit along with periodic indebtedness and

Table 1
Area and Population of Proposed Extractive Reserves in Acres and Amazonas

Name of Seringal	State	Area (ha)	Number of Colocacoes	Number of Families[a]	Area/family (ha)
Cachoeira Santa	Acre	25,000	43	67	372
Quiteria	Acre	41,000	136	212	193
São Luis do Remanso	Acre	39,000	102	159	245
Macauan	Acre	103,000	343	535	192
Antimari	Amazonas	335,000	1,118	1,744	192

[a] The number of families per seringal is approximate, except for Seringal Cachoeira.

Source: Personal communication with Interamerican Development Bank, June 1, 1988.

suggests that either soils are no better for agriculture than the average for the region or that there are important variations in extractive survival strategies among rubber tappers. Nevertheless, the diversity of sources of income make long term occupation of the seringal feasible, and indeed, from the point of view of the overwhelming majority of the families there, worth defending. Part of this manifest desire to remain on the Seringal and invest in improvements there is undoubtedly linked to considerations that are difficult to quantify: rubber tappers value the forest, their diet is more balanced than that of urban populations–they eat game, cultivate or manage some 50 fruits, palms and other trees, and use many more forest species (see Appendix A).

While it is presently impossible to say precisely how much land per family is required to sustain one rubber tapper household in the Amazon overall, the average area occupied per family on Seringal Cachoeira (373 hectares) is high by regional standards, implying a more land-extensive strategy. The average area occupied per family on the four seringals proposed as extractive reserves in the region is about 200 hectares (see Table 1). This discrepancy suggests that Seringal Cachoeira may not be typical of those areas proposed by the government for extractive reserves. Accordingly, my survey results should be regarded as preliminary.

The actual return on labor in this system is difficult to calculate, since many activities using family labor not uniformly valued in the labor market are involved in daily production. An approximate (and preliminary) calculation of two scenarios of labor invested in rubber and Brazil nut production, the main income-generating activities, follows: The labor investment (of adult man-days) in rubber and Brazil nut production ranges between 142 days per year and 268 days per year. This includes preparation of trails for rubber extraction, and collecting rubber, as well as gathering and breaking the outer husks of Brazil nuts. Processing rubber must also be considered. On Cachoeira, latex is left to coagulate into "biscuits" which are then pressed into blocks. Total labor time (man-days per year) in rubber and Brazil nut production range from 12 to 18 days preparing 6 rubber trails, 90 to 180 days extracting latex, 12 to 24 days in latex processing and 40 to 70 days collecting Brazil nuts. The average total labor expenditure for latex collection and Brazil nut gathering were 142 and 57 days respectively. Taking 200 hectares as the average area occupied per family in the region (see Table 1), labor investment per hectare/year in rubber and Brazil nut production ranges between .71 days/ha./yr. and 1.34 days/ha/yr. The value of this labor is open to discussion. Wage labor is rare on the seringal. In the city of Rio Branco CZ$4,000 per month was a high salary, earned by men fortunate enough to find work in the government, for example. At six work days per week, four weeks per month, the daily formal sector wage rate is about $2.60. At this rate, the low labor cost in extraction on the Seringal is about $1.60 per hectare/year, and the high labor cost is about $3.50 per hectare/year. Recalling that cash income from rubber and Brazil nuts averaged $960 per year, or $4.80 per hectare/year, for an average household, there is a positive return on labor of at least 37% per hectare/year.

Rubber Policy and the Subsidy for Native Rubber Production

It has been argued that the major flaw in the extractive reserves proposal is the costly Brazilian price subsidy protecting "primitive" methods of domestic natural rubber production. The subsidy is in fact an import tax on rubber paid by industry on imported rubber, natural and synthetic, protecting Brazilian rubber producers against lower world market prices. This tax, the Rubber Market Organization and Regulation tax (TORMB), established by law 5.459 of 6/21/68, art. 22, paragraph 1, keeps the price of imported rubber equivalent to domestic industry production costs, thereby, guaranteeing national rubber a market and providing the Superintendency for Rubber Development (SUDHEVEA) with a budget. Since Brazil only produces about 35% of the natural rubber used in industry and imports the rest, (see Table 2) considerable income is generated through the TORMB. If it were not for the subsidy, so the argument goes, there would be no rubber tappers, and so no extractive reserves. It is undoubtedly true that rubber price

Table 2
Rubber Prices and Amazonian Native Rubber Production

Year	Brazil Controlled Price (US$/kg)	World Market Price (US$/kg)	Domestic Amazonian Rubber Production (000 m.t.)	Natural Rubber Imports by Brazil (000 m.t.)
1980	2.13	1.37	23.2	56.2
1981	2.52	1.08	24.3	44.5
1982	2.23	0.75	26.3	38.1
1983	1.58	0.95	28.2	35.2
1984	1.55	0.90	28.5	59.2

Sources: SUDHEVEA (1984, 1985); Dean (1987).

policy has reflected a long history of special pleading and political deal-making (Dean 1987), but this hardly seems exceptional in a region where virtually all economic activities have been subsidized. It is also true that rubber price supports have done little if anything to improve the situation of rubber tappers, since price increases for rubber are rapidly overtaken by corresponding or greater increases in the price of the market goods that rubber tappers buy.

Rubber is one among several sources of household income. In our sample, for example, Brazil nuts represented an average 50% of cash income, and could surely be further exploited. This is not however, an argument to eliminate the "subsidy," or reduce rubber tapper cash income. As Noronha's (1983) study suggests, income can be increased, and the cost of production of native rubber lowered, by improved marketing and access to market goods on better terms for rubber tappers.

Furthermore, in the Amazonian context, where several land uses are often in direct and violent conflict, it is important to see rubber pricing in relation to policy toward other sectors. The total value of the subsidy on native Brazilian rubber produced on average between 1980 and 1984, averaged about 25 million dollars a year (Table 2). This was less than half of the import tax (TORMB) actually collected (in 1985, $54 million) (SUDHEVEA 1984, 1985). The TORMB is also levied on imported synthetic rubber, and national rubber. If the purpose of the import tax policy were merely to support Amazonian rubber production, it could be done much more cheaply by means of a direct subsidy to the rubber tappers. More importantly, the "rubber subsidy" is relatively minor in comparison to various subsidies to other sectors competing for land in the Amazon. The government's tax credits to corporate cattle ranches in the Amazon, for example, represented a cost of more than $1 billion between 1975 and 1986, or over 90 million dollars a year for 527 projects alone (Binswanger 1987). These projects show a negative return on invested resources, and in many cases have not been implemented as planned (Ibid). These government subsidized cattle projects alone have caused up to 4 million hectares of deforestation (Ibid). In this light, the rubber price subsidy, as it relates to native rubber is relatively insignificant. Elimination of government subsidies may be a reasonable policy goal, but elimination of the rubber price support while maintaining subsidies for the livestock sector would heavily favor a demonstrably unproductive and resource destructive land use (Hecht et al. in press) over one that employs more people, conserves the natural environment and is being defended by organized local constituencies that appreciate the economic value of the rainforest.

Another issue in considering the Brazilian rubber pricing policy and subsidy concerns the factors that condition the world market for rubber. Plantation rubber from southeast Asia since the 1920s has been cheaper than native rubber produced in the Amazon. But exogenous factors have had significant effects on production and export of rubber from Southeast Asia as well. From 1971 to 1980, the World Bank loaned $676.4 million to Indonesia, Malaysia, Thailand, Cameroon and other natural rubber producing countries for rubber development projects or rubber components of projects (World Bank 1982). The Bank financed an average of 50% of total project costs and total investment (by the Bank and governments) was about $1.06 billion over nine years, or $117 million a year, directly supporting production and processing of natural rubber for export. It is then an oversimplification to conceive the Brazilian rubber policy problem as subsidized rubber production versus the unrestrained free world market. The issue is, in both cases, colored by government fiscal policy and the investment behavior of multilateral lending institutions.

The central issue here is that native rubber production in the Amazon has been discussed largely in the context of the Brazilian rubber industry's demand, and the failure of rubber policy to resolve a chronic supply deficiency. Yet, nowhere in the world is natural rubber produced at an export-scale that is unsubsidized. Amazon native rubber, subsidized or not, will not supply Brazil's needs for natural rubber. But maintaining a guaranteed market for rubber tappers may help to diminish deforestation, provide employment, and maintain a productive population on a fragile land.

Social Movements and Resource Management

Perhaps the most important point about extractive reserves as a strategy for the sustainable use of "fragile lands" is that the proposal embodies the aspirations of a social movement—autonomous, unionized rubber tappers. It is necessary to describe household income generation and resource management in order to understand the role of sustainable natural resource extraction in Amazonian rural economies. These are necessary but insufficient conditions to explain the appearance of the extractive reserve concept in regional development planning. The creation of a legal mechanism for reserves, and the institutional support won for this proposal are results of the organized pressure the rubber tappers' movement brought to influence state and federal agencies as well as multilateral lending institutions that invest in Amazonian development. Because the proposal was created by a social movement, its implementation does not depend exclusively on government agencies, which in the Amazon often have little political power, or administrative and technical capacity (Schwartzman and Arnt 1988). The rubber tappers, nevertheless have made government agencies respond to their demands.

Conclusion

The creation of extractive reserves represents a new way of integrating conservation and rural economic development in the Amazon. For the rubber tappers promoting this concept, the two issues are inextricably linked, and therein lies the strength of the proposal. The local organizations involved have made enormous progress since the idea emerged in 1985, and this momentum will continue. The fragile land use strategies of autonomous rubber tappers furnish them an income that puts them above half of the economically active population of the region. The higher economic value of extraction, compared to other land uses (e.g. some forms of cattle ranching and agriculture), is another way of approaching the economic viability of extractive reserves (Hecht and Schwartzman 1988). The viability of extractive reserves, does not necessarily depend on the rubber price subsidy; it depends on development policy for the Amazon, including incentives for livestock and other activities, and the institutional means of government to address the needs and aspirations of Amazonian populations. What is perhaps most novel, and most important in this proposal is that forest communities have put their own model before the government and multinational lending institutions as a potential strategy for the sustainable development of some of the Amazon's fragile tropical forest lands.

Acknowledgments

This article continues research jointly initiated in 1985 with Mary Helena Allegretti of the Institute for Amazon Studies. Survey data for this paper were collected in 1987 with the assistance of Paolo Chiesa, also of the Institute of Amazon Studies. I am indebted for much of my understanding of Rubber Tapper and other extractive populations to Ms. Allegretti and Mauro Almeida. Dr. Susanna Hecht made fundamental contributions to the research design of this project and Dr. John Browder's comments and criticisms were extremely useful. Any errors are of course my own.

Notes

1. From *seringa,* "rubber," also the root of seringueira, "rubber tree," seringal, "rubber estate," seringueiro, "rubber tapper," seringalista, "patron" owner or claimant of a rubber estate; rubber baron.

2. All prices are as of November 1987.

3. This figure is derived from a count of cattle, pigs, horses, donkeys, and sheep on the 31 households for which we have information. Prices were derived from conservative estimates based on reported sale prices within the seringal or in the town of Xapuri: cattle were valued at Cz$5,000 a head, pigs at Cz$1,000, donkeys and horses at Cz$6,000 and sheep at Cz$2,000. Cattle prices are particularly conservatively estimated, since some families had more valuable breeds (such as Nelore) which sold for Cz$10,00-15,000 a head, but it was assumed that all cattle were *pe duro,* the lowest value classification. Chickens and ducks, the most common domestic animals, were not counted.

References

Almeida, Mauro Barbosa de. in press. Seringais e trabalho na amazonia: o caso do alto Jurua. Anuario Antropologico. *Universidade da Brasilia.*

Binswanger, Hans. 1987. Fiscal and Legal Incentives With Environmental Effects on the Brazilian Amazon. Discussion paper, Research Unit, Agricultural and Rural Development Dept. OPS World Bank.

Branford, Susan, and Oriel Glock. 1985. The Last Frontier: Fighting Over Land in the Amazon, Zed Books, London.

Dean, Warren. 1987. Brazil and the Struggle for Rubber, ed. 1, Cambridge University Press, Cambridge.

Fearnside, Philip. 1986. Spatial Concentration of Deforestation in the Brazilian Amazon. Ambio 15:74–81.

Hecht, Susanna B., et al., in press. "The Economics of Cattle Ranching in Eastern Amazonia." Interciencia.

————. 1987. "Contemporary Dynamics of Amazonian Development: Reanalyzing Colonist Attrition." UCLA Graduate School of Urban Planning Working Papers.

———— & Stephan Schwartzman. 1988. The Good, the Bad and the Ugly: Extraction, Colonist Agriculture and Livestock in Comparative Economic

Perspective. UCLA Graduate School of Architecture and Urban Planning Working Papers.

IBGE (Instituto Braziliero Geografico e Estatistico). 1980. Censo Demografia: Mao de Obra.

———. 1984. Annuario Estatistico do Brasil.

Malingreau, Jean-Paul, and Compton J. Tucker. 1988. Large Scale Deforestation in the Southeastern Amazon Basin of Brazil. Ambio 17:49–55.

Noronha, Jose Ferreira de et al. 1983. Custo de Produção da Borracha natural em seringais nativos. SUDHEVEA, Brasilia.

Schwartzman, Stephan, and Mary Helena Allegretti, in press. Extractive Production and the Brazilian Rubber Tappers Movement. *In* S. Hecht and J. Nations eds. The Social Dynamics of Deforestation: Processes and Alternatives. Cornell University Press, Ithaca.

& Ricardo Azambuja Arnt. 1988. Mapeamento de Agéncias Ambientáis, organizações Não-governamentáis e Pesquisadores. Ford Foundation, Brazil.

Setzer, Alberto W., and M.C. Pereira, A.C. Pereira, Junior, S.A. de Oliveira Alameida. 1987. Relatorio do projeto IBDF-INPE "SEQE," Instituto de Pesquisas Espacias, Ministerio da ciencia e Tecnología, Brasilia.

SUDHEVEA. 1984. Relatorio de Atividades. Superintendencia de Borracha, Brasilia.

———. 1985. Projeção da Arrecadação da TORMB para o periodo 1985–1986. Superinténdencia de Borracha, Brasilia.

Weinstein, Barbara. 1983. The Amazon Rubber Boom 1850–1920, Stanford University Press, Stanford, CA.

Wood, Charles H. and John Wilson. 1984. The Magnitude of Migration to the Brazilian frontier. *In* Schmink and Wood, (eds.), Frontier Expansion in Amazonia, University of Florida Press Press, Gaineville.

World Bank. 1982. Natural Rubber Sector Policy Paper. Washington D.C.

———. 1986. Statement of Loans. Washington D.C.

Appendix A
Tree and Fruit Species Planted and Managed by Rubber Tappers

Portuguese Name	English Name	Latin Name
Cultivated fruit trees		
Laranga	Orange	*Citrus aurantium*
Lima	Lime	*Citrus* sp.
Limão	Lemon	*Citrus aurantifolia*
Limão galego		*Citrus medica*
Tangerina	Tangerine	*Citrus reticulata*
Graviola	Soursop	*Annona muricata*
Cupuaçu		*Theobroma grandiflora*
Caju	Cashew	*Anacardium occidentale*
Biribá		*Rollinia mucosa*
Mamão	Papaya	*Carica papaya*
Banana	Banana	*Musa* sp.
Comprida		
Macã		
Torinha		
Roxa-branca		
Roxa		
Prata		
Chifre de bode		
peroa		
Chifre de boi		
Manga	Mango	*Mangifera indica*
Abacate	Avocado	*Persea americana*
Goiaba	Guava	*Psidium guajava*
Jaca	Jackfruit	
Fruta pão	Breadfruit	
Azeitona		
Ciriguelo		
Jambu		
Cutiribá		
Coco de bahia	Coconut palm	*Cocos nucifera*
Abacaxi	Pineapple	*Ananas comosus*
Café	Coffee	*Coffea arabica*
Cana de açucar	Sugarcane	*Saccharum officinarum*
Genipapo		*Genipa americana*
Urucum		*Bixa orellana*
Castanhola		
Bacuri		*Platonia insignis*
Cacau	Cocoa	*Theobroma cacao*
Maracuja	Passion fruit	*Passiflora edulia*
Apurui		
Caja		*Spondias dulcis*
Abiu		*Lucuma caimito*
Fruta macã		

(Continued)

Appendix A (Continued)
Tree and Fruit Species Planted and Managed by Rubber Tappers

Portuguese Name	English Name	Latin Name
Palms and other wild species		
Açai		*Euterpe precatoria*
Bacaba		*Oenocarpus bacaba,*
		Oenocarpus distichus,
		or both
Patoá		*Oenocarpus batua*
Buriti		*Mauritia vinifera*
Tucumã		*Astrocaryum tucuma*
Ouricuri		*Attalea excelsa*
Paxiúba		*Socratea exhorrhiza* (?)
Jarina		
Ubim		*Geonoma sp.*
Murumuru		*Astrocaryum murumuru*
Pupunha	Peach palm	*Bactris gasipaes*
Seringueira	Rubber tree	*Hevea sp.*
Castanha	Brazil nut	*Bertholletia excelsa*
Copaiba		*Copaifera sp.*
Quina-quina		
Aguano	Mahogany	*Sweitenia macrophylla*
Cumaru de chiero		*Dipteryx oderata*
Cumaru ferro		
Cedro		*Cedrela fissilia*
Amarelão		*Apuleia praecox*
Canelão		*Nectandra sp.*
Maçaranduba		*Manilkara huberi*
Andiroba		*Carapa guianensis*
Piquiá		*Caryocar villosum*
Itauba		*Mezilaurus itauba*
Breu		*Caesalpinia sp.*
Marfim		*Aspidoderma eburneum*

11

Indigenous Soil Management in the Amazon Basin: Some Implications for Development

Susanna B. Hecht

Introduction

During the last 20 years, more than 20 million hectares (ha) of lowland forests have been converted to other land uses in the Amazon basin (INPE 1988). The potential long term global impacts include changes in the global carbon balance, atmospheric moisture recycling, hydrological resources, and in genetic diversity. While these effects are speculative and the subject of much debate, the most consistently documented impact of deforestation is the degradation of soil resources once the nutrient flush from conversion of forest to pasture or agriculture is over. The main forms of regional agriculture that follow forest conversion are very unstable and declining soil fertility is frequently cited as a factor in agricultural failure (Buschbacker, 1986; Fearnside, 1982, 1984, 1986; Hecht, 1982a, 1982b, 1985; Sanchez, 1976; Sanchez and Benites, 1987; Sanchez et al. 1982; Smith, 1982). As soil nutrients become exhausted, and the costs of weeding increase, farmers and ranchers abandon old areas and clear new ones and thus create an ever-expanding front of forest removal and land degradation.

This paper focuses on two main issues. First it discusses the indigenous versus modernization approaches to soil resource management in Amazonian research and development strategies. The production systems of the Kayapó Indians of southern Pará state are compared with those that inform current regional agricultural programs. While indigenous systems are complex, the principles that underlie them are not. Native land management models could be adapted by development planning agencies in a fuller way. Second, the outcomes of Kayapó and

Table 1
Main Soil Constraints in the Amazon Under Native Vegetation

Soil Constraint	Million Hectares	% of Amazon
Phosphorus deficiency	436	90
Aluminum toxicity	353	73
Drought stress	254	53
Low potassium reserves	242	50
Poor drainage/flood hazard	116	24
High phosphorus fixation	77	16
Low cation exchange capacity	64	13
High erodibility	39	8
No major limitations	32	7
Slopes of over 30 percent	30	6
Laterite hazard if subsoil exposed	21	4

Source: Adapted from Sanchez (1985).

conventional colonist and livestock systems are compared in terms of soil fertility and yields.

Amazon Soils and Research Approaches: From Transnational to Tribal Paradigms

The dynamics of agricultural and pasture failure in the Amazonia are extremely complex and are not uniquely determined by soil parameters (Hecht, 1985; 1988). What is clear, however is that Amazonian soils for the most part are extremely poor, and soil constraints are severe for many crops grown under conventional cropping systems. As Table 1 indicates, more than 90% of Amazonian soils are deficient in phosphorous and nitrogen, while more than 50% are deficient in potassium, have serious problems of aluminum toxicity, or low levels of calcium and magnesium. Only about 7% of the soils of the Amazon basin exhibit no major agricultural constraints. The problems inherent in conventional crop-soil management in areas with such poor soils have given tropical zones a reputation for "fragility." This perception ignores the resiliency of many tropical forest formations and overlooks the fact that indigenous Amazonian populations have developed complex systems of agriculture and intensive soil management that have been able to overcome these difficulties.

The dramatic nature of soil degradation after forest conversion is recognized in much of the regional research on tropical agronomy (Falesi, 1977; Sanchez, 1976; Sanchez et al. 1982; Tropsoils 1985; CIAT, 1987). Research related to soil management is a central focus of most agronomic research stations in the humid tropics, and probably more than 60% of tropical agronomic research budgets involve surveying, mapping and classifying soils, and fertilizer and management trials. This research, along with climatic data and germplasm selection is viewed as essential for developing the scientific basis for technical transfer of improved crops and cropping systems. In the main, these results argue that soil constraints, often considered to be the most critical agronomic limitation, can be overcome by the application of fertilizers and other modern inputs (Sanchez et al. 1982; CPATU, 1984; CIAT, 1984, 1987). One of the arguments used to justify conventional soil research is the idea that if production systems, especially annual production systems could be stabilized through the use of modern inputs, then the migration and deforestation linked to cropping failures would be diminished.

The Yurimaguas Model

The most famous Amazonian example of modern soil management research is that developed by Sanchez's group in Yurimaguas, Peru. Following the U.S. Land Grant College model of agronomic research and development, soil and crop management strategies focus on target crops or soil problems, with minimal reference to local knowledge systems and indigenous land use practices. This kind of approach has generated useful results but as a strategy it concentrates primarily on what scientists have been able to learn through the application of scientific techniques to narrowly defined pedological/agronomic problems. The overriding response to the soil management problems has emphasized agronomic techniques rooted in temperate zone agricultural intensification models that consist principally of fertilizer applications (Sanchez et al. 1982, Sanchez 1985, Sanchez and Benites 1987). In approaching soils issues in this manner, a large body of local knowledge about soil potential and management has been ignored.

There are a number of reasons why a soil management approach based on chemical fertilizers, such as the Yurimaguas model, is open to question. Some of these issues have been outlined elsewhere (Fearnside, 1987) but include *agronomic issues* such as: 1) soil nutrient imbalances, and micronutrient deficiencies that cannot be easily monitored by most Amazonian peasants; 2) pest outbreaks that can reduce yields regardless of soil management; 3) erosion problems; and 4) physical changes in soil properties. *Institutional issues* include: 1) the availability of inputs at the proper time; 2) access to inputs; and 3) adequate quality of inputs. Finally there are *market factors* such as: 1) adequate return, 2) affordable transport costs; and 3) affordable credit. Broader structural questions that impinge on the use of such technologies may include the very low annual incomes of most Amazonian inhabitants, about US $1,000 and less. The high costs of fertilizer, about $250–300 per ha, represent almost one third of an average household's income and are, therefore, beyond the reach of most Amazonians. While credit is usually proposed as the solution to this impasse, only about 4% of Amazonian peasants receive credits. The inherent riskiness of annual crops often reduces the use of high technology packages (Scott, 1978), and the opportunity costs of labor and cash in annual cropping systems limit the adoption of such crop/soil technologies. The Yurimaguas approach has undergone several modifications over the years and increasingly incorporates practices that are less input demanding (Sanchez and Benites, 1987).

Some analysts are beginning to argue that tropical land use models should be based on land management methods developed by local populations that are presumably more closely integrated into the dynamics of tropical ecological systems and more reflective of the needs of local populations (Altieri, 1987). Researchers increasingly recognize the role of native populations in the development of ecologically sound, productive land uses. However, indigenous soil management techniques have received little attention in spite of the enormous budgets devoted to tropical pedology and agronomy. One might well ask why such a central issue in tropical development has so systematically ignored local knowledge systems. A bag of fertilizer is not inherently a "bad" technology for Amazonian soil management, but it is not the only one available. The real issue is how to define the range of appropriate technical options for the Amazon. Existing native practices may suggest useful development strategies that could be tested under experiment station conditions. Indigenous systems could be used as a springboard for incorporating the best of both systems.

The Kayapó Model

The Gorotire Kayapó inhabit a region characterized by a complex geology and geomorphology in southern Pará, Brazil. Lying at the interface between the Precambrian Brazilian shield and more recent metamorphic and sedimentary formations, several major soil orders are found within short distances. Most Kayapó agriculture is carried out on four main soil types: a high fertility alfisol, a relatively high fertility ultisol, a low fertility ultisol and a low fertility oxisol. Because the four soil orders managed by the Kayapó are similar to more then 80% of the Amazonian soils the principles, the techniques and the impacts of Kayapó management could have wider implications for tropical soil management in the Amazon Basin.

Table 2
Kayapó and Yurimaguas Production Systems

	Kayapó	Yurimaguas
Soil classification	Yes	Yes
Clearing	Slash & burn	Slash & burn
Crop diversity	High	Low
Medium cycle (crops: 2–4-yr. production periods)	Yes	No
Arboreal species	Yes	Rarely
Polyvarietal planting	Yes	No
Plant structure	Concentric ring	Pure stand monocultures
Nutrient inputs	Yes – ash, mulch, termite nests, litter, palm fronds	Yes – 30kg N, 22kg P, 48kg K
Residue return	Yes – rice, corn stover, banana leaves, vines of yam, sweet potato, manioc peelings	Yes – rice and cowpea stover
Cultivation practices		
Intercropping	Yes	Rarely
Relay planting	Yes	Yes
Mulching	Yes	No
Continuous planting	Yes	No
In-field burning	Yes	No
In-field mulch pits	Yes	No
Weed control		
Manual	Yes	Yes
Fire	Yes	No
Mulch	Yes	Sometimes
Allelopathy	Possibly	No
Scandent crops	Yes	No
Herbicides	No	Yes
Fallow	5 – 10 years	Yes – kudzu 1 – 2 years

The characteristics of the Kayapó and Yurimaguas systems are outlined in Table 2. This table shows the rich array of techniques and strategies for managing relatively low fertility soils and the points of intersection between the modernization and indigenous models. The Kayapó system includes a soil taxonomy, selection for varietal diversity, a complex spatial planting pattern of concentric rings (Hecht and Posey, in press; Stocks, 1983), intercropping, continuous planting for certain crops, relay planting, and successional strategies. Several soil conserving practices are incorporated within these physical and temporal frameworks. These include the use of spatial segregation of plantings, multiple

Table 3
Agriculture Formations of the Kayapó

Village gardens
1. Household gardens
2. Swidden plots (Puru)
3. Successional plots derived from swidden
4. Grave sites
5. *Marantaceae* gardens on hill slopes (Krāi kam puru)

Planting associated with travel
6. Trails between villages and gardens
7. Trails between villages
8. Hunting/trekking trails
9. Planting around old camp sites

Forest planting
10. Natural ecosystem gaps (Bá kre tí)
11. Man-made gaps
12. Plantations in mature forest (viz *Euterpe, Bertholetia*)
13. Fruit groves "in memory of the dead"

Cerrado plantings (Apête)

Source: Adapted from Hecht and Posey (in press).

cropping systems, crop rotations, crops with scandent habits, concentrated tillage, direct additions of nutrients in the form of applications of ashes, mulches, residues, dung and enriched soils, complex coplanting, transferring forest litter, composting, and controlled periodic, infield burning. There are clearly points of similarity in the Yurimaguas/Kayapó systems in the use of crop residues, relay planting, nutrient additions and short fallows. However, the active "arsenal" of the Kayapo agricultural system is much richer, and requires no purchased inputs.

The Kayapó designate 14 types of land us as "agriculture" (Table 3). These various land uses are complex, and include ceremonial planting, reforestation, trek gardens, as well as swidden plots. The Kayapó practice concentric ring/crop segregation agriculture based on sweet potatoes, manioc, yams, and perennials, periodically intercropped with maize, beans, cucurbits, introduced rice, and numerous other minor crops and ritual plants. Kayapó swiddens stay in active root crop production for about five years and continue to contribute these products at reduced levels for as long as eleven years. This is an exceptionally long production period before an agricultural plot goes into fallow. This protracted production period is a function of a 8 main factors:

1) A mixture of short and long cycle cultigens and cultivars;
2) Sequential harvesting and replanting;
3) Root crop cultivars well adapted to fire (including fire tolerant manioc, sweet potatoes, yams, marantaceaes);
4) Systematic, differential, periodic burning within the agricultural field for the entire production sequence;
5) Mulching;
6) Nutrient additions;
7) Agriculture structure;
8) Manipulated fallows.

Informants indicate that concentric zones facilitate the creation or manipulation of in-field microvariability that "fine tunes" soil nutrients to crop demands. Considering the dominant physical and chemical properties of the regional soils, slight lateral changes in those properties can be strongly reflected in the growth and productivity of most annual and bienniel crops. Concentric field architecture permits the use of specific soil nutrient management techniques in a controlled manner. For example, the frequent use of in-field burning throughout the agricultural cycle requires that particular crops be separated from others to control nutrient additions, and to minimize fire damage. Mulch application, specific nutrient additions, soil aerating etc., can be more effectively practiced when crops are spatially segregated.

Researchers should also recognize that there is a complex intellectual system that underlies the native management of soil resources, the ensemble of which is "ethnopedology." Ethnopedology includes the study of native land classification systems, management techniques and their variability, and how the practical and theoretical knowledge is developed, expanded, encoded and reproduced.

Kayapó land uses reflect the relative capabilities of soils and practical techniques of crop selection and soil management. Folk soil taxonomies are widespread (although generally underinvestigated) and tend to correlate well with discernable quantitative differences among soil types (Behrens, in press; Carter, 1969; Christanty, 1987; Conklin, 1957; Hecht and Posey, In prep; Johnson, 1982; Toledo and Barrera-Bassals, 1984). Crop genetic selection and experimentation is impressively widespread in Amazonia (Boster, 1984; Chernela, 1986; Kerr and Posey, 1984). An emerging body of ethnobiological work in Amazonia suggests that native populations developed complex systems of resource management that are ecologically sustainable, yield well, and generate levels of income that exceed the regional average (Anderson et al. 1985; Clay, 1988; Denevan and Padoch, 1988; Hecht and Schwartzman, 1988).

The study of soil management has many advantages: 1) soil properties can be more precisely specified than vegetation processes; 2) edaphic data from one area can illuminate the probabilities of land use outcomes on similar sites more clearly than vegetation data; 3) soil data are particularly useful for evaluating and comparing the impact of land management over time. In addition, insights from millenia of tropical land management experience that have survived the test of time and the vagaries of environment can help inform new strategies and shape testable hypotheses. Given the power of soil analysis, it is rather surprising that so little serious attention has been paid to native land management techniques. If Kayapó techniques can sustain productivity on a given site by maintaining soil fertility, or increase output through soil modification and crop management, these techniques could serve as the foundation for sustainable agricultural models for small scale farmers in Amazonia.

In the next section, Kayapó agricultural yields and soil dynamics are compared with the two dominant regional land uses: livestock and colonist agriculture.

Comparing Kayapó Agriculture with Colonist Agriculture and Livestock in the Eastern Amazon

The dominant forms of land use in the Amazon are pasture and short cycle agriculture, both notorious for their lack of sustainability and low rates of economic return (Browder, 1988; Fearnside, 1980, 1986; Hecht, 1985, 1988; Hecht et al., 1988; Moran, 1982). The features of these systems are described elsewhere in the literature and will not be elaborated here except in summary form. The features of Kayapó agriculture are outlined and compared with these two other land uses in Table 4. There are structural differences in these production systems ranging from field pattern, use of arboreal species, harvest patterns, to degree of agricultural integration into the larger market economy. Table 4 suggests a gradient of management intensity, ecological complexity and declining labor allocation per hectare from Kayapó to conventional livestock systems. Because these systems are so different the following analysis focuses on production yields and proteins.

The edible harvest and protein yields for each of the land uses are outlined in Table 5 for periods of five and ten years.[1] The Kayapó yields per hectare over five years are roughly 200% higher than colonist systems, and one hundred and seventy five times that of livestock. Colonist agriculture rarely continues beyond five years, hence there is no comparison between the Kayapó and colonist in the ten year period. However, over ten years animal production is a mere 700 kilos per

Table 4

Comparison of the Structure of Kayapó, Colonist and Livestock Production Systems

	Kayapó	Colonist	Livestock
Clearing	Slash & burn	Slash & burn	Slash & burn
Clearing size	About 1 ha	2-5 ha	Up to 20,000 ha
Planting patterns			
Cropping zonation	Yes	Rarely	No
Continuous cropping	Yes	Sometimes	Yes
Continuous planting	Yes	Rarely	No
Relay cropping	Yes	Yes	No
Monocropping	No[a]	Often	Usually
Intercropping	Yes	Sometimes	No
Polyvarietal crops	Yes	Rarely	No
Arboreal species	Yes	Rarely	Rarely
Cultivated Species			
in field	10-42	5-10	1-5
Harvest pattern	Continuous	Pulsed	Pulsed
Soil conservation			
practices	Yes	Rarely	Rarely
Main crops	Sweet potato, yams, manioc, maize, musa, beans, squash	Rice, manioc	*Panicum, Brachiaria*
Labor	40 md/ha	25 md/ha	4.5 md/ha

[a] Parts of the Kayapó system are monocultured in the concentric field, but the entire field is not monocropped.

hectare in conventional livestock systems compared to more than 84,000 kilos/ha of Kayapó product.

The data follow the same trends when protein production is analyzed. Kayapó protein yields from vegetable sources are roughly double those of colonists and more than 10 times the protein production of livestock systems. The protein per 100 grams of beef is roughly 30 grams (USDA, 1981). If the "dressed-out" animal, (that is one with hide, bones and offal removed—usually about 40% of live animal weight) is used as the basis of the analysis, the kilos of pure protein produced over five years are a scandalous 63 kilos per ha. In ten years, using these calculations, 1 ha of pasture has produced less than a ton of meat and slightly more than 100 kilos of protein, or roughly 5% of the protein generated by the Kayapó system. Incidently, Kayapó gardens in their later phases become habitats for animals such as agouti, peccaries and deer, and thus producers of animal protein during the fallow (Redford and Richards, 1987). This protein production is not taken into account in this study.

Table 5
Production in Kilograms and Proteins per Hectare of Kayapó, Colonist and Livestock Systems over Time

Production System	Five Years	Ten Years
Kayapó		
Production of all crops		
(kg/ha)[a]	61,750	84,050
Protein (kg/ha)[b]	1,248	1,704
Colonist		
Production of all crops[c]	21,800	–
Protein	602	–
Livestock		
Production (kg/ha)	350	700
Protein[bd]	105	210
	(63)	(126)

[a] Estimates based on in-field measurement, area/harvest weights, household harvests, and informant estimates. The crops here include sweet potato, yam, manioc, plantains and bananas, maize, beans, squash, and peanuts. Many other minor crops such as *Colocassia* and other tubers, papayas, watermelons, peppers, mangoes, and pineapples are not in the calculation.

[b] Protein estimates derived from Dufour (1988), USDA (1981).

[c] Based on average yields of rice, maize, and manioc in colonist agriculture in Amazonia.

[d] Assumes that virtually the entire animal, including the hide, is consumed and is roughly 30% protein. If the animal is dressed out it weighs about 60% of its liveweight. This protein yield is indicated in parentheses.

The Kayapó system is largely based on root crops, especially sweet potatoes which are very productive in the tropics. The sheer volume of production assures carbohydrate adequacy and with minor supplements, protein sufficiency. While these crops are often reviled for their low protein contents (Gross, 1975), nutritional studies by Huang (1983) on adult Yami tribesmen show that diets were nutritionally adequate when subjects eat 2.5 kilos of sweet potatoes a day. Several studies in New Guinea show that protein content varies significantly between cultivars (Hayward and Nakikus 1981), and that intestinal flora of some groups of New Guinean sweet potato eaters may have been able to fix nitrogen (cited in Huang and Lee 1979).

Soil Effects

The next issue is what impact the high productivity of the Kayapó system has on soil properties compared with colonist and livestock systems. Soil samples were taken on sites with similar soil characteristics, in this case dystrophic paleudults. Adjacent forest sites were used

Table 6
Changes in Soil Fertility Elements in Kayapó, Colonist and Livestock Systems

	Forest	Year One	Year Five	Year Ten
Kayapó				
Ph	4.70	5.40	5.60	5.40
N%	0.05	0.07	0.03	0.06
P ppm	1.00	5.00	3.00	3.16
K	0.17	0.37	0.23	0.33
Ca	0.75	1.55	1.31	1.90
Mg	0.31	0.89	0.97	1.67
Colonist				
Ph	4.80	5.40	5.40	–
N%	0.12	0.10	0.06	–
P ppm	1.20	6.00	1.00	–
K	0.12	0.32	0.09	–
Ca	1.09	2.10	1.30	–
Mg	0.34	0.59	0.42	–
Livestock				
Ph	4.70	5.50	5.20	5.00
N%	0.10	0.07	0.06	0.06
P ppm	2.00	7.00	2.00	1.00
K	0.10	0.17	0.10	0.05
Ca	1.30	1.70	0.92	0.64
Mg	0.42	0.65	0.60	0.30

Source: Data derived from soil samples taken at Gorotire (Kayapó), Nixdorf Fazenda, located near Rendencao (livestock), and colonist agriculture of squatters on the Nixdorf Ranch. Colonist and livestock agriculture sampled in 1982.

as "controls" and samples were collected on areas in the first, fifth, and tenth years of production. Sampling areas were roughly 1 ha in size, and the samples were collected randomly. Ten samples were taken per "treatment" area.

Table 6 suggests several important trends. First, pH tends to improve with burning, and this effect persists over time in all the systems, mainly as the result of decomposition of larger boles. In the Kayapó case, higher pHs are maintained for a longer time, probably due to the continuation of field burning, cooking within the fields themselves, and importing wood for cooking fires. Nitrogen (N) levels are very low in all three systems, but the importance of low nitrogen is less pronounced in Kayapó agriculture because of its emphasis on root crops rather than grains for most of the production cycle. For example, rice requires about 23 kgs of nitrogen per ton, while manioc and sweet potato remove 3.7 and 4.3 kgs per ton respectively, and require little nitrogen for good production (Sanchez, 1976). Phosphorous (P) levels are low in all the soils but Kayapó production maintains higher levels of P over time. Potassium (K) is a very labile element, it is easily leached in tropical conditions and one which is closely associated with productivity in root crops like manioc and sweet potatoes. The use of high K mulches such as *Maximiliana* leaves, crop residues, cooking ash additions (See Hecht and Posey, 1988) maintain K levels in the Kayapó system where K level decline in both colonist and livestock systems. This element stays at levels equal to the first year of production because of these mulching practices. Calcium (Ca) and magnesium (Mg) levels are also maintained in the Kayapó system over time. Kayapó land management produces higher yields and more protein than either livestock or colonist systems. While the labor demands are greater in this system it does assure the reproduction of human subsistence and the tropical forest. Tropical soils are difficult, but not impossible to manage. The Kayapó have much to teach us about how this can be done.

Conclusion

This paper has emphasized two main points. First, indigenous knowledge systems and the agriculture on which they are based are rich in management information about nutrient poor tropical soils. Second, these systems are better producers of calories and proteins than any of the alternatives without damaging the resource base.

The real question becomes why do some production systems prevail over others. The livestock story has been the subject of a spate of recent articles (Browder, 1988; Buschbacher, 1986; Fearnside, 1986; Hecht, 1982a, 1985; Hecht et al., 1988), and colonist migration figures prominently the Amazon's 20th century history. These land uses and the deforestation associated with them are driven by an array of social and economic factors ranging from government policy, credit incentives, land speculation, rural violence among others. The political economies of accumulation and subsistence associated with the new occupation of the Amazon drives the destructive and low productivity patterns that we see. These patterns are related to processes that have very little to do with questions of technological adequacy, in spite of the discourse that posits production failure and land degradation as the central driving force behind deforestation. For these reasons, neither the Yurimaguas nor indigenous models will be very effective at altering this particular deforestation process.

This does not make exploration of sustainable management systems a trivial exercise. There are technological questions about land management in the Amazon that could increase production or at least maintain it a bit longer. However, hundreds of millions of dollars have been funneled into surveys and experiments which have not made colonist agriculture more stable, or livestock systems more productive. At the same time, the total budgets for exploring indigenous Amazonian soil management which is based on locally available inputs, and whose principles are straight-forward, probably have not exceeded $40,000.

Finally, the populations which have created the cultivars and sustainable land resource management techniques are under extraordinary pressures. Our society pays for libraries, universities, research facilities of all types. It should be prepared to protect the producers of sustainable Amazon land use systems and the cultures that support them. No investment in research and development is likely to have greater return.

Acknowledgments

Funds for this project were generously provided by the Wenner-Gren Foundation, Resources for the Future, the U.S. Fulbright, and World Wildlife Fund. The Kayapó field work was carried out with Darrell Posey through the Kayapó Project.

Notes

1. The Kayapó data were derived from yield measurements of crops in the field, household harvests, and informant estimates. Because Kayapó planting and harvests are continous and our field presence was not, the numbers cited are probably underestimated. Colonist production data was derived from field interviews, and estimates from the Conceição de Araguaia census office (IBGE), as well as generalized estimates on colonist agricultural productivity derived from government and academic literatures (Butler, 1985; Kitamura and Muller, 1984; Moran, 1982; Smith, 1982). Livestock data were derived from field research. The livestock and colonist field work was undertaken 25 Km from Redenção in the direction of Gorotire. The Kayapó work has been underway since 1984. The other data were collected in 1982.

References

Altieri, M. 1987. Agroecology: The scientific basis of alternative agriculture. Westview, Boulder, Colorado.

Anderson, A., A. Gely, J. Strudwick, G. Sobel, and M. Pinto. 1985. Un sistema agroflorestál na várzea do estuário amazonico Acta Amazonica 15(1):195–224.

Behrens, C. In press. The relation between Shipibo and western soil classification. American Ethnologist.

Boster, J.S. 1984. Classification, cultivation and selection of Aguaruna cultivars of *Manihot esculenta*. Advances in Economic Botany 1:34–48.

Browder, J.O. 1988. The social costs of rainforest destruction. Interciencia 13(3):115–120.

Buschbacher, R. 1986. Tropical deforestation and pasture development. Bioscience 36(1):22–28.

Butler, John R. 1985. Land, gold, and farmers: Agricultural colonization and frontier expansion in the Brazilian Amazon. Ph.D. thesis, University of Florida, Gainesville.

Carter, J. 1969. New lands, old traditions. University of Florida. Gainesville, Florida.

Chernela, J. 1986. Os cultivares de mandioca na area do Uaupes. Suma étnologica brasileira. Vózes, Sao Paulo.

Christanty, L. 1987. Shifting cultivation and tropical soils. pp. 226–239. In: G. Marten (ed.) Traditional agriculture in southeast Asia. Westview, Boulder, Colorado.

CIAT (Centro international de agricultura tropical) 1987. Informe annual del programa de pastos tropicales. CIAT, Cali.

———. 1984. Relatorio annual. CIAT, Cali.

Clay, J. 1988. Indigenous models of agriculture and forest development. Cultural Survival Report #27.

Conklin, H. 1957. Folk classification, Yale University, New Haven.

CPATU (Centro de pesquisas agropecuarias tropico umido). 1984. Relatorio annual. CPATU, Belem.

Denevan, W. and C. Padoch. 1988. Swidden fallow agroforestry in the Peruvian Amazon. Advanced Economic Botany. Volume 5.

Dufour, D. 1988. Composition of some foods used in northwest Amazonia. Interciencia 13(2): 83–86.

Falesi, I. Ecossistema de pastagem cultivada. 1977. CPATU, Belem.

Fearnside, P.A. 1987. Rethinking continuous cultivation in Amazonia. Bioscience 37(3):209–213.

———. 1986. Human carrying capacity of the Amazon rainforest. Colombia Press. New York.

———. 1984. Brazilian Amazon settlement schemes. Habitat Intern. 8:782–137.

———. 1982. Deforestation in the Amazon Basin. How fast is it occuring? Interciencia. 782–788.

———. 1980. Effects of cattle pasture on soil fertility. Topical Ecology. 21:125–137.

Gross, D. 1975. Protein capture and cultural development in the Amazon Basin. American Anthropologist. 77:526–549.

Hayward and Nakikus. 1981. Protein, energy and nutrition in Papua New Guinea. Papua New Guinea Food Crops Conference. Port Moreley, New Guinea.

Hecht, S. B. 1988. Reanalysing colonist attrition. World Development (submitted).

――――. 1985. Environment, development and politics: the livestock sector in the eastern Amazon. World Development 13(6):663–685.

――――. 1982a. Deforestation in the Amazon Basin: magnitude, dynamics and soil resource effects. Studies in Third World Societies 13:61–101.

――――. 1982b. Cattle ranching development in the eastern Amazon: Evaluation of a development policy. Ph.D. Thesis. University of California, Berkeley.

―――― and D. Posey. In press. Preliminary analysis of Kayapó soil management. Advanced Economic Botany.

――――, R. Norgaard and G. Possio. 1988. The economics of cattle ranching in eastern Amazonia. Interciencia. 13(5):233–240.

―――― and S. Schwartzman. 1988. The good, the bad and the ugly: Extraction, colonist agriculture and livestock in comparative perspective. Graduate School of Architecture and Urban Planning. Working Paper.

―――― and Posey. In Preparation. Kayapó soil taxonomy.

Huang. 1983. Nutritive value of sweet potato. International Symposium on Sweet Potato. Taiwan.

――――. and N. Lee. 1979. Evidence of no intestinal N. fixation in sweet potato eaters. American Journal Clinical Nutrition. 32:1741.

INPE (Instituto nacionál de pesquisas espaciáis). 1988. Relatório de atividades do projeto IBDF-INPE. São José dos Campos, São Paulo.

Johnson, A. 1982. Ethnoecology and planting practices in a swidden agricultural system. pp. 49–67. In: D. Brokensha, D. Warren, O. Werner, eds. indigenous knowledge systems and development. USA Press. Washington, D.C.

Kerr, W. and D. Posey. 1984. Additional notes on Kayapó agriculture. Interciencia. 9(6):392–400.

Kitamura, P.C. and G. Muller. 1984. Análise econômica do pequeno produção do norte do Pará. Empresa Brasileira de Pesquisa Agropecuaria, Belém.

Moran, E. 1982. Developing the Amazon. University of Indiana Press. Bloomington, Indiana.

Redford, K. and J. Richards. 1987. The game of choice. American Anthropology. 89(3):650–667.

Sanchez, P.A. 1985. Management of acid soils in the humid tropics. Paper presented at Acid Soils Network Inaugural Workshop. Brasilia, Brazil.

――――. 1976. Properties and management of tropical soils. Wiley Interscience, New York.

―――― and J. Benites. 1987. Low input cropping systems for acid soils of the humid tropics. Science. 238:1521–1527.

――――, D. Bandy, J. Villachica and J. Nicolaides. 1982. Soils of the Amazon and their management for continous crop production. Science. 216:821–827.

Scott, G. 1978. the moral economy of the peasant. Yale Press, New Haven.

Smith, N. 1982. Rainforest corridors. University of California Press, Berkeley.

Stocks, A. 1982. Candoshi and Cocamilla swiddens in eastern Peru. Human Ecology (1):69–84.

Toledo, V. and J. Barrera-Bassals. 1984. Ecologia y desarrolo rural en Patzucuaro. Instituto de Biologia, Mexico.

TROPSOILS. 1985. Tropsoils: the first three years. North Carolina State University. Raleigh, North Carolina.

USDA. (United States Department of Agriculture). 1981. Nutrient value of foods. USDA, Washington, D.C.

12

An Economic Analysis of Huastec Mayan Forest Management

Janis B. Alcorn

Introduction

In this paper, I describe and evaluate a type of "social forestry" system (sensu Gregersen and McGaughey, 1987) currently used by indigenous farmers living at a density of 100 persons per square kilometer in a zone of "fragile lands" in northeastern Mexico. This zone can be classified as fragile for several reasons. It is a zone where bare soil is easily damaged by heavy rains and hot sun (Nye and Greenland, 1960; Sánchez, 1976; others). It is a zone of slopes subject to erosion by runoff from the heavy rains. The land use I describe is not limited to the specific physical or social conditions of my study site. Systems similar to that of the Huastec have been described from other areas (Alcorn, 1989b) and could be applied by trained smallholders living in any forested area, regardless of forest type or slope. In Mexico, for example, the majority of farmers are smallholders; only 5% of farm families operate more than 25 hectares (ha) (Yates, 1981). Forest is the natural cover of 29% of the Mexican land surface, 40,500,000 hectares (Toledo et al., 1985; García Rocha, 1983). Pastures and other often degradative land uses have replaced much of this natural cover, but in some areas forest could be regenerated from existing patches or through the use of nurse trees (Uhl, 1988). An estimated 350,000 ha of Mexican forest are currently managed by Huastec and other small farmers (Fuentes Flores, 1979).

The advantages of this system are that it complements production from other farm subunits, gives farmers access to subsistence goods, produces commercially valuable products, conserves wild genetic resources of forest species, and protects soil.

Research Setting

Huastec farmers manage lands in the foothill region of the Mexican physiographic province of the Sierra Madre Oriental, in the southeastern part of the state of San Luis Potosí. The type of forest management I describe is primarily found at altitudes from 700 feet to 1500 feet. The area has Karst topography formed from Cretaceous limestone (Muir, 1936). The Rendzina type soils range from slightly acidic (pH 6.6) to alkaline (pH 7–9)—the more acidic soils lie under forested areas, and the more alkaline soils are those near the tops of exposed slopes. A sample of soils from my study site were low in phosphorus and nitrogen, but high in calcium, zinc, manganese, and extractable copper (Alcorn, 1984a). The potassium content was highest under forest areas (284 ppm) and lowest on exposed slopes (108 ppm). Soils under forested areas tend toward black clays, and those on exposed slopes are yellowish silt loams. Soils under forest were more moisture retentive, richer in nutrients, and more acidic than soils under other types of land use. Because the Rendzina soils are relatively young soils, trees function to enrich surface soils by bringing up nutrients from lower strata.

The region lies in the Sierra Madre Oriental floristic province. The land use I describe is carried out within the Bosque Deciduo Templado (cloud forest) and Bosque Tropical Perennifolio (rainforest) vegetational types as described by Rzedowski (1963, 1966, 1978), Puig (1976), and Gómez-Pompa (1973). Annual rainfall amounts vary widely (Alcorn, 1984a) but average around 2300 mm per year. Rainfall distribution is one of the most variable in Mexico (Rzedowski, 1978), primarily because of the effects of hurricanes. The wettest months are usually June through September; the least rain falls December through March. Rain waters drain from the sierra through many seasonal creeks into the Pánuco-Tamesi River basin system which carries the second greatest volume of water of any drainage system in Mesoamerica (Sanders, 1978). Climatically the region has been classified in the Koeppen system as Cwag and Awg (Rzedowski, 1966), a hot humid region with little extended dry periods. Average annual temperature is 23.5 degrees C, but over the year, temperatures range from near 0 degrees C to 45 degrees C (Alcorn, 1984a).

The forest management strategy upon which I focus is an indigenous practice of the Huastec Mayan Indians (population approximately 60,000) who have probably occupied this region for at least 3,000 years (Wilkerson, 1979). Like over three quarters of the Mexican rural population (De Rouffignac, 1985), Huastec families operate farms on communally owned lands (*comunidades* and *ejidos*), henceforth referred to as communities. Most families live on their own landholdings which generally range from one to fifteen hectares, and average six hectares. Despite the existence of individual landholdings, however, use rights to land are shared to a certain extent. In addition, some land is held by the school, a communally-owned parcel the profits from which are used for community purposes such as maintenance of the school and other required buildings.

The population density supported by the Huastec system is difficult to determine as records are not easily available. Data from two municipios (a municipio being the equivalent of a county or parish) of the eight occupied by Huastec in San Luis Potosí (S.L.P.) are probably indicative of densities generally. In Huastec communities in San Antonio municipio, S.L.P., there is approximately one hectare per person (100 persons per square kilometer). Stresser-Péan (1967) reported a density of 100 persons per square kilometer on Indian lands in the neighboring Santos de Tancanhuits municipio, S.L.P.; given population increases, that density would now be higher.

Huastec Production

The Huastec have a mixed economy; they produce goods for a market and buy goods with cash, while at the same time producing directly other goods for their own consumption. Their primary source of cash income is the sale of raw sugar produced with farmgrown sugarcane and household labor, although in some areas coffee is the major source of income. Huastec also derive cash income from short-term jobs (usually outside the community), and the sale of honey, fruits, and a variety of other minor products (milk, eggs, poultry, wood, etc). Products produced for direct consumption include maize (for making the staple bread, the tortilla), a wide variety of domesticated and wild foods, construction materials, herbal medicines, craft materials, and firewood. Firewood is harvested from managed forest plots and from fallowed maize fields of the milpa swidden system, a sort of sequential agroforesty system that integrates secondary successional forest with maize production in Middle America. The Huastec primarily use a short fallow, or "bush fallow" form of milpa. The secondary regrowth is slashed back, firewood is harvested, and the remaining slash is burned. After the maize is planted, secondary regrowth is slashed back only once (when the maize is 6 weeks old), and then it is allowed to grow freely for three to four years when it is again slashed back for firewood harvest. Maize production from these fields meets less than half of the family's needs. But this level of production is deemed important for its "insurance" function so the family can continue to eat when working members are ill. They supplement the maize grown on their land with purchased maize. Further details on the Huastec agricultural system are available in Alcorn (1984a).

The Huastec are similar to peasant farmers in other parts of the world. The primary unit of production and consumption is the household (although the community also functions as a unit), and risk-spreading strategies are used to maintain a margin of safety (Durrenberger, 1984; Hunt, 1979; Roseberry, 1976; Scott, 1976). The Huastec-managed agroecosystem meets farm family needs for subsistence goods and cash. At the same time, it also retains the capacity for forest regeneration and protects natural resources for future use by developing a mosaic comprised of patches of older forest, secondary forest swidden-fallow cycled fields, and more permanent fields.

The Huastec system of forest management could, with local modifications, be integrated as a farm component of smallholders using forested lands anywhere in the world. In fact, similar systems have been reported among farmers in many parts of the world (for reviews, see Alcorn, 1989b; Olofson, 1983). The factors limiting its continued use in the Huasteca region, or the extension of its use elsewhere, include: government classification of land under such management as "unused" (e.g., Dewalt, 1982), government subsidies to modify land-use practices in ways that damage the forest's ability to regenerate, severe population pressure on a land base where people have no alternative employment or other means of supporting themselves, and the attitudes of the farmers themselves (see Moran, 1979, for a discussion of colonists' attitudes in Amazonia, for example).

Huastec-Managed Forest Groves

Huastec forest management creates patches of "te'lom." These managed forest plots contain elements of primary and secondary forests as well as introduced species. A given household's te'lom grove ranges from as small as 0.25 ha to 3 ha or more. (Larger te'lom size correlates with steep topography, larger landholdings, and increased off-farm employment.) From a community perspective, however, the te'lom patches are more extensive, because one farmer's te'lom tends to border another farmer's te'lom, thus creating irregularly-shaped, managed forest groves of 25 or more ha, often stretching along creeks and down steep slopes. In a typical community of 406 ha (Tamjajnec, San Antonio municipio, San Luis Potosí), 27% of the land is under te'lom. Most te'lom groves have been present within living memory (i.e., at least 80 years old), but some have been established more recently, and some parts of te'lom are cycled into milpa swiddens. This age indicates that the land use is sustainable. However, if land on ridges or steep slopes taken out of te'lom to be put into milpa is not returned to te'lom quickly (i.e., if it is kept in short fallow milpa for many cycles), the land becomes degraded to the extent that te'lom cannot be re-established, according to informants (a problem ascribed to a change in soil structure and color). On the other hand, in one community (San Pedro, S.L.P.), te'loms were slowly being created by allowing natural succession to proceed in pastures established by the mestizo largeholder from whom the land was taken. The extent to which te'lom can be established in deforested areas needs further study. The proximity of the seed sources in te'loms in nearby communities probably makes reestablishment of te'lom in these pastures an easier undertaking than it would be in large deforested areas.

Te'lom groves are created and maintained by casual management (Plate 1). For the most part, work is done a little at a time, whenever it is convenient for household members. Despite the casual nature of most care, attention is paid to each individual plant at sometime during a given year. Te'lom management harnesses the natural regenerative processes of the forest as a subsidy from nature (Alcorn, 1989a). As one informant put it:

> To have all these benefits, all you have to do is weed it, so it will grow quickly under good conditions. That's one of the advantages of the te'lom. After 15 to 20 years you can get house construction materials and firewood. But the longer you let it develop, the better it is—the more things you can harvest from a small area.

The basic technique used is selective weeding (Plate 2). Seedings arise where seeds are dispersed naturally; seeds are "planted by the bats and the birds" according to farmers. Then, on the basis of their priorities, farmers selectively remove individuals that are not wanted: usually those that would reduce the production of a nearby useful individual, those that are too tall and might be felled by winds and thereby harm other neighboring useful individuals, or those that are unproductive or unhealthy. Priorities are shaped by a variety of factors including access to other sources of similar resources, topographical considerations, and access to markets. Native trees, regardless of species, are valued for the ecological services they provide by their presence (e.g., canopy over coffee for temperature control, erosion control, water protection). If desired species do not volunteer, seedlings are transplanted or propagules are planted where they are wanted. Such planted species include cultigens and native species, including those which are rare, as well as useful species native to other ecological zones. Different areas of a farmer's te'lom can be dedicated to different purposes. For

Plate 1   A Huastec farmer, walking a path between his sugarcane field and a fallow, brings home livestock forage cut in his te'lom grove (J. Alcorn, 1983; reprinted by permission from *Biótica*).

Plate 2 A Huastec woman applies the technique of selective weeding in a te'lom grove. Relying on her knowledge of native trees, she spares saplings and seedlings of useful species.

example, one area may have a high concentration of coffee bushes while another may be high in construction resources. But in all such subzones, native species are tolerated and encouraged. On the sunny edges of the grove and along open trails, small gardens of cacti, bananas, and manioc are sometimes maintained as well.

A typical te'lom grove contains over 300 species. Construction materials are derived from 33 species; utilitarian items (tools, baskets, furniture, musical instruments, firewood) are derived from 65 species; food is derived from 81 species; medicine is derived from 221 species; and livestock feed is derived from eight species. In total, 90% of the plant species occuring in Huastec te'lom grove have use values. (For lists of the useful species see Alcorn, 1983, 1984a, 1984b).

The main commerical product of these groves is coffee. In some areas where coffee growing conditions are especially good (particularly in Aquismón municipio, S.L.P.), the coffee bushes are regularly spaced under native trees and carefully tended to maximize production. In other areas, such as in San Antonio municipio, S.L.P., where sugarcane production is more important, coffee bushes are scattered through the te'lom like any other useful tree. In the coffee producing region of the state of San Luis Potosí (the area occupied by Huastec, Nahuatl, Pame,

Otomi, and other indigenous peoples), 7,500 hectares are managed by 4,733 smallholders (Instituto Mexicana del Cafe, 1975). The average coffee production area is 2 ha per farm family. Almost all of this area is under management as te'lom-type groves, sometimes referred to as "rustic" or "traditional" fincas (Fuentes Flores, 1979). Within Mexico, 350,000 hectares are dedicated to coffee production, and it is estimated that most of this area is under traditional management by smallholders (Fuentes Flores, 1979). Annual coffee yields from such systems range from 4 to 1400 kg per hectare (Fuentes Flores, 1979).

The te'lom also yields other products sold on a more limited basis. The market for fruits (avocado, mango, orange, sapote, mamey, and others) is poorly developed. While some are sold in local markets, at least half of the fruits produced go unharvested. Firewood, medicines, and construction materials are occasionally sold, although they are primarily harvested for the farmer's own use. Hand sawn lumber from *Cedrela odorata,* tropical cedar, is sold locally. Parlor palm (*Chamaedorea elegans* Mart.) and other ornamentals are grown in te'lom shade for sale to traveling buyers or to housewives in the few large towns in the area.

The te'lom grove alone could not support a family. Its success as a viable land use depends on its integration as a subunit of a larger diversified farmstead. Alone, it produces a wide variety of important subsistence goods that would otherwise be expensive or unavailable to the farmer. It provides nutritionally important additions to the diet— thus preventing the deterioration in diet quality that tends to accompany the shift to commercial agriculture (Dewey, 1981; Flueret and Flueret, 1980). It produces a variety of marketable goods to supplement farm income. It supports the production of farmyard livestock (often an important source of cash for women). It serves important ecological functions that farmers value. And it functions to protect the region's genetic diversity by providing a place for native species to reproduce so they will be available for future generations (Figure 1).

A Financial Analysis of the Huastec Farmstead

Because the te'lom system functions as an integral part of a diversified farmstead, I will attempt to analyze the entire farm enterprise: milpa, sugarcane, te'lom, and livestock. Table 1 outlines the characteristics of the major production components of the Huastec farmstead. Such peasant systems are not easy to study, and researchers often choose instead to focus on single segments of the enterprise, "fractured pieces of the whole" (Morrison 1979:633). But farm decisions and resource allocations for a given unit of a farm are partially based on

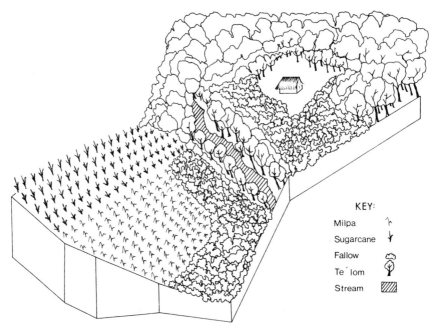

KEY:

Milpa

Sugarcane

Fallow

Te´lom

Stream

Figure 1   Schematic diagram of typical Huastec farmstead.

the requirements of other units and the ways each unit is integrated into the entire system. If we are to evaluate indigenous technologies accurately, we must assess them within their context (Michie, 1986).

Because labor, land use rights, and harvest rights are shared to varying extents among families, and because every farmstead's management is somewhat different, my analysis focuses on production at the community level rather than on production by specific, individual farms or households. The community being analyzed is Tamjajnec, S.L.P. (population 500). Tamjajnec contains 406 ha and supports 98 families.

My figures are derived from interviews during 1978-1980 with 18 informants, 12 of whom responded to a lengthy, formal interview schedule about agricultural production and problems, and from written correspondence with two of these same informants during 1987 and 1988. The interviews were designed to determine which factors should be included in a shorter instrument for surveying the entire community at a later date. Monetary values of labor and goods are based on prices in late 1987. My effort to evaluate the Huastec farming enterprise from a financial perspective should be viewed as preliminary, based on a limited data set from a complex farming system. The limitations of the data are outlined in the discussion of each Appendix table.

Table 1
Main Characteristics of Huastec Farmstead

Component	Valued Uses	Labor Timing	Economic Assessment
Milpa	Insurance, firewood	Flexible	Risky (weather)
Sugarcane	Cash	Spring–summer	Reliable
Grove[a]	Firewood, construction materials, fruit, cash, medicinals, recreation	Flexible	Varies: coffee risky (weather) but high value, rest reliable
Livestock	Meat, eggs for diet, ceremonial and festival uses, cash for women, beast of burden	Flexible	Risky (disease)

[a] Te'lom.

Table 2
Estimated Labor Input on Huastec Farms

	Mandays[a]/ha/yr		Mandays/community/yr
Milpa (62 ha)	93		5,766
Beans (1 ha)	40		40
Garden (20 hh[b])	46	mandays/hh/yr	920
Sugarcane (110 ha)	250		27,500
Te'lom (110 ha)	60		6,600
Livestock care (98 hh)	46	mandays/hh/yr	4,508
Firewood gathering (from milpa & te'lom)	24	mandays/hh/yr	2,352
Total mandays input			47,686 (or 486 mandays/hh or 117 mandays/ha/yr)[c]
Horse sugar labor[d]	125	horsedays	13,750
Burro & horse transport			2,600
Total animal labor input			16,350 horsedays

[a] Manday equals 7 hours if continuous labor, but 8 hours for sporadic work of firewood gathering, livestock care and gardening.
[b] hh = household.
[c] 47,686 ÷ 406 ha in community = labor input/ha/yr, = 106.5 mandays/ha/yr.
[d] Horse labor is required for turning sugarcane press. Burros and horses are also used for carrying sugar, coffee, and other items to market once a week on average. But every household does not own a horse or burro. Horses and burros are generally borrowed from neighbors living inside or outside the community.

Table 2 shows the labor input into the different components of the Huastec system. Labor is primarily done by household members. Households often contain more kin than just the nuclear family and kin living in separate houses often help one another. The work that children do casually or work done at night (such as guarding the milpa as ears ripen) is problematic and is not included, although young teenagers regularly gather firewood. Households do pay wages for some work done by non-household members. Weeding jobs are usually given to poorer community members, especially women or teenagers, and therefore these labor opportunities have a special value for those members of the community. The work done to maintain the household labor force (cooking, carrying water, washing, marketing, etc.) has not been included, although one of the peasant farm's major functions is to maintain the labor force. Community labor projects have not been included either. Each household is required to contribute one day's labor per week to community projects (e.g., working school lands, repairing community buildings, etc.)—a communal labor input of 5,096 mandays per year. Although much of this time is not spent in active labor, the requirement keeps men from taking advantage of other employment opportunities.

Because of their isolated location, the Huastec must invest substantial time in noneconomic activities. In addition to one day per week donated to communal labor, another day must be invested in making purchases in the market each week. Trips for other purposes (e.g., to visit a doctor/curer with a sick child or to take sugar into town for sale) also usually require a full day. There is no regular bus or other transport service, and many hours are spent either walking to one's destination and/or waiting for transportation. Therefore Huastec have less time available for doing remunerative activites. Overall the Huastec community devotes about 117 mandays/ha/year of labor in directly productive activities.

Table 3 summarizes the estimated costs of the different components of the Huastec production system (see Appendix A for detailed justification). This table does not include the interest paid on loans taken out to buy seed or purchase equipment. For loans from local merchants (patróns of the typical Latin American patrón system), farmers must pay interest of 10% of the total original amount of the loan per month until the total amount has been repaid (i.e., annual rate 120%). Sugarcane presses and horses are the major items of equipment. They are necessary for the production of sugar. Approximately half of the households own a press and/or a horse, and the other half borrow them.

Assigning monetary values to labor is problematical. Most of the work is done by household members. Some of the labor (particularly clearing and planting maize fields) is exchange labor done by work parties who are fed lunch but not paid. In addition, the extra value that should be assigned to work that can be done at odd times (such as weeding the te'lom or feeding farmyard livestock) is difficult to assess economically, as is the added value of wage labor opportunities for the poorer members of the community. Most importantly, the wage figures are misleading for comparative purposes, because peasant un-waged domestic labor lowers local wages (De Rouffignac, 1985). Wages paid tend to run at 50% of the official minimum wage in the Huasteca and elsewhere in rural Mexico. In the Huasteca, this situation is further complicated by the two-tiered wage structure based on higher wages to mestizos than to Indians. The wages paid by Huastec to each other for working on Huastec lands is higher than that paid Huastec for working on local mestizo lands.

For the state, from a capitalist point of view, unwaged domestic labor has a value that is not evident from the analysis limited to the Huastec community. Workers can be paid only seasonally when needed, yet be maintained year-round without further expense. Capital is thus freed to be used in more profitable ways (De Rouffignac, 1985), e.g., for urban/industrial development.

The te'lom itself requires low capital inputs aside from the labor costs for harvesting coffee. And maintenance is an activity that can be done a little at a time or put off for many months if jobs need to be done elsewhere. I have not included the costs of establishing te'lom in a milpa fallow, but there would be a period of some 15 years between initiation and significant harvesting of products. In the Huastec case, almost all te'lom groves have been present during informants' lifetimes, although a few households were actively initiating te'lom plots in milpa fallows during my fieldwork.

Total annual cash outlays for the Huastec community are about U.S. $51 per hectare. Annual non-cash inputs represent a value of about U.S. $111 per hectare given estimated shadow prices.

The monetary value of Huastec production is outlined on Table 4 and detailed in Appendix B. The values in this table are problematic and must be viewed as a rough estimate. Where possible, shadow pricing has been used to assign values to products consumed by the household or used on the farm. Of the estimated total value of production of about $760 per ha, 83% is sold for cash while the balance is consumed by the Huastec community.

No one was willing to estimate fruit production, but informants consistently reported that over half of the fruit produced rots on the ground due to lack of market. Therefore I have valued the fruit based on local consumption. I have assumed that each person consumes an

Table 3
Estimated Production Inputs of Huastec Farms[a] (pesos/community/yr[b])

	Non-Cash Input (shadow price)	Cash Input	Total
Milpa	9,424,000	3,187,830	12,611,830
Sugarcane	59,125,000	4,768,577	63,893,577
Te'lom	7,700,000	5,500,000	13,200,000
Livestock	23,142,000	32,300,000	55,442,000
Total inputs	99,391,000	45,756,407	145,147,400
Inputs/ha/yr (US$)[c]	111.27	51.22	162.50

[a] See Appendix A for detailed justification.
[b] Based on total area of 406 ha in the community of Tamjajnec.
[c] Based on late 1987 exchange rate of 2,200 pesos per US$ and 406 ha in the community of Tamjajnec.

Table 4
Estimated Value of Huastec Production[a] (pesos/community/yr[b])

Component	Consumed	Sold	Total
Milpa (and fallow)	29,880,000	306,000	30,186,000
Sugarcane	–	243,375,000	243,375,000
Te'lom	69,554,000	293,228,000	362,782,000
Livestock	14,817,600	27,760,000	42,577,600
Total value	114,251,600	564,669,000	678,920,600
Value/ha/yr (US$)[c]	128.00	632.00	760.00

[a] See Appendix B for detailed justification.
[b] Based on total area of 406 ha in the community of Tamjajnec.
[c] Based on late 1987 exchange rate of 2,200 pesos per US$.

average of 1/4 kg of fruit per day (from diet diaries and informants' statements), and I have merged the value of the entire gamut of fruits to get average fruit value. Fruits are for the most part, like many other te'lom products, freely available to other community members and kin who do not have te'lom groves.

Farmers also have other sources of income. Teenagers and young adults (male and female) often work outside the community. This situation of semi-proletarianization is common in Latin America (Ortega, 1986). Girls take jobs as maids in distant urban centers, but they often thereby just support themselves. Boys and young men regularly work four to six weeks a year doing agricultural labor outside the

Table 5

Economic Return on Cash and Non-Cash Investment from Huastec Production (pesos/community/yr[a])

Component	Total Inputs	Total Benefits	Net Return
Milpa (and fallow)	12,611,830	30,186,000	17,574,170
Sugarcane fields	63,893,577	243,375,000	179,481,430
Te'lom	13,200,000	362,782,000	349,582,000
Livestock	55,442,000	42,577,600	(12,864,400)
Total	145,147,407	678,920,000	533,773,200
Value/ha/yr (US$)[b]	162	760	598

[a] Based on total area of 406 ha in the community of Tamjajnec (98 households).
[b] Based on late 1987 exchange rate of 2,200 pesos per US$.

community (usually near Tampico), and some of their earnings are contributed to the farmstead operation. A few young people join the military or move to the city to seek work. They occasionally send money home. The intra-community paid labor opportunities generally provide cash income for women and teenagers from more impoverished families. Women also earn pocket money in a variety of ways: e.g., the sale of eggs, fruits, garden produce, cooked food, and pottery, or by sewing garments for neighbors. In households that maintain bees, the men sell the honey, and women make candles for sale. In addition, some households operate small stores or radio repair services out of their homes.

Table 5 summarizes the economic returns to the community from farmstead production. These, I feel, are conservative estimates. Much of subsistence production has not been assigned any value. My analysis indicates that the average Huastec household earns a net benefit equivalent to U.S. $2,477 per year from farm production. As a community, this estimated 1987 benefit represents a net return on investment equivalent to U.S. $598 per hectare. The management of Huastec te'loms represents U.S. $391/ha (65%) of total net return on investment with coffee production. Without coffee production, total net returns on investment are U.S. $290/ha, to which te'lom management contributes U.S. $84/ha (29%).

There are four comments I wish to make here. First, I have used the figures for a good coffee yield. When coffee production is good, the return from the te'lom is the highest of any farm component. But during many years, coffee production is very low. Sugarcane gives the second highest return, but it is the most reliable. From the farmer's point of view, the sugarcane is the basic income commodity (limited by the available labor). The milpa is important for firewood production, livestock pasture, and insurance levels of staple food. But planting maize ("making milpa") is seen as the riskiest venture. It requires cash input but it does not generate a cash profit. The te'lom is primarily seen as necessary for fruits, firewood, medicines, and construction materials. It is also recognized as the only land use that can be sustained on steep slopes, and its ecological services are appreciated by the Huastec. In Tamjajnec, the income from coffee during good years is an added boon. In other communities, especially those in Aquismón municipio where coffee growing conditions are better, coffee is a reliable income producer.

Secondly, the economic return from sale of raw sugar could be higher if communities could sell directly to the large commercial users (primarily liquor production plants, according to local middlemen) instead of having to sell it to local mestizo patróns. For example, while the current price paid to farmers for pilón sugar is 300 to 350 pesos per kg, pilón reportedly sells for 1,000 to 1,500 pesos per kg in Monterrey.

Thirdly, I should point out the return per hour from the different field types. Huastec get 1.5 kg of maize per hour invested, 4.2 kg of sugar per hour invested, and 2.4 kg of coffee per hour invested. Maize and sugar have similar prices (currently close to 300 pesos per kg for each), but coffee has a cash value about seven times higher (currently 2,200 pesos per kg).

Not evident in the numbers shown in the Tables is the value of the social security provided by the subsistence production from this system, a system which guarantees family survival when farmers are disabled or when absent family members return home during periods of unemployment. Huastec value the security provided by direct production of subsistence goods. This form of social security or unemployment insurance also has value for the state, although it is largely unrecognized. Subsistence agriculture has been castigated as backward and eradication of subsistence farming is a goal of "development." Farmers are viewed as workers to be manipulated to produce a surplus for generating foreign exchange. But in this process, the valuable social contributions of subsistence production are overlooked. Not only does farmers' direct subsistence production contribute to the well-being of farmers, but it also subsidizes a partially employed labor force (Ortega, 1986).

The te'lom is an important component of Huastec production from an economic perspective. There are important non-economic values of the te'lom recognized by Huastec farmers as well (Appendix C). Some farm families regularly harvest only enough coffee for their own consumption from their te'lom plots. These families still see the te'lom as a valuable component of their farm. It is attractive to farmers because it maintains the farm family's access to a diverse array of important, free goods, it provides supplemental income, and it serves as a "bank"—conserving species and products that can be "cashed" in at a later date. Its establishment and its maintenance are compatible with smallholder management strategies, production needs, limitations, and priorities (Barlett, 1980; Hunt, 1979; Richards, 1985).

Conservation Functions and Their Values

Unlike the other components of the Huastec farm, the te'lom is a major reservoir of genetic resources. With over 300 species, it is a seed bank for individual species as well as the seed bank for future forest communities. The economic valuation of genetic resources is problematic (Oldfield, 1984). But the lack of prices on which to base economic values should not bar consideration of the value of maintaining these resources.

Willingness to pay (WTP) values have not been established for the vast majority of individual species, or for the te'lom forest grove as a unit. For the Huastec, over 90% of te'lom species have "use values." And Huastec farmers do perceive that the te'lom has an "option value," because they believe that its constituent species may have some future use not known today. It also seems that Huastec give the te'lom some "existence value" in their land use decisions in so far as (1) they give traditional respect to the Earth and its vestment of plants, and (2) the comfortable prosperous Huastec farmer is seen as one who has a te'lom on his farmstead. (See Randall, 1986:83–85 for a definition of these values).

Farmers recognize that the te'lom also provides ecological services. The valuation of these services is also problematic. Farmers recognize that deforesting hilltops and hillsides sets site-destructive processes into motion. The te'lom functions to prevent erosion of valuable soil. Forest roots bring nutrients up from subsoil and make them available to other plants. Forest plants also hold nutrients so that they are not leached from the site. Some of them also participate in nitrogen fixation or form mycorrhizal associations which further improve the nutrient status of the site. The forest cover protects the soil structure so that the land remains useful. In the Huastec zone, the canopy of native trees serves to protect coffee from occasional near-freezing temperatures (Barradas and Fanjul, 1984). But these functions, while valued by farmers (Alcorn, 1989a) are difficult to evaluate from an economic perspective (Westman, 1977; Oldfield 1984). The "replacement cost" approach to evaluating these services by making them equivalent to the cost of fertilizer to replace the lost nutrients each year, soil conditioners, and labor to replace lost soil is inappropriate, because the (uncertain) repair process would not be so simple. Te'loms also protect watersheds. This function, likewise, is difficult to include in a cost-benefit framework.

Huastec farmers are providing a valuable service to the State by retaining forest patches, but they receive no compensation from the State for maintaining genetic resources, for protecting watersheds, or for protecting soil resources for future use.

Conclusion

The benefits of low-input sustained yield land use systems that do not degrade fragile environments compared to short-term, high yield systems cannot be overlooked (Southgate and Disinger, 1987). It is important to mention the divergence in land use valuation criteria applied by different sectors of the population (de la Peña cited in Grindle, 1981). Commercial producers use profit to determine the best use of land; while small farmers value a land use by its ability to meet their own needs (both directly and indirectly through cash generated by farm products). In Mexico, land is also valued as leverage in conflicts between the rich and the poor. Unable to win wage improvements, rural workers have been able to win land though land reform; the high value given land by small farmers has been validated in the political arena (De Rouffignac, 1985). Few farmers in the world today, however, are truly producing *only* at subsistence levels; for example, in Mexico only 15% of smallholders are judged to be subsistence farmers (Yates, 1981). As consumers of purchased goods, peasants have become participants in the capitalist exchange economy. Smallholder land use reflects these two divergent sets of values (self sufficiency and cash profit).

The Huastec case demonstrates that real farmers will dedicate part of their lands to low labor intensive, resource conservative structures that provide them with free access to subsistence goods and variable income, *if* reliable, profitable, labor intensive crops are part of a farm. The major advantages of including a forest grove component in a farmstead lie not in predictably high financial and potentially high economic returns, but in the conservation and subsistence benefits that are appreciated by small farmers.

Systems mixing commercial and subsistence concerns should form the essential basis for rural development programs. Programs could be designed to build on farmers' existing efforts to mix these two concerns. Development planners who recognize the need for subsistence production to complement cash crops have overlooked te'lom-like groves and instead have promoted the home garden, probably because it is traditional in temperate zone small farms. Home gardens can fulfill family needs for nutritious fruits and vegetables (DeWalt, 1983; Fleuret & Fleuret, 1980). But it is short-sighted to overlook the advantages of groves which meet other needs in addition to those met by gardens. Huastec, for example, have chosen to maintain gardens and groves.

The te'lom system has potential for improvement. It is an old, widespread system of forest management developed by peasants to meet their needs (Alcorn, 1988). It is a flexible system into which new crops such as coffee have been fit without reducing its subsistence support functions. Other high profit, low labor and low capital intensive perennial crops with markets could be introduced to improve income production from these groves. For example, nursery plants and orchids could easily be produced if market connections were developed. In the Huasteca, one specific improvement would be improved access to marketing networks. Access to markets would enable farmers to take advantage of the 50% of their existing fruit production that now rots on the te'lom floor for lack of buyers. The object of such improvement, however, would not be to transform the te'lom into an intensively managed modern agroforestry system with complex and risky market relationships. Striving after such a goal could result in the loss of the conservation and subsistence functions of the te'lom.

Efforts to improve smallholders' commercial productivity should primarily focus upon other components of their farms. The te'lom grove would be retained as the component with a strong subsistence function. In the Huastec area, for example, farmers consistently ask for help growing beans and improving their maize yields. Both of these goals are consonant with recent national interest in reducing imports of basic food crops by increasing production within a given nation's borders (e.g., Bailey, 1981; Browne and Hadwiger, 1986; Grindle, 1981; Toledo et al., 1985). Huastec farmers would, however, most welcome more productive sugarcane. At present, they eagerly bring home cuttings of sugarcane they find growing in plantations outside the region for assessment under Huastecan growing conditions. Honey production could also be promoted by creating a better infrastructure for marketing honey to private buyers. Improving labor-intensive production in other farm components will also serve the added function of reducing pressure on forests as population increases. Loans for improving other components of the farmstead should have provisions requiring the retention of forest groves.

In order to develop diversified farmsteads having a grove component appropriate for introduction or encouragement in other areas, existing systems should be studied, and resident farmers should be involved in the process at all levels. Similar grove systems are found elsewhere in

Latin America and in other parts of the world (Alcorn, 1989b; Olofson, 1983), but they are poorly documented. In Latin America, coffee extension agents probably have the best knowledge of the distribution of these systems. Depending on their abilities, they could probably also identify areas ecologically and socially amenable to development if the criteria were clearly explained to them.

Agronomists, agricultural extension agents, coffee extension agents, and colonists must be educated about the values of including forest groves within the farm landscape. Given modern attitudes, without such education, forests are seen primarily as an impediment to agriculture, something which must be transformed into a more "civilized" use. Forests must be recognized as land use especially in areas redistributed under agrarian reform policies. Forests and their products must be valued by society for colonists to be expected to leave stands of forests on their newly acquired land or for young Huastec farmers to follow their parents' land use pattern. Among the Huastec, for example, having a te'lom confers traditional status upon the farmer as one who can provide for his family, one who has a comfortable life with cool, fresh breezes and plenty to eat. This traditional value judgement continues to carry weight in land use decisions.

To prepare colonists for farming fragile forested lands, colonists must be educated about the forest. Indigenous residents have traditionally learned this knowledge as part of their enculturation. Colonists from outside the region cannot be expected to have any ecological knowledge of a new environment. Colonists should be taught the values of forest species (e.g., which ones produce marketable goods and which ones produce items of use by the family) and the ecology of forest species, so they are able to manage them successfully. Colonists should be given status for having forest groves on their lands. They should also be taught why their lands are fragile and how the forest can help them to create and maintain a productive farmstead for themselves and their children.

Acknowledgments

The data presented here were gathered during 15 months fieldwork among the Huastec between 1978 and 1983 and from postal correspondence with informants between 1983 and 1988. I am grateful to the Huastec farmers who guided my research, especially Cándido Hernández Vidales and Francisca Vidales Medina. I thank John Browder, Annette Citzler, Barbara Edmonson, and Margery Oldfield for information, comments and suggestions related to this manuscript and Lauren Wunsh for preparing a graphical illustration. Research among the Huastec from 1978 to 1983 was supported by NSF Dissertation Improvement Grant DEB 78–05968, a Social Science Research Council International Doctoral Research Fellowship, and E.D. Farmer International Fellowship, The University of Texas Institute of Latin American Studies, The University of Texas Office of Graduate Studies, The University of Texas International Student and Faculty Exchange Office, and a Tinker postdoctoral fellowship administered through the Mesoamerican Ecology Institute of Tulane University. I alone, however, retain responsibility for the contents of this paper.

References

Alcorn, J.B. 1983. El te'lom huasteco: Presente, pasado y futuro de un sistema de silvicultura indígena. Biótica 8:315–331.

———. 1984a. Huastec Mayan ethnobotany. University of Texas Press, Austin.

———. 1984b. Development policy, forests, and peasant farms: Reflections on Huastec-managed forests' contributions to commercial production and resource conservation. Economic Botany 38:389–406.

———. 1988. Indigenous agroforestry strategies meeting farmers' needs. Paper presented at the Symposium on Alternatives to Deforestation, 39th Brazilian Botanical Congress, Belem, Brazil.

———. 1989a. Process as resource: The agricultural ideology of Bora and Huastec resource management. In press *in* D.A. Posey and W. Balée (eds.), Resource management in Amazonia: Indigenous and folk strategies, Advances in Economic Botany, Volume 7, New York Botanical Garden, Bronx, New York.

———. 1989b. Indigenous agroforestry systems in the Latin American tropics. In press *in* M. Altieri and S. Hecht (eds.), Agroecology and small farm development, CRC Press, Boca Raton, Florida.

Bailey, J. 1981. Agrarian reform in Mexico: The quest for self-sufficiency. Current History 80 (469):357–360, 391–392.

Barlett, P.F. 1980. Adaptive strategies in peasant agricultural production. Annual Review of Anthropology 9:545–573.

Barradas, V.L. and L. Fanjul. 1984. La importancia de la cobertura arborea en la temperatura del agroecosistema cafetalero. Biótica 9:415–521.

Browne, W.P. and D.F. Hadwiger, eds. 1986. World food policies: Toward agricultural interdependence. Lynn Rinner Publishers, Boulder.

De Rouffignac, A.L. 1985. The contemporary peasantry in Mexico. Praeger, New York.

Dewalt, B. 1982. The big macro connection: Population, grain and cattle in S. Honduras. Culture & Agriculture 14:1–12.

Dewalt, K. 1983. Nutritional strategies and agricultural change in a Mexican community. UMI Research Press, Ann Arbor.

Dewey, K.G. 1981. Nutritional consequences of the transformation from subsistence to commercial agriculture in Tabasco, Mexico. Human Ecology 9:151–187.

Durrenberger, E.P., ed. 1984. Chayanov, peasants, and economic anthropology. Academic Press, New York.

Fleuret, P. and A. Fleuret. 1980. Nutrition, consumption, and agricultural change. Human Organization 39:250–260.

Fuentes Flores, R. 1979. Coffee production systems in Mexico. Pages 60–72 *in* G. de las Salas (ed.), Agroforestry systems in Latin America, CATIE, Turrialba, Costa Rica.

García Rocha, O. 1983. Importancia del uso del suelo forestal en el desarrollo rural de México. Pages 318–324 *in* Relación campo-ciudad: La tierra, recursos estratégico para el desarrollo y la transformación social, XIV Congreso Interamericano de Planificación de la Sociedad Interamericana de Planificación (SIAP), 1982, Ediciones SIAP, Mexico City.

Gómez-Pompa, A. 1973. Ecology of the vegetation of Veracruz. Pages 73–147 in A. Graham (ed.), Vegetation and vegetational history of northern Latin America, Elsevier, New York.

Grindle, M.S. 1981. Official interpretations of rural underdevelopment: Mexico in the 1970s. Working Papers in US-Mexican Studies No. 20. University of California, San Diego.

Gregersen, H. and S. E. McGaughey. 1987. Social forestry and sustainable development. Pages 7–20 *in* D.D. Southgate and J.F. Disinger (ed.), Sustainable development in the Third World, Westview, Boulder.

Hunt, D. 1979. Chayanov's model of peasant household resource allocation. Journal of Peasant Studies 6:247–285.

Instituto Mexicano del Cafe. 1975. Perfil cafetalero del Estado de San Luis Potosí. INMECAFE, Mexico.

Michie, B.H. 1986. Indigenous technology and farming systems research: Agroforestry in the Indian desert. Pages 221–244 *in* J.R. Jones and B.J. Wallace, eds., Social sciences and farming systems research, Westview Press, Boulder.

Moran, E.F. 1979. The Trans-Amazonica: Coping with a new environment. Pages 133–159 *in* M.L. Margolis and W.E. Carter (eds.), Brazil, anthropological perspectives, Columbia University Press, New York.

Morrison, B.M. 1979. The persistent rural crisis in Asia: A shift in conception. Pacific Affairs 52:631–646.

Muir, J.M. 1936. Geology of the Tampico region, Mexico. American Association of Petroleum Geologists, Tulsa, Oklahoma.

Nye, P. H. and D.J. Greenland. 1960. The soil under shifting cultivation. Commonwealth Agricultural Bureau, Harpendon, England.

Oldfield, M.O. 1984. The value of conserving genetic resources. U.S. Government Printing Office, Washington, D.C.

Olofson, H. 1983. Indigenous agroforestry systems. Philippine Quarterly of Culture & Society 11:149–174.

Ortega, E. 1986. Peasant agriculture in Latin America: Situations and trends. Pages 245–293 *in* R.P. Misra and N.T. Dung (eds.), Third world peasantry, Sterling Publishers Private Ltd., New Delhi.

Puig, H. 1976. Végétation de la Huasteca, Mexique. Mission Archéologique et Ethnologique Française au Mexique, Mexico City.

Randall, Alan. 1986. Human preferences, economics, and the preservation of species. Pages 79–109 in Bryan G. Norton (ed.), The preservation of species: The value of biological diversity. Princeton University Press, Princeton,

Richards, P. 1985. Indigenous agricultural revolution. Westview, Boulder, Colorado.

Roseberry, W. 1976. Rent, differentiation and the development of capitalism among peasants. American Anthropologist 78:48–58.

Rzedowski, J. 1963. El extremo boreal del bosque tropical siempre verde en Norteamérica continental. Vegetatio 30:173–198.

———. 1966. Vegetación del estado del San Luis Potosí. Actas Cientificas Potosinas 5:1–191.

———. 1978. Vegetación de México. Editorial Limusa, Mexico City.

Sanchez, P.A. 1976. Properties and management of soils in the tropics. J. Wiley and Sons, New York.

Sanders, W.T. 1978. The lowland Huasteca archaeological survey and excavation 1957 field season. Museum of Anthropology, University of Missouri, Columbia, Missouri.

Scott, J.C. 1976. The moral economy of the peasant. Yale University, New Haven.

Southgate, D.D. and J.F. Disinger (ed.). 1987. Sustainable development in the Third World, Westview, Boulder.

Stresser-Péan, G. 1967. Problèmes agraires de la Huasteca ou région de Tampico (Mexique). Pages 201–214 in Les problèmes agraires des Amériques Latines, Colloques Internationaux du Centre Nacional de la Recherche Scientifique, Paris, France.

Toledo, V.M., J. Carabias, C. Mapes, and C. Toledo. 1985. Ecología y autosuficiencia alimentaria. Siglo Veintiuno Editores, Mexico City.

Uhl, C. 1988. Barreiras ecológicas a regeneracão florestal em pastagens altamente degradadas (municipio de Paragominas, Estado do Para, Brasil). Paper presented at the Symposium on Alternatives to Deforestation, 39th Brazilian Congress, Belém, Brazil.

Westman, W.E. 1977. How much are nature's services worth? Science 197:960–964.

Wilkerson, S.J.K. 1979. Huastec presence and cultural continuity in North-Central Veracruz, Mexico. Actes du XLII Congres International des Americanistes IXB:41–55.

Yates, P.L. 1981. Mexico's agricultural dilemma. University of Arizona Press, Tucson.

Appendix A
Production Inputs (pesos/community/yr)

	Non-Cash Input (shadow prices)	Cash Input
Milpa		
Maize seed[a]	992,000	–
Fertilizer (burned fallow)	?	
Paid labor [bc]	–	3,100,000
Nonwage labor[d]	8,432,000	–
Bean seed	–	7,830
Bean labor	–	80,000
Milpa total	9,424,000	3,187,830
Sugarcane		
Nonwage labor	55,000,000	–
Firewood (own)	4,125,000	–
Sugar press[e]	–	2,640,000
Horses & burros[f]	–	2,128,577
Sugarcane total	59,125,000	4,768,577
Te'lom		
Paid labor[g]	–	5,500,000
Nonwage labor[h]	7,700,000	–
Te'lom total	7,700,000	5,500,000
Livestock[i]		
Shelter	6,566,000	–
Nonwage labor	9,016,000	–
Forage[j]	7,560,000	–
Maize for feed	–	32,300,000
Livestock total	23,142,000	32,300,000
Total inputs	99,391,000	45,756,407

[a] Usually farmer uses seed produced on his own farm.
[b] Labor valued at 1987 value of 2,000 pesos per manday as paid within the community. One hour is allowed for eating a lunch provided by the landowner, but I have not assigned a financial value to the lunch.
[c] 25 mandays.
[d] 68 mandays.
[e] At 1987 cost, amortized straight-line over 20-year period of use.
[f] Amortized straight-line over 7-year useful life. Horses are said to be the riskiest investment because they tend to have health problems. (There are currently 37 horses and 13 burros in the sample community.)
[g] 35 mandays.
[h] 25 mandays.
[i] Does not include minor cost of tick sprays or veterinary supplies occasionally purchased for horse or cow.
[j] Estimated at cost of forage for 105 head if purchased. Very difficult to quantify.

Appendix B
Value of Huastec Production (pesos/community/yr)

	Consumed	Sold[a]	Consumed and Sold
Milpa			
Maize	18,600,000	–	
Beans	–	306,000	
Fallow			
Firewood	3,720,000	–	
Forage from fallow[b]	7,560,000	–	
Milpa – fallow total	29,880,000	306,000	30,186,000
Sugarcane			
Sugar	–	243,375,000	243,375,000
Te'lom			
Coffee	–	242,000,000	
Fruits[c]	45,625,000	45,625,000	
House materials[d]	2,303,000	2,303,000	
Medicine[e]	11,760,000	–	
Lumber for sale	–	3,300,000	
Livestock shade[f]	6,566,000	–	
Livestock feed[g]	?	–	
Firewood	3,300,000	–	
Te'lom total	69,554,000	293,228,000	362,782,000
Te'lom total without coffee or fruit sold			75,157,000
Livestock[h]			
Pork[i]	10,584,000	–	
Lard	–	10,584,000	
Milk	–	3,000,000	
Eggs	1,176,000	1,176,000	
Poultry	3,057,600	–	
Calves	–	9,000,000	
Piglets	–	4,000,000	
Colts[j]	?	–	
Horse labor[k]	–	?	
Livestock total	14,817,600	27,760,000	42,577,600
Total production	14,251,600	564,669,000	678,920,600

(Continued)

Appendix B (Continued)
Value of Huastec Production (pesos/community/yr)

ª A small percent of the production labeled as "sold" is kept for home consumption.

ᵇ Estimated from cost of purchased forage (6,000 pesos per head per month). Part of this should be assigned to the te'lom. See below.

ᶜ Amount sold is unknown. Estimate is from statements that half of production that could be sold is not because of lack of market.

ᵈ Based on one building/5 years (= 1/5 material cost), and every family putting up one building every 5 years and having to buy the materials half the time.

ᵉ Based on cost of doctor's visits (10,000 pesos per visit in 1987) if 12 visits/family/yr. Some medicine can be gotten from garden or dooryard, but te'lom contains the greatest range of medicines.

ᶠ Figured at the value of 1 shed built every 3 years by every family. People without te'lom tie their animals in their neighbors' te'lom groves.

ᵍ Included in fallow value. Pigs, chickens, and horses eat significant quantities of te'lom products, but I have no basis on which to estimate the amounts consumed, their values, or their proportion of animals' total diet.

ʰ Figured per household, not per hectare.

ⁱ Pig meat is given away at festivities, although a live pig is occasionally sold if money is needed. If the animal is butchered, only the lard is sold. Value and disposal of pigskin unknown.

ʲ Includes horses and burros. Horses are very valuable, but the sale of colts, horses, or burros is complex. Mestizo patróns can take them as interest on loans, etc.

ᵏ The value of labor done by horses and burros is unknown. Horses and burros are generally borrowed without direct payment.

Appendix C
Non-Monetized Values Assigned by Huastec Farmers to Te'lom Forest Groves

---

Direct access to products
  Access to firewood
  Access to fruits
  Access to medicines
  Access to construction materials
  Access to items that may be needed in the future
Labor advantages
  Low, sporadic labor requirements
Quality of life provided
  Cool place to rest
  Clean air to breathe
  Clean water to drink
  Protects the Earth
Services provided
  Improves site for planting maize
  Prevents erosion
  Protects soil from degradation

PART THREE

Strategies for Sustainable Agriculture in the Andean Highlands

13

Agricultural Terraces in Peru's Colca Valley: Promises and Problems of an Ancient Technology

John M. Treacy

Introduction

Agricultural terraces are among the most distinctive and widespread features of the Andean highland landscape. In the pre-Hispanic era, terraces built by indigenous societies supported large populations, primarily in the arid valleys of the western Andes (Donkin, 1979), but also on the moist eastern Andean flanks (Lathrop, 1970). During the age of the Incas, terracing became an essential ingredient of a state-organized political economy based upon the stable production of foods, especially maize, which circulated through imperial redistributive networks. Today, no one knows how many ancient terraces remain in the Peruvian Andes, however they may total up to 500,000 ha (W.M. Denevan, 1988: pers. comm.). Up to 75 percent of these terraces are now abandoned and crumbling.

Few who gaze upon ranks of unused agricultural terraces in highland Peru fail to imagine them rebuilt and glimmering with crops. Such visions have inspired Andeanist scholars and development consultants to advocate the revival of pre-Hispanic technologies, especially terracing and raised fields, to expand agricultural production in the Andes, and to counter the increasing rate of land degradation (Morlon et al., 1982; Portocarrero, 1986; Torre and Burga, 1986; Guillet, 1986; Erickson, 1986). The keen interest in terracing is in great measure the result of a growing appreciation of the ecological soundness of traditional farming methods (Altieri, 1982; Denevan, 1980). Rebuilding abandoned terraces and constructing new ones, proponents argue, would stimulate production in the neglected Andean heartland. In the long run, terracing would also curb highland emigration and shift the locus of agricultural investment away from the coast and eastern forest regions which receive the bulk of Peruvian funding. In addition, direct investment supporting terrace construction in highland communities would be an inexpensive alternative to costly irrigation schemes in coastal valleys, such as Arequipa's massive billion dollar Majes project designed to bring highland waters to irrigate coastal lands.

As a result of the new enthusiasm for ancient technologies, state-funded programs are underway in Peru to restore and extend agricultural terraces. A major participant, PRATVIR (*Programa de Acondicionamiento Territorial y Vivienda Rural*) sponsors terrace reconstruction projects by offering communities low-interest loans or seeds and other inputs to restore large areas (up to 30 ha) of abandoned terraces. Others, such as PNCSACH (*Programa Nacional de Conservación de Suelos y Aguas en Cuencas Hidrográficas*) primarily work with individual farmers through extension programs. Other Peruvian and foreign agencies also work to expand terrace agriculture.

Most of what we know of Andean terracing has been derived from archaeological and geographical research, which has tended to focus upon the architectural and functional aspects of terracing. As a result, we still know relatively little about the social circumstances in which terracing arose, or about how terraces are built and managed. Such knowledge would be helpful in discovering how to restore the social practice of terracing. The salient question is: How can the ancient technology of terracing be successfully reintroduced into contemporary agricultural systems within contemporary socioeconomic frameworks? The purpose of this paper is to examine how farmers in the Colca Valley of Peru manage and rebuild agricultural terraces, and to understand the present agronomic and social contexts of terracing and how the practice may contribute to future Andean farming strategies.

Ecological and Economic Fragility in the Andes

What I call the promise of agricultural terraces emerges from their ecological virtues: moisture-retentive, erosion-proof soils of good tilth; advantageous micro-climatic features; and efficient systems of gravity irrigation. Terrace agriculture is demonstrably sustainable: many terraces in the Colca Valley appear to have been in constant use since the Inca period. Terraces counteract erosive forces that make the highlands a particularly fragile environment. Rainfall is highly seasonal in the Andean region, and on most slopes, erosion is not slow and continuous but occurs rapidly during heavy storms and off-year bursts of rains (Williams et al., 1986:46–47). While 58 percent of the region's soils experience only light to moderate rates of erosion and appear remarkably intact despite centuries of farming (due, perhaps, to sectorial fallowing systems), 16 percent suffer serious erosion as evidenced by gullying and earthslides (Alfaro, 1986:56–57). As agriculture intensifies and fallowing times decrease due to expanding populations and commercial farming (Mayer, 1979; Orlove and Godoy, 1986), erosion accelerates accordingly. Programs to encourage terracing could fight erosion along two fronts; (1) terracing some existing lands in cultivation may halt or drastically reduce soil erosion; and (2) restoring terraces or building new ones to expand the farming frontier may take pressure off unterraced fields which may be fallowed for longer periods.

The notion of fragility also applies to the enterprise of agriculture in the Andes where success is in constant jeopardy not only from erosive forces, but also from frequent droughts, floods, hailstorms, and frosts. The risks to agriculture are great, and yields may fluctuate greatly from year to year because of environmental disturbances. This translates into social and economic fragility caused by the unpredictable nature of highland climates. Failure to harvest sufficient amounts of food, either for consumption or for sale, forces people to abandon farming and seek employment elsewhere. For farmers, reducing agricultural risk is a basic imperative, permitting them not only to survive, but also to safely experiment with new crops and pursue commercial production. Terracing, as we shall see, reduces the risks of farming and therefore appears to be particularly appropriate for small farmers whose livelihoods and futures are often at risk to begin with.

Nonetheless, reestablishing the practice of terracing is problematic and demands working within contemporary socioeconomic contexts. Above all, it demands working within the local contexts of Andean communities where abandoned and future sites may be located. The extent to which terrace construction and reconstruction is consonant with household and community economic goals, local irrigation capacities, and land tenure patterns may in large measure determine the ultimate success of new terrace agriculture.

Much of the material on Andean agricultural terracing presented herein stems from fieldwork during 1985–1986 in the village of Coporaque, one of several in the Colca Valley of southern Peru. Additional information is culled from the current and growing literature on agricultural terracing and terrace construction in the Andes. Observing the beginnings of a reconstruction project in Coporaque sponsored by PRATVIR provided an opportunity to record data on terrace construction.

Land and Agriculture in the Colca Valley

The deeply-incised valley of the Colca River is 100 km north of the city of Arequipa in the southern Peruvian Andes. The Colca region, like many in the Andean highlands, lies within a belt of great climatic uncertainty. The central valley is within the semi-arid Montane Steppe climate according to the Holdridge system (ONERN, 1973), roughly corresponding to the "arid (desert or dry) puna" biome described by Troll (1968). These dry lands extend from the western flanks of southern and central Peru, through central Bolivia, and into northern Argentina and Chile. Numerous sites of cultivated and abandoned terraces lie within the region (Donkin, 1979; Field, 1966; Wright, 1963). In the Colca Valley, rainfall averages 433 mm annually. Rain is seasonal; 75 percent falls between November and March. Yearly variability is great: some years have abundant amounts approaching 700 mm; others are calamitously droughty with less than 200 mm. Fluctuations in the temperature of the Peruvian current, termed *El Niño* events, affect climates throughout Peru, and produce drought in the southern Andes (Caviedes, 1984).

An additional element of uncertainty and danger to crops is frost caused by nighttime radiational cooling under clear skies, and katabatic (downslope) movements of cold air into valley floor areas. Though frosts normally occur during the cold, dry months of the Andean winter, some may fall during summer nights early in the growing season, severely damaging young shoots. Hailstorms that topple grains and shred leaves are common in years of abundant rain.

Despite unfavorable climatic conditions, Colca Valley landforms and soils offered pre-Columbian farmers opportunities to practice permanent agriculture in an environment few Westerners would consider hospitable to farming. Snow-covered peaks flanking the valley are permanent repositories of moisture, and farmers capture snow melt during the planting season using complex systems of canals and channelized streams. Slopes between series of ancient alluvial plains are heavily terraced to take advantage of the thermal belt between higher cold regions and the lower frost-prone alluvial plains. Soils are derived from weathered volcanic colluvium and alluvium on slopes, or from more recent alluvial depositions of volcanic material on ancient floodplains. Thick soils, rich in nutrients and well-structured, combined with abundant cobbles scattered on slopes, were natural pre-adaptations for building stone-walled, irrigable terraces.

There are approximately 6000 ha of irrigated fields under cultivation in the valley, and two-thirds of them are terraces (Denevan and Hartwig, 1986). There are two basic types of terraces: narrow valley-side

Plate 1   Bench terracing in the Colca Valley. Narrow terraces are valley-side bench terraces on steep slopes; wider broadfield terraces are on gentle slopes or at footslope breaks (from the Shippe and Johnson expedition, ca. 1929; courtesy of the American Museum of Natural History).

bench terraces on steep slopes made by cut-and-fill methods, and wider broadfield terraces on shallow slopes or slope breaks made by normal slope processes and plowing (Plate 1). Both forms are called *andenes* in the valley. Bench terraces commonly measure approximately 50 m in length, between 4 m and 6 m in width, and 1 m and 3 m in height. Broadfield terraces have lower walls than bench terraces, but are much wider. Both variations are essentially linear contour, irrigable terraces according to Spencer and Hale's terrace typology (1961:10). Very broad valley floor terraces with walls less than a meter high, and naturally level, unterraced fields confined to wide, low alluvial plains are termed *pampas*, and are considered by farmers to be conceptually distinct from *andenes*.

Irrigation is the driving force behind Colca Valley agriculture. By moistening their fields during September and October to prompt seed germination before the onset of the December rains, farmers extend the growing season and manage to harvest before the June frosts. Virtually every functioning field in the region has access to irrigation water. In order to manage scarce supplies and maneuver water easily upon their fields, ancient farmers carefully terraced and leveled them. Terraces, therefore, are hydraulic features in the Colca Valley. Erosion control was probably an ancillary bonus of terracing, as were the slightly warmer temperatures on terrace platforms produced by energy re-radiation from terrace walls.

There appear to have been historical reasons for the development of sophisticated agriculture in the valley, although the archaeological sequences needed to clarify the valley's history are not yet well defined. Coporaqueños believe the genesis of terracing in the valley was due to the need to create level surfaces to irrigate maize. Symbiotic relationships of dependence and exchange between agriculturalists and camelid pastoralists surrounding the valley in large numbers in the pre-Columbian period may have prompted intensified cultivation. Food exchanges between the groups still occur today. Food policies under Wari or Inca rule may also have fostered agricultural intensification to produce maize, which had an important role in the political ecology of Andean empires (Murra, 1975).

Over 40 percent of all agricultural fields in the Colca Valley are abandoned, and two-thirds of all abandoned fields are terraces, supporting widespread speculation that similar percentages of terraces elsewhere in the Andes are now uncultivated (Denevan and Hartwig, 1986). Discovering why terraces are abandoned bears heavily on the future of reconstruction efforts. Post-conquest depopulation, Spanish resettlement policies, loss of irrigation management skills, crop changes, and climatic change are possible causes of terrace abandonment in the Colca region (Denevan, 1986), and these may also apply to other areas of abandoned terracing.

The Coporaque data indicate abandonment was not unicausal nor within one historical epoch. The demographic collapse following the Spanish conquest, when the pre-Hispanic population of over 70,000 dwindled to less than 5,000 by the mid-eighteenth century, has been documented by Cook (1982). There is compelling reason to believe agricultural production also diminished substantially. Since current population levels in the Colca Valley have yet to reach pre-Hispanic levels, land loss may be linked to demographic collapse. In support of this argument is the apparent correlation of land restoration with recent population increases, and improved access to local markets for surplus crops. Yet even during the darkest days of the early colonial period, not all of the valley's terraces appear to have been selectively abandoned. Ethnohistoric data for Coporaque suggest many of the most fertile and well-watered maize terraces were under continuous cultivation, and may have been in intensive cultivation up to the present.

Local people believe that lack of water is the root cause of terrace abandonment; if more water were available, they assert, uncultivated fields would be cheerfully restored for cash cropping regardless of local population levels. Climatic change may have contributed to land use shifts from unirrigated fields to irrigated ones well before the Inca period, but there is no evidence that irrigable lands are permanently abandoned because of lower amounts of rainfall. Forced colonial resettlement in nucleated centers, and the restructuring of political boundaries may have severed Coporaque from headwater canal sources thus prompting land abandonment. Short term droughts account for most water shortages today (Guillet, 1987).

Farmers in Coporaque own land privately, and their many small plots are scattered throughout the cultivation zone, reflecting a common Andean strategy to decrease the risks of owning and planting fields clustered in one ecological zone. One-third of Coporaque's fields are valley-side bench terraces and broadfield terraces, and most families have access to some combination of terraces and other types of *pampa* fields. The major crops in Coporaque and other valley towns are barley, alfalfa, maize, broad beans (*Vicia faba L.*), accompanied by smaller amounts of quinoa, potatoes, wheat, and peas. Most production is destined for household consumption, but farmers strive to market surpluses, and some crops, especially barley for the Arequipa brewery, are grown only for cash. Sales of barley and potatoes to Arequipa are increasing, as are purchases of bread, noodles, and other consumption goods. Alfalfa is planted to feed cattle for market; the crop is rapidly growing in popularity in the Colca region, and it appears frequently on terraces.

The Agro-Ecology of Terracing in Coporaque

One of the primary agro-ecological functions of Colca Valley terraces is to control and absorb irrigation water. Reducing the slope of the fields (1) reduces surface runoff; (2) allows irrigators to guide water to each plant (the Quechua term in Coporaque for such controlled irrigation is *yaku yachachi,* or "teaching water"); and (3) allows water to percolate through soils slowly to charge them with moisture. In general, leveled fields tend to absorb and retain more moisture than sloping fields. Valley-side bench terraces may drain slightly faster than valley floor fields because they are on slopes and therefore prone to gravity flow through, but also because they drain internally through artificial interior soil horizons made of cobbles and pebbles. The internal features are necessary because poorly drained bench terraces may be vulnerable to collapse by waterlogging following heavy rains or careless irrigation.

Terraces are invariably owned in vertical rows so water can pass from one to another through drop canals and elaborate systems of stone offtake valves and chutes. Irrigators use shovels to coax flowing water through scratch canals on terrace platforms to nurture each plant. Terraces slope slightly forward to pass water from one terrace to the next through gravity water drops, or to one side so water enters a drop canal connected to terraces below. It takes one farmer from one half hour to one hour to irrigate a regular sized bench terrace (approximately 250 m^2), but with high velocity canal flow and extra laborers, work goes much faster. It requires more time to irrigate valley floor fields, partly because they are larger than terraces (up to 5000 m^2), but also because it takes more time to "teach" water to flow over them. Irrigation records from Coporaque suggest a day's ration of water goes farther for irrigating terraces than for irrigating valley floor fields, perhaps because several terraces may be irrigated simultaneously and farmers can manage water in a coordinated fashion.

Valley side terraces are located in belts of favorable temperatures. Terraces on steep slopes above the Colca River's edge (3350 m) enjoy warm temperatures engendered by low elevations. In contrast, the wide alluvial *pampas* above (3500 m) often register daily temperatures 3–4 degrees celsius cooler, and are susceptible to morning frosts. Temperatures rise again by 1–2 degrees celsius on valley-side terraces above the *pampas* to an elevation of approximately 3600 m. The effect is produced by the drainage of cold air which glides over valley-side terraces and settles upon valley floor areas. Constructing terraces within the frost-free upper slopes took advantage of a micro-climatic temperature inversion to create agricultural space for sensitive plants.

According to local informants, plants on terraces are also less likely to be infested with blights. Wind turbulence, which also disrupts cold air sinking upon terraced fields, may remove excess, blight-promoting moisture from plant leaves.

Maize thrives on terraces year after year because of excellent soils, studied in detail by Sandor (1987), from which the following material is a summation. Most Coporaque terrace soils are within the Mollisol order (Haplustolls, Argiustolls), with dark, organic-rich surface horizons and high base cation content (Soil Survey Staff, 1975). Terrace soil structure, consistence, microporosity, and extensive root permeation indicate good tilth; there is little evidence of compaction. The loamy-textured soils hold water well. The majority of the soils have organic matter and macronutrient nitrogen levels comparable to soils in the fertile U.S. midwest. Soils of many abandoned terraces are of similar quality, requiring only additional nitrogen to equal the quality of cultivated soils.

Terrace soils, especially those in cut-and-bench terraces, have carefully made anthropic horizons. Builders packed small boulders, cobbles, and pebbles in layers 50 to 80 cm deep behind terrace walls to form a lower fill horizon. The fills may have economized on the amount of earthen fill needed to raise terraces, and lessened the weight of soil behind the walls, but they also served as drainage horizons. Farmers today believe these horizons protect against wall collapse caused by waterlogging. Similar drainage horizons have been noted in terraces in the Cuzco and Ayacucho regions of Peru (O.F. Cook, 1916; Bonavia, 1967–8).

The upper cultivated surfaces have been substantially enriched by manure, which in the past was obtained from *puna* camelid herders, to form plaggen-like horizons. Today, camelid manure is no longer used, but some maize terrace soils receiving annual inputs of sheep and burro manure have organic material levels and macronutrient nitrogen levels comparable to U.S. Mollisols.

Echoing a pre-Columbian pattern, terraces continue to be associated with specific crops. Farmers almost exclusively plant maize on terraces, and tend to plant broad beans on them as well (Table 1). Both are water-demanding and sensitive to frost (especially maize). Both are also staple crops even though small amounts of each may be marketed. Peas, grown for consumption and for market, often appear on terraces, intercropped with broad beans. Farmers seed alfalfa and barley on "extra" terraces: those which are left over after maize and broad bean terraces are planted. Heavy doses of manure and ashes permit farmers to plant maize year after year in the same fields, although occasional rotations with broad beans or alfalfa (both soil-enriching legumes) occur.

In effect, terraces are the backbone of Coporaque agriculture because they enhance subsistence security. Although the overall spatial pattern of cropping shifts annually as farmers adjust to new household and market needs, a general trend towards planting sensitive staple crops on terraces persists. Farmers assert terraces are necessary for growing maize, and promote secure harvests of broad beans. In years when water may be lacking (people appraise early rains and depth of snowpacks to predict annual supplies before planting), local authorities limit the total number of hectares planted. Families usually sacrifice barley and other market crops planted on level fields, but must seed subsistence maize and broad beans on terraces.

Terrace Construction Techniques

Terrace building requires little specialized knowledge and the techniques are easy to learn (Treacy, 1987). Since Colca Valley terraces are

Table 1
Crops Planted in Coporaque (1985 – 1986), as Percentages of Total Crop,
Percentages on Terraces, and Use[a]

Crop	Percentage of Total[b]	Percentage on Terraces	Use
Barley	28.8	16.3	M, C
Alfalfa	19.7	16.1	M, C
Pasture	14.2[c]	*[d]	M, C
Broad beans	12.4	55.0	C, M
Maize	11.0	93.3	C, M
Quinoa	4.9[e]	17.5	C
Potatoes	3.4	21.3	C, M
Wheat	3.1	18.6	M, C
Peas	0.9	31.0	C, M
Oats	0.6	30.1	C, M
Others[f]	1.0	*	*

[a] M = marketing; C = home consumption. Order of letters indicates relative importance of use.
[b] Total area cropped approximately 520 ha.
[c] Category could include well-grazed alfalfa plots.
[d] * = data not available.
[e] Quinoa is invariably intercropped with broad beans or peas.
[f] Includes small amounts of onions and garlic and unidentified fields. Crops in family house gardens not included in totals.

Source: Fieldwork mapping and air photo interpretation.

invariably irrigated, canal construction precedes or accompanies terrace construction to assure that fields can receive water. Builders begin terracing from the bottom of a slope and proceed upward, using gravity to help move soil down behind the new walls. The base of a terrace wall is a row of stones placed upon indurated subsoils some 50 cm below the soil surface (Plate 2). In Coporaque, natural elluviation of silica from upper soil horizons formed a soil duripan upon some slopes, making the task of setting terrace walls easier. The rubble fill horizon forms a pocket behind the base. Completing the terrace above the base and fill involves digging into the slope, moving soil down towards the wall, and packing it tightly while building the wall higher to retain the soil. Not everyone in the village is an experienced wall mason, but there are many who know how to fit and balance rough cobbles and stones to form a sturdy retaining wall.

Since an irrigated terrace on a valley-side slope must be level or nearly so to control water, builders moved the soil themselves during construction, not waiting for natural erosion to fill terraces slowly. Moving topsoil down and behind the wall may expose subsoil at the

Plate 2 Rebuilding abandoned agricultural terraces in Coporaque, Arequipa, Peru, by placing new wall base stones and building the wall upwards to retain the soil.

rear of the new terrace if the original topsoil is thin. If that occurs, organic material may be worked into the new exposed soil surface.

Most often, a terrace is damaged when waterlogged soil bursts the retaining wall and spills forth. Careless wall repair hastens further wall failure. Builders blame poor masonry techniques or dry soil construction for broken walls. Builders prefer to terrace with wet soil since dry soil is porous and will quickly become saturated following heavy rains, thus provoking sudden, early bursting. Common mistakes cited include not fitting wall stones together tightly, or failure to press stones tightly against the earthen fill behind. In the latter case, a gap forms between the wall and fill causing the wall to collapse.

Terrace reconstruction duplicates the labor techniques of construction, except that soil spilled from ruptured walls has to be thrown back upslope and re-walled. Workers trench down to the original base to remove the fallen and buried stones from the original wall. The wall is rebuilt while the fill stones and soil are carefully re-packed in behind the wall and tamped down. Building bench terraces from scratch may not require a great deal more time than rebuilding abandoned ones. When reconstructing fields, masons replace up to 80 percent of the ancient walls, and must laboriously throw spilled soils upslope, which demands more effort than moving soils downslope for new terraces.

Field observations indicate no clear relationship between worker-days expended, male/female worker combinations, and the progress of work. Men, in general, are more productive earth movers and masons than women, although some older women excel at those tasks. Women and older children normally gather and stack stones next to masons as they fill and raise terrace walls. Differences in terrace size and degree of erosion, as well as labor efficiency, determine the rhythm of work.

The tasks of shoveling down soil and raising walls is an initial heavy investment of work. Succeeding tasks—carefully levelling the platform, installing irrigation devices, and working organic material into the soil—are usually accomplished over time. Coporaque farmers often spend several days each during planting seasons tinkering with walls, canals, and soils in a constant process of fine-tuning their fields.

The Economic Aspects of Terracing

The paramount economic contribution of terraces to the people of Coporaque is agricultural security. In periods of frost or drought, the difference between planting on terraced or non-terraced fields may be the difference between harvest or serious losses. Another contribution is the radically broadened agricultural options that terraces permit because of their microclimatic and hydraulic advantages. Terraces converted large areas of the Colca Valley into maize lands, and the crop would not have survived there without them. Once built, the annual costs to families to maintain their terraces are minimal and may be accomplished with family labor, or with assistance acquired through reciprocal labor exchange networks or hired workers.

Terrace construction or reconstruction costs are labor costs since few tools other than picks and shovels are needed. Work may be accomplished in a piecemeal fashion by family labor, or by massing labor to rebuild entire ranks of terraces. In the former case, labor measurements indicate two men can rebuild 7.2 m² wall in one day (1 day herein equals 6 hours). Assuming a common size terrace wall measures 1.8 m high and 50 m in length, two men could restore an entire terrace in two weeks, or build an entirely new one in a slightly longer period of time. Most terraces in the valley today are built individually by household labor groups.

Preliminary results of a terrace reconstruction effort in Coporaque with massed labor indicate that 610 worker-days were required to rebuild 2,781.3 m² (slightly less than one third of a hectare) of valley-side terraces, with 1,030.8 m² of new wall (Treacy, 1987). At that rate it would require 2,000 worker-days to complete 1 hectare. The pace of work was uneven, however, and during the most productive week with the greatest number of workers in attendance (19 men and 13 women with a total of 177 worker-days for the week), 1,239.4 m² of platform were restored, with 254.5 m² of new wall. This suggests that 1 hectare could be completed with an investment of 1,416 worker-days, since progress improves greatly with more workers.

Comparative data on other terrace projects in Peru show many are less labor demanding (Table 2). Differences in terrace size, soils, degree of erosion, and the organization of work no doubt account for some of the disparities. Many of the figures, especially those for Puno (and perhaps for Coporaque) may be sorely exaggerated since most projects pay an inflated daily wage, creating an incentive for workers to proceed slowly (C. Erickson, 1988: pers. comm.). Araujo (1986: 283) reports costs of between U.S. $468 and U.S. $1,162 for projects near Lima (see Table 2). Assuming a daily rural wage of U.S. $1.50 and 1,266 worker-days per hectare (an average of the figures on Table 2), it could cost approximately $1,900 to restore 1 hectare of Andean terraces.

Long term data on the yields and economic returns of terrace restoration or construction are still unavailable since most projects are very new. First year yields data from the Peruvian Ministry of Agriculture for new bench terraces (converted from non-terraced sloping fields) suggest yields rise significantly with terracing (Table 3). Ministry personnel attribute the improvement to enhanced moisture retention (Alfaro, 1986:108-109). For individual farmers, restoring small areas of terraces or building new ones may also represent positive returns since the investment yields a net creation of arable land. New production could either augment household consumption or provide marketable surpluses.

Compared with the per hectare costs of opening unfarmed coastal or forest lands, terrace reconstruction costs in the highlands may be competitive. They are comparable or lower than the average costs of bringing new coastal desert lands under production. ($2,500–6,000 per hectare), but often higher than the costs of opening new cultivable lands in the eastern tropical forests ($1,000 per hectare) (Zamora, 1986:123–24).

A key issue in terrace economics is the practice of providing incentives for farmers to build them. Agencies almost invariably report difficulties with direct incentives: people participate for no other reason than to receive food or cash (Coolman, 1985), incentives slow down the pace of work, they create needless dependencies (PNCSACH, 1984:62–63), and they effectively dissuade farmers from voluntary terracing (Williams et al., 1986:62). Communities demand incentives when

Table 2

Per Hectare Labor Requirements for Terrace Reconstruction in Peruvian Villages

Project	Worker Days/ha	Source
Puno	3750[a]	Coolman, 1985:40
Coporaque	2000	Treacy, 1987:55
Lari (Colca Valley)	1320[b]	Guillet, 1987:412
Cajamarca	800 – 1000	Araujo, 1986:283
PNCSACH	336 – 1181[c]	PNCSACH, 1984:88
Puno (Asillo)	622[d]	Ramos, 1986:236
Porcón	500[e]	Araujo, 1986:283
San Pedro de Casta (Lima)	350[f]	Masson, 1986:213

[a] Average of over 30 sites in the Department of Puno.
[b] Extrapolated from farmers' calculations, not measured directly.
[c] Range of values from 12 areas in highlands.
[d] Reported total costs per hectare of US$1121.
[e] Reported total costs per hectare of US$468.
[f] Reported total costs per hectare of US$1162.

Table 3

First Year Per Hectare Yields of Crops on New Bench Terraces, Compared to Yields on Sloping Fields (kg/ha)

Crop[a]	Terraced[b]	Non-Terraced[c]	Percent Increase	N[d]
Potatoes	17,206	12,206	43	71
Maize	2,982	1,807	65	18
Barley	1,910	1,333	43	56
Barley (Forage)	23,000	15,865	45	159

[a] All crops treated with chemical fertilizer.
[b] Water absorption terraces with earthen walls and inward platform slope.
[c] Fields sloping between 20 and 50 percent located next to terraced fields for control.
[d] N = number of terrace/field sites.

Source: Ministry of Agriculture (Peru), *Programa Nacional de Conservación de Suelos y Aguas* (See Alfaro, 1986:108 – 109).

they realize that many agencies are willing to pay to achieve their own priorities and timetables. Direct payments to farmers to practice new land management techniques are not new; the U.S. Soil Conservation Service paid farmers some bonuses to build drainage ditches and practice contour plowing in Wisconsin during the 1940s. However, complete subsidies to build terraces seem to be necessary when farmers see no pressing need to terrace, or fail to perceive the benefits.

The Socioeconomic Contexts of New Terracing

From the point of view of agricultural development, there is much to say in favor of terracing. They reduce agricultural risk, a basic requirement of a successful farming innovation. They prevent soil erosion and create new habitats for crops, and require no costly technological inputs. The challenge of restoring the practice of agricultural terracing is now to design flexible programs that extend or recover terraces by giving farmers reasons to build them. Terracing became a highly developed form of land management in the Andean past because there were ecological and economic contexts which required that cultivators invest in permanent irrigated agriculture. There are socioeconomic contexts in contemporary rural societies that, while different from the past, may be equally supportive of terrace agriculture.

The outstanding ecological advantage of terraces is that they halt erosion, and one of the prime promotional approaches of restoration programs has been soil conservation. The long-term economic importance of conserving soil resources is unimpeachable and not easily factored into conventional economic planning. Appeals based upon the anti-erosion values of terracing alone, nonetheless, may be insufficient to propel terracing campaigns in the field. First, most of the terraces in the Andean area (and elsewhere) appear not to have been constructed specifically to counter erosion; they were built with other purposes in mind (Spencer and Hale, 1961; Donkin, 1979). Certainly in the Colca Valley, the motives for terracing were the need to build irrigation platforms, and the wish to cultivate maize. Second, reports from terrace extension programs indicate that small farmers are just as interested in yield improvements as they are in soil conservation, and in some cases more so (Williams et al., 1986:75–77; PNCSACH, 1984:55–57). There is no suggestion here that farmers are heedless of erosion. Williams (Williams et al., 1986:87–88) advances the interesting argument that soil conservation interests are strongest among poor farmers, and are of less importance to wealthier farmers. The point I wish to make is that resting the case for terracing upon the equally firm ground of economic benefit as well as soil conservation (both are clearly related in the long run) may be a more compelling argument to many small farmers.

This suggests that terracing may be best advanced by forms of co-innovation: re-introducing the technique of terracing as an adjunct to other inputs into agricultural systems that make them more productive. Irrigation is one example, since many terraces were built expressly for irrigated agriculture. In Coporaque, farmers have restored terraces under population pressure coupled with a desire to market surplus crops to buy food and other goods, including elaborately embroidered clothes (Femenias, n.d.). But finding new sources of water must precede land restoration since water availability determines the rate at which abandoned terraces are restored. In decades past in Coporaque, farmers rebuilt terraces spontaneously by reconstructing adjacent unused canals with communal labor. Therefore, an indirect and less expensive approach to restore terrace agriculture in irrigated or irrigable areas may be to: (1) overhaul or introduce irrigation systems; and (2) provide markets for new production.

Communities with access to water, or with excess water, may be good targets for terracing projects. The relative hydraulic efficiency of terraces may prompt terrace construction in areas with scarce supplies. Linking terracing with irrigation may also help avoid the misuse of water resources that often are diverted for cattle pasture instead of for planned agricultural programs (Wilkenson et al., 1984:E-18).

Recalling that many terraces were built in prehistory for a special crop suggests that they be built or rebuilt for special crops, especially marketable ones, to offset the increased costs of terracing. The best, albeit extreme, demonstration of spontaneous terracing is that of eastern Peru and Bolivia for coca plants grown illegally. There are more felicitous examples. Migrants in the Rimac Valley above Lima build terraces on barren hillsides to plant flowers sold in the city at good prices. The terraces of Sabandia and Paucarpata near Arequipa are renowned for producing alfalfa for the local dairy industry. Terraces also offer sufficient micro-niches for clever, labor-intensive polycropping. Well-protected terraces near the Colca River's edge in Coporaque have become highland agroforestry plots with apple and pear trees planted over an alfalfa cover on the platforms, and with oregano, flowers, and prickly pear (*Opuntia ficus indica*) ensconced in the walls. Close links with markets could justify intensive commercial terrace horticulture. The geographic factor of distance to markets may help select prime candidate areas for terrace development, and mapping projects underway now in Peru to identify terrace sites may be of assistance.

To counter the high labor inputs required by some forms of terracing, a processual or accretional construction approach may be appropriate, especially for terracing fields already under cultivation. One method is termed the controlled erosion terrace system whereby temporary walls are erected upon slopes; behind the wall, soil is allowed to accumulate by natural slope processes, until leveling or near leveling occurs and a new, higher retaining wall is added. The system is admirably described by Williams (Williams et al., 1986) and Doolittle (1984). The method will not result in an immediate major reduction in slope, and will not provide the immediate benefits of a leveled surface (Williams et al., 1986). However, controlled erosion terraces may be more convenient for making wide terraces which would otherwise require labor-intensive hand shoveling of soils.

Although the most pressing problems in terrace extension programs are social and economic, the search for additional useful terrace technologies should continue. In areas with a shortage of available stone for walls, terrace batters of earth seeded in pasture grass may be sufficient (cf. Arledge et al., 1985). Mitchell (1985) reported spotting traditional terraces in Ayacucho, Peru faced with adobe.

Terraces are not necessarily incompatible with modern technological inputs. Many Andean farmers are interested in technically advanced cultivation methods, and are wary of continually being cast in the subordinate role of "peasants." In the Colca Valley, people sum up their aspirations to be yeomen farmers by stressing proudly they are *agricultores* (farmers) and not *campesinos* or *comuneros* (peasants). There is interest in light, hand operated, gas-powered tillers, called *mulas mecánicas* in Peru, which are portable enough to plow narrow terraces, and inexpensive enough to be within the grasp of some farmers.

Finally, working within Andean communities in terrace restoration requires the sociological or anthropological perspicacity to realize that terraces, in the eyes of farmers, are also instances of land. In the Colca Valley, the notion of "development" or "progress" largely means improving the circumstances by which individuals may enhance incomes. One pathway to higher income is to acquire more land, since land represents wealth and the ability to accumulate more wealth. People regard terraces much the same way they regard any other class of field: they are stocks of social capital. Adding new stocks implies land redistribution and resolving questions of secure tenure and water rights, and handling these social issues should be an integral component of terrace promotion campaigns.

Conclusions

Ancient societies built agricultural terraces because they were good habitats for select crops, and farmers value them today because they help to reduce agricultural risk. There are few if any insuperable technical problems involved in building them. Some skill is required, but terrace reconstruction projects report that farmers usually master the techniques quickly. People who build houses of earth and stone have little difficulty learning how to build terraces of the same materials. Terraces require maintenance, but a well-built and tended terrace may last for centuries.

Agricultural terracing could be integrated into the conventional repertoire of development techniques, which to date consists largely of improved crop varieties, fertilizers, irrigation, crop rotations, and access to markets. It is an appropriate complement to irrigation needed in many arid areas of the highlands, and could lend itself well to sensitive crops with good market prices.

Terracing, however, is only a technology—a useful method for managing the environment to enhance agricultural productivity—and therefore only one dimension of farming. Terracing is not an agricultural system in itself; systems have social, political and economic contexts as well as environmental ones (Brush and Turner, 1987). In order to appraise the role of terraces in agricultural systems, they must be placed within a perspective which includes local perceptions of utility and potential.

Acknowledgments

Field work in Peru was funded by a Fulbright-Hays Doctoral Dissertation Research Abroad Grant during 1985 and 1986. I thank Lourdes Izaguirre, Pedro Romero, John Earls and other members of PRATVIR for the opportunity to study and discuss terrace restoration projects. William Denevan, Clark Erickson, Kay Candler, Blenda Femenias, B. L. Turner II, and John Browder made many helpful suggestions for the text.

References

Alfaro, Julio. 1986. Conservación de suelos y desarrollo rural en los andes peruanos. Pages 51–153 in Andenería, conservación de suelos y desarrollo rural en los andes peruanos. See Portocarrero.

Altieri, Miguel A. 1983. Agroecology: The scientific basis of alternative agriculture. Division of Biological Control, University of California, Albany.

Araujo, H. 1986. Civilización andina: Acondicionamiento territorial y agricultura prehispánica. Hacia una revaloración de su tecnología. Pages 277–300 in Andenes y camellones en el Perú andino. See Torre and Burga.

Arledge, J.E., L. Chang-Vavarro L. and A. Vasquez V. 1985. Manual técnico de conservación de suelos. Programa Nacional de Conservación de suelos. Programa Nacional de Conservación de Suelos y Aguas en Cuencas Hidrográficas. Ministerio de Agricultura, Lima.

Bonavia, D. 1967–1968. Investigaciones arqueológicas en el Mantaro medio. Revista de Museo Nacional, Lima, 35:211–294.

Brush, S.B. and B.L. Turner II. 1987. The nature of farming systems and views of their change. Pages 11–48 in B.L. Turner and S.B. Brush (eds.)

Caviedes, C.N. 1984. El Niño. Geographical Review 74:267–90.

Cook, N.D. 1982. The people of the Colca Valley: A population study. Westview Press, Boulder.

Cook, O.F. 1916. Staircase farms of the ancients. National Geographic Magazine 29:474–534.

Coolman, B. 1985. De la consultoria de la evalucación del sub-proyecto "recuperación y desarrollo de andenes y terrazas," PIRR-Puno, 1983–1985. Unpublished manuscript.

Denevan, W.D. 1980. Latin America. Pages 217–244 *in* G.A. Klee (ed.), World systems of traditional resource management. Halstead Press, New York.

———. (ed.) 1986. The cultural ecology, archaeology, and history of terracing and terrace abandonment in the Colca Valley of southern Peru. Technical report to the National Science Foundation and the National Geographic Society (manuscript). Department of Geography, University of Wisconsin, Madison.

———. and L. Hartwig, 1986. Measurement of terrace abandonment in the Colca Valley. Pages 99–115 *in* The cultural ecology, archaeology, and history of terracing and terrace abandonment in the Colca Valley of southern Peru. *See* Denevan (ed.), 1986.

Donkin, R.A. 1979. Agricultural terracing in the aboriginal new world. Viking Fund Publications in Anthropology 56.

Doolittle, W.E. 1984. Agricultural change as an incremental process. Annals of the association of American geographers 74:124–137.

Erickson, C.L. 1986. Agricultura en camellones in la cuenca del Lago Titicaca: aspectos técnicos y su futuro. Pages 331–350 *in* Andenes y camellones in el Perú andino. *See* Torre and Burga.

Femenias, Blenda. 1987. Regional dress of Colca Valley, Peru: A dynamic tradition. Paper presented at the Symposium on Costume as Communication: Current Issues in Ethnographic Cloth and Costume for Middle America and the Central Andes of South America, Haffenreffer Museum of Anthropology, Brown University, Bristol, RI.

Field, C. 1966. A reconnaissance of southern Andean agricultural terracing. Ph.D. dissertation, University of California, Los Angeles.

Guillet, David. 1986. Paleotecnolgías hidraúlicas en el altiplano peruano y su potencial económico. América Indígena 46:331–48.

———. 1987. Terracing and irrigation in the Peruvian highlands. Current Anthropology 28:409–430.

Lathrap, D. 1970. The upper Amazon. Praeger, New York.

Masson, L. 1986. Rehabilitación de andenes en la comunidad de San Pedro de Casta, Lima. Pages 207–16 *in* Andenes y camellones en el Perú andino. *See* Torre and Burga.

Mayer, Enrique, 1979. Land use in the Andes: Ecology and agriculture in the Mantaro Valley of Peru with special reference to potatoes. Centro Internacional de la Papa, Lima.

Mitchell, William P. 1985. On terracing in the Andes. Current Anthropology 26:288–89.

Morlon, P. B. Orlove and A. Hibon. 1982. Tecnologías agrícolas en los andes centrales; perspectivas para el desarrollo. Coporación Financiera de Desarrollo (COFIDE), Lima.

Murra, J. V. 1975. Maíz, tubérculos, y ritos agrícolas. Pages 45–57 *in* Formaciones econónicas y políticas del mundo andino. Instituto de Estudios Peruanos, Lima.

ONERN 1973. Inventario, evaluación y uso racional de los recursos naturales de la costa: Cuenca de Río Camaná-Majes. Oficina Nacional de Evaluación de Recursos Naturales, Lima.

Orlove, B. and R. Godoy. 1986. Sectorial fallowing systems in the central Andes. Journal of Ethnobiology 6(1):169–204.

PNCSACH. 1984. Impacto de la conservación de suelos y aguas en el desarrollo del agro en la sierra peruana. Programa Nacional de Conservación de Suelos y Aguas en Cuencas Hidrográficas, Ministerio de Agricultura, Lima.

Portocarrero, J. (ed.) 1986. Andenería, conservación de suelos y desarrollo rural en los andes peruanos. Asociación Naturaleza, Ciencia, y Tecnología para el Servicio Social (NCTL), Lima.

Ramos, C. 1986. Reconstrucción, refacción y manejo de andenes en Asillo (Puno). Pages 225–239 *in* Andenes y camellones en el Perú andino. *See* Torre and Burga.

Sandor, J. 1987. Initial investigation on soils in agricultural terraces in the Colca Valley, Peru. Valley. Pages 163–192 *in* W.M. Denevan, K. Mathewson and G. Knapp (eds.), Pre-Hispanic agricultural fields in the Andean region. British Archaeological Reports, International Series 359 (i), Oxford.

Shippee, R. 1932. A forgotten valley of Peru. National Geographic 65:110–132.

Soil Survey Staff. 1975. Soil taxonomy. U.S. Dept. Agr. Handbook No. 436. U.S. Govt. Printing Office Washington.

Spencer, J.E. and G.A. Hale. 1961. The origin, nature, and distribution of agricultural terracing. Pacific Viewpoint 2:1–40.

Torre, C. de la and M. Burga (eds.). 1986. Andenes y camellones en el Perú andino. Concejo Nacional de Cienca y Tecnología (CONCYTEC), Lima.

Treacy, J.M. 1987. Building and rebuilding agricultural terraces in the Colca Valley of Peru. Pages 51–57 *in* M.A. Works (ed.), Yearbook, proceedings of the conference of Latin Americanist geographers 13, Louisiana State University, Department of Geography and Anthropology, Baton Rouge.

Troll, C. 1968. The cordilleras of the tropical Americas. Pages 15–56 *in* C. Troll (ed.), Geo-Ecology of the Mountainous Regions of the Tropical Americas, Bonn.

Wilkerson, J.L. McKean & R.E. Meyer, 1984. Peru: Improved water and land use in the sierra. AID project impact evaluation no 54, U.S. Agency for International Development, Washington.

Williams, L.S. Cooperband and B.J. Walter. 1986. Agricultural terrace construction: The Valles Altos project of Venezuela as an example for AID. Cooperative Agreement on Human Settlements and Natural Resource Systems Analysis. Clark University International Development Program, Worcester.

Wright, A.C.S. 1963. The soil process and the evolution of agriculture in northern Chile. Pacific Viewpoint 4:65–74.

Zamora, C. 1986. La frontera agrícola: aprovechamiento y potencial. Pages 103–144 *in* A. Figueroa and J. Portocarrero (eds.), Priorización y desarrollo del sector agrario en el Perú. Pontificia Universidad Católica del Perú and Fundación Friedrich Ebert, Lima.

14

Raised Fields and Sustainable Agriculture in the Lake Titicaca Basin of Peru

Clark L. Erickson and Kay L. Candler

Introduction

Many non-western traditional agricultural systems have been proven to be highly productive, ecologically sound, and sustainable (Altieri 1983; Denevan 1980; Wilken 1987). Although they supported hundreds of generations of farmers, many of these systems have not survived into historic times (Denevan 1970, 1983; Turner and Harrison 1983). While most of the surviving systems continue because of their resilience and ecological stability, many others have or are in the process of disappearing in the face of major social, economic, and political changes occurring in developing countries (Altieri 1983; Denevan 1980; Wilken 1987).

The reconstruction of raised fields in the Lake Titicaca Basin illustrates the role archaeology can play in developing alternative technologies. Because raised field agriculture was completely abandoned in the Andes, archaeological methods provide the only means to understand the history of the system and to develop models for its proper rehabilitation. Excavation indicates that the prehistoric abandonment of the raised fields was due to socio-political changes rather than environmental limitations or change. This implies that, with proper consideration of the contemporary socio-economic context and the ecologically sound prehistoric models, raised field agriculture has productive potential for the future of development in the Lake Titicaca Basin (Erickson 1988; Candler and Erickson 1987).

This paper presents a summary of the results from 5 years of raised field reconstruction by the Proyecto Agrícola de los Campos Elevados, in conjunction with the 5 Quechua communities in and around the District of Huatta, Peru (Figure 1). Raised fields are a highly productive

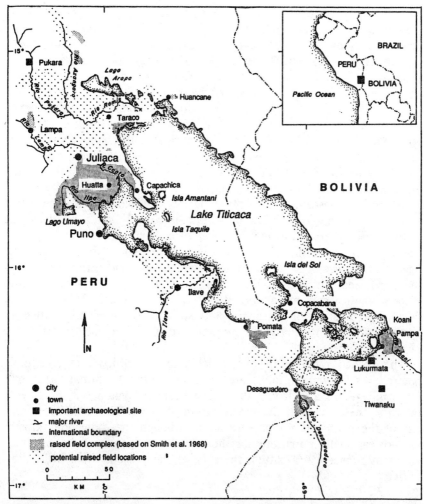

Figure 1 Map showing the location of prehistoric raised fields (based on Smith et al., 1968) and areas potentially cultivated by raised field farming.

alternative to the various capital intensive agricultural schemes being introduced by development agencies in the area. Raised field agriculture is compared to a government-sponsored irrigation project that would destroy the remains of thousands of potentially recuperable raised fields.

The Agro-Environment of the Lake Titicaca Basin

The Lake Titicaca Basin, located about 3800 meters above sea level, is a difficult environment for agriculture because of irregular rainfall, poor and degraded soils, and frequent and severe frost during the short growing season (Erickson 1988). Prehispanic farmers developed sophisticated methods to overcome these limitations, including diverse and well-adapted crops, highly efficient agricultural tools, and intensive agricultural systems such as terraces (*andenes*), sunken gardens (*gochas*), and raised fields (*campos elevados, camellones,* or *waru waru*) (Donkin 1979; Erickson 1987, 1988; Flores and Paz 1987; Garaycochea 1987; Kolata 1986; Lennon 1982; Marion et al. 1982; Smith et al. 1968; Torre and Burga 1986). In addition to agricultural technology, complex social mechanisms were developed to minimize risk and land degradation by dictating sectorial fallow and crop rotation and to efficiently organize labor.

Today, the descendants of these farmers employ an impoverished agricultural technology. Land in Huatta is roughly categorized as one of two types: *cerro* (hillslope) or *pampa* (lacustrine and riverine plain). The *cerro* lands continue to be cultivated intensively, but without the benefit of the sectorial fallow system (which was discontinued in living memory), and with very reduced benefit from the ancient terrace and erosion control systems on the slopes. These structures have generally fallen into a state of disrepair, and some have been dismantled to permit cultivation of larger contiguous areas and to facilitate the use of yoked oxen.

The eroded remains of raised fields in the *pampa* are essentially ignored. As the *pampa* lands are more vulnerable to climatic extremes (especially flood and frost), they have been cultivated only in a very desultory manner, with little expectation of profit. The major economic use of the *pampa* is for pasture land; although the indigenous grasses are not especially nutritious for the introduced species of domesticated ruminants (sheep and cattle), there is, at the present time, little alternative.

The Altiplano as a Fragile Environment

The landscape of Huatta, as in most of the low-lying parts of the Lake Titicaca Basin, can be seen as two poorly-articulated parts (the *cerro* and the *pampa*) in a single system of economic exploitation. The hillslope is essentially vulnerable to soil impoverishment through overcropping and erosion; unfortunately the present-day economic patterns accelerate rather than reduce this vulnerability. While the *pampa* lands themselves cannot be considered "fragile" to the same degree as the hillslopes, in that they are not subject to ecological degradation, their under-utilization in the present-day economic system has contributed to the degradation of the *cerro,* and therefore to the system as a whole.

While the disruption of the sectorial fallow system and the decay of the erosion control systems on the *cerro* have led to reduced fertility, the erosion of the raised fields has not caused a similar deterioration in *pampa* ecology. However, when these remains are viewed as a part of the system's potential resources for agricultural production, the active destruction of raised fields poses a dilemma. Some 15,000 hectares of raised fields have been destroyed in the Huatta *pampa* area alone (Garaycochea 1983). It is ironic when raised field remains are destroyed as a result of projects intended to increase agricultural production in the *altiplano*.

Two examples merit discussion. The first is "Irrigación Buena Vista y Illpa," sponsored by USAID and the Corporation of Puno to develop much of the raised field-covered zone (ONERN-CORPUNO 1984:118–120). This project would construct an earthen dam (4 meters tall and 1.1 kilometers long) upstream on the Rio Illpa near Lago Umayo that would control a large reserve of water (110 million cubic meters) and, theoretically at least, prevent flooding of the *pampa* during the wet season. This water would also be used to irrigate the *pampa* when necessary, and a proposed network of canals (covering approximately 800 hectares for Buena Vista and 5,000 hectares for Illpa) would permit the mechanized cultivation of improved pasture crops. Much of the expensive infrastructure, including the dam earthworks, has already been constructed. However, the project has not yet been fully implemented because of conflicts among the communities in the areas it encompasses. Ironically, the project area is covered by well-preserved raised fields with a network of sophisticated pre-Columbian water-management structures (Lennon 1982; Erickson 1988). If the project continues, these ancient raised fields will be leveled or inundated by the reservoir. If the new capital-intensive system works at all, it will probably benefit only the government cooperative and the experimental agricultural station.

A second government project, directed by the National Agrarian University, plans to test a design based on blocks of raised platforms with encircling ditches developed by their engineers. *Altiplano* farmers will then be encouraged to adopt this technology. These modern engineers recognize the advantages of the technology for minimizing the effects of flood and frost, but are apparently unaware that a similar solution was discovered in prehistoric times. The new earthen structures will be constructed with heavy machinery. These modern fields will, at great capital expense, destroy the ancient raised field system and replace it with a technology that is beyond the means of the average farmer. In the sense that raised field remains are becoming increasingly vulnerable to eradication by Western technology, they may be considered "endangered landforms," important resources to preserve and rehabilitate.

Raised Field Agriculture: Definitions and Functions

Raised fields are defined as "any prepared land involving the transfer and elevation of earth in order to improve cultivating conditions" (Denevan and Turner 1974:24). Raised field agriculture has been documented in many areas of the Americas, and appears to have provided an important economic base for New World civilizations (Darch 1983; Denevan et al. 1987; Denevan 1970, 1983; Farrington 1985; Harrison and Turner 1978).

Remains of raised fields are found throughout the vast lake and river plains or *pampa* of the Lake Tititcaca Basin; some 82,000 hectares of raised fields have been observed in aerial photographs and limited ground survey (Smith et al. 1968), but it is believed that their original extent was actually much larger, possibly double that figure (Erickson 1988). The largest continuous block of raised fields in the basin (56,000 hectares) lies in the Huatta area, where our archaeological and experimental research was conducted.

Although the raised fields of Huatta were abandoned, we have been able to document many technological details and functions of raised fields, in addition to the crops cultivated (Erickson 1985, 1986, 1988; Garaycochea 1986a, 1986b, 1987; Denevan and Turner 1974). These functions are summarized as:

The Concentration, Production, and Recycling of Soil Nutrients. The construction of raised fields doubles topsoil thickness on the planting surface, while the canals produce "green manure" in the form of rapidly-growing aquatic plants, and organic matter and other nutrients produced by the decomposition of animals. The canals also act as sediment traps for the recapture of topsoil eroding from the platforms and also from the nearby hilltops.

Improvement of Crop Microclimates. We have demonstrated that raised fields improve microclimates by slightly raising ambient temperature during radiation frost episodes. This is effected through the effective capture and noctural release of solar energy in canal water.

Water Control and Conservation. The canals can be used either to provide drainage or to conserve water, depending upon hydraulic needs.

Minor Functions. Raised field canals could also be used for aquaculture and pisciculture, serve as barriers to crop pests and grazing animals, and provide routes of transportation and communication.

The major functions of raised fields are exactly tailored to overcome the limitations to agriculture in the lake basin. Soil depletion, which has become critical on the over-cultivated hillslopes, is not a problem in functioning raised fields. At the same time, the effects of climatic extremes on rainfall and temperature are ameliorated by the raised fields' morphology.

Applied Archaeology in Huatta: 1981–1986

Raised field experiments were conducted between 1981 and 1986. Eroded raised fields were reconstructed according to models developed from archaeological excavations in prehistoric raised fields (Erickson 1985, 1986, 1987, 1988; Garaycochea 1987). The first plots were built on privately owned land. In 1982 the project expanded to include the reconstruction of raised fields by local members of farmer organizations of Huatta on their communal lands. By the end of 1986, about 30 hectares of raised fields had been reconstructed in 10 different communities. In Huatta alone, over 500 families were involved. A large part of the success of the project was due to community participation and the development of effective teaching materials and a video program (Brinkmeier 1985; Candler and Erickson 1987; Garaycochea 1987: pers. com.). After 1986, the raised field project was subsumed under a Peruvian government program, and since then has been expanded to include over 30 *altiplano* communities where an estimated 50 hectares of raised fields have been rehabilitated (Garaycochea 1987: pers. com.).

Field Reconstruction

Construction began with measuring the surface of the ancient field remains to determine the proper spacing of canals and raised field platforms. A ratio of 1:1 was usually maintained between the widths of the reconstructed platforms and canals. The borders between the canals and platforms were then marked to guide the construction. The *chakitaqlla* (Andean footplow) was used to cut sod blocks (rich in organic matter) from the canals, first for rebuilding retaining walls along the platform edges, and then for the fill of the field. The elevation of the reconstructed raised fields varied between 20 and 50 cm. The final height of the platforms depended upon both the depth of good agricultural soil in the canal (excavation generally stopped when a hard clayey horizon was encountered) and the local farmers' estimates of how high the water level rises during a typical growing season.

Our approach was oriented to the technology currently employed by the local farmers; we used common implements such as *chakitaqllas, waqtanas*, ("clod buster"), *rawkanas* (indigenous hoe), picks, and shovels rather than attempting to promote mechanization of raised fields. The *altiplano* has an over-abundance of available labor, and the maintenance and capital needed for mechanization is not presently available to most small farmers. It would be theoretically possible to mechanize certain aspects of raised field farming, particularly the initial construction of fields, but this is not practical given the present socio-economic context of the small farmer in the *altiplano* (Plates 1–4).

Social Organization of Labor and Land

Labor for raised field reconstruction was organized at the individual family, multifamily, and communal levels. Several individual families constructed raised fields on their privately-held plots of land. Labor for these fields was generally provided by the nuclear family or an extended family group. Small blocks of fields were easily constructed using this form of labor organization.

Most of the raised fields were constructed through communal labor on community-owned land. Huatta is currently organized into 4 *parcialidades,* or semi-independent communities, based loosely on the traditional Andean *ayllu* (a localized landholding group, whose members are generally related by common descent). It already has been observed that, in living memory, a sectorial system of cultivation was followed on the *cerro.* Although the actual plots were privately held, their cultivation was communally controlled. It also has been mentioned that the land in the *pampa* has been used primarily for grazing animals, with only occasional cultivation. In this context, some developments of recent years have been highly significant. Under pressure of legal suits brought by the community, and threatened by "restructuring" (in effect, dissolution), the government cooperative (Sociedad Anónima de Interés Social [SAIS] Buenavista) which controls most of the *pampa* surrounding Huatta has released various plots of *pampa* land to the District of Huatta. This land was then distributed among the four *parcialidades,* as there is no mechanism for the distribution of land among private individuals. Some of these land "donations" have been outright concessions, while others have been temporary "loans," with somewhat vague terms of usufruct. Most of the *parcialidades* consider it politically expedient to demonstrate that they are making more productive use of the land than the SAIS Buenavista did. In effect, this means that they must make an attempt to cultivate these *pampa* lands (Candler and Erickson 1987). Therefore, when research began in 1981, sizable blocks of *pampa* land covered with raised field remains were controlled by communal organizations. Moreover these organizations wanted to cultivate the *pampa* lands as a political expedient, whether or not it would be economically rewarding. While previously

Plate 1 Manual reconstruction of raised fields using the *chakitaqlla*, or Andean footplow, to cut and remove organic-rich sod blocks from sediment-filled canals. Chojnocoto, Huatta, Peru, November 1986.

Plate 2 Final construction and leveling of the raised field planting platform. Chojnocoto, Huatta, Peru, November 1985.

Plate 3 Young potato plants on raised fields at Viscachani Pampa. Community of Segunda Collana, Huatta, Peru, January 1986.

Plate 4 Mature potato plants on raised fields at Viscachani Pampa during the end of the rainy season, February 1986.

Table 1
Comparative Labor Calculations for Raised Field Construction[a]

Example	Depth of Fill (cm)	Area of Platform Constructed (m²)	Fill for ha r.f. & Canal (m³)	Rate of Construction (m³/person/ day)	ha r.f. & Canal (person- days/ha)
Erickson[b]	20	1,943	1,000	5.0	200
Garaycochea[c]	20	642	1,000	4.0	250
Garaycochea[d]	20	1,351	1,000	3.2	310
Garaycochea[e]	20	66,801	1,000	1.3	786
Ramos[f]	24	8,613	1,752	1.9	900
Denevan[g]	20	na	1,000	2.6	769

[a] One day = 5 hours.
[b] Based on Erickson (1985).
[c] Based on Garaycochea (1986a, 1987b).
[d] Based on Garaycochea (1986b), converted to a 5-hour day.
[e] Based on Garaycochea (1987b).
[f] Based on Ramos (1986b).
[g] Based on Denevan (1982).

there were some communal structures associated with cultivation of *cerro* lands, there was not a tradition of *pampa* cultivation at all, much less communal cultivation on the *pampa*. Fortunately for our project, the situation described above which motivated the *parcialidades* to become involved in communal cultivation of *pampa* lands also engendered a lively interest in raised field reconstruction.

Labor Requirements of Raised Field Agriculture

The person-hours necessary to reconstruct and maintain raised fields were recorded during several events between 1981 and 1986 (Erickson 1986, 1988; Garaycochea 1986a, 1986b, 1987b). Table 1 summarizes the labor figures derived from these data. The labor used in the initial construction of the raised fields was highly variable, from 200 to 1,000 person-days/ha (Andean "day" = 5 hours) (Erickson 1988). It is estimated that the initial construction, rebuilding every ten years, and annual planting, weeding, harvest, and maintenance of raised fields planted in potatoes requires 270 person-days/ha/year (see Table 2).

Production of Raised Field Agriculture

The reconstructed raised fields produced impressive harvests. In 1981–1982, the average potato yield on the initial test plots was 8

Table 2
Estimated Annual Labor Costs for Raised-Field Activities

Activity	Person-Days/ha/year Raised Fields and Canals	
Preparation of soil[a]	20	
Seeding[b]	50	
Aporque (potato banking)[c]	100	(twice/yr)
Irrigation		
normal year[d]	0	
short drought	20	(4 splash irrigation)
long drought	100	(once/week for 5 months)
Harvest[e]	100	(potatoes)
Total (minus irrigation)	270	

[a] Preparation of the soil is not necessary following tuber harvest and is minimal after the harvest of grains. If the raised fields were rebuilt every 10 years (which is probably excessive), the annual labor costs would be 20 person-days/yr (based on 200 person-days/10 yrs for original construction or rebuilding). Fields with year-round water-filled canals would be "mucked," a more laborious procedure. These cases would be rare since most canals dry out periodically during the dry season or during droughts.

[b] This figure is based on planting potato seed and other tubers. Much less time would be needed for most other crops.

[c] The figures for aporque are based on potatoes and other tubers. Traditionally in Huatta, other crops are banked only in exceptionally wet years. Aporque also incorporates weeding.

[d] Irrigation is relatively easy to do because of the close proximity of the water to the field surfaces. General "splash" irrigation was 4 times faster than bucket irrigation of individual plants (5 person-days/ha vs. 20 person-days/ha).

[e] This figure depends upon the amount to be harvested. The figure presented is based on a year of excellent harvest.

metric tons/ha (Erickson 1986).[1] Potato production on larger field blocks was measured during 1983–1986. Data from these years indicate a sustained yield of 8–14 metric tons/ha/year, with an average of 10 metric tons/ha (Garaycochea 1987; Erickson 1988). These figures contrast favorably with the average production of 1–4 metric tons/ha in the Department of Puno (Erickson 1988; Garaycochea 1986b), which is somewhat lower than the Peruvian national average of 5.3 metric tons/ha (Christiansen 1967). Potato production rates on raised field experiments conducted in Asillo, north of Lake Titicaca, are similar to those we calculate for Huatta (Ramos 1986a).

It is to be expected that raised fields constructed on "virgin" or long-fallowed soils would produce high yields the first year. However, our plots also demonstrated sustainable yields; some plots have been continuously cultivated for 6 years without a decline in production (Erickson 1988). As field block size increases, we predict that yields will also increase, due to the improved micro-climate and reduced "edge effects."[2] In addition, some fields produced higher yields in the second to fourth years, possibly because of the increased availability of nutrients formed by the decay of "green manure." Increased yields are also expected after certain crops become adapted to the conditions of the raised fields, as the well-adapted genetic material that would certainly have developed during prehistoric times has, since then, disappeared.

The potential carrying capacity of raised field agriculture is 37.5 persons per hectare (Erickson 1988). Using Denevan's (1982) conservative figures for the extent of prehistoric remains of raised fields, and the assumption that 100% of them are in use (which is highly unlikely), 1.5 million people could be supported in the Lake Titicaca Basin (Erickson 1988). Because of the complexity of the variables affecting the flow of water through the system—ultimately dependent on the highly irregular seasonal rainfall in the Lake Titicaca watershed—it is impossible, at present, to determine a likely percentage of the total field area which could, theoretically, be productive in any one year. However, this figure gains meaning when it is compared to the present population of the Department of Puno, which is 890,000. This is even more provocative in light of the surprising fact that during most of the early 1980s Puno actually had to import potatoes from other parts of Peru and overseas.

The Success of Raised Field Agriculture: Will It Be Adopted?

Andean farmers of the Lake Titicaca region are, like many farmers, very conservative; they do not readily adopt new techniques (although they may experiment, on a small scale, with surplus time and seed). Raised fields are adaptable in that farmers have been able to maintain traditional crops, tools, and social organization against the onslaught of introduced western technology, which is very often economically and socially unsound for the *altiplano,* no matter how well-intended. The unsuitability of numerous recent development projects (introduction of rapeseed, expensive mechanized irrigation projects, and capital-intensive mechanized agriculture) was not recognized until after attempts to introduce them in the *altiplano.* The traditional farmers' reluctance to adopt unproven techniques has insulated them against development fiascos.

Raised field technology, although an ancient indigenous technique, had been completely forgotten; thus, it is a new technology to the present-day farmers. Because of its simplicity and efficiency, raised field agriculture is relatively easy to teach. Both informal and formal means of communication were used to spread information about raised field agriculture between 1981 and 1986 (Brinkmeier 1985; Erickson et al. 1986). One of the most significant aspects of the project was that the farmers themselves collaborated in developing and adapting this ancient technology for their present-day use. While the archaeologist suggested guidelines based on his research, it was the farmers themselves who, from experience and experimentation on their own, refined the construction techniques and developed new approaches. This process generated an active interest in the raised field experiments, while at the same time, it produced a technology especially suited to the present local, social, and economic environments. As a result, some 30 communities were practicing raised field agriculture by early 1987 (Ignacio Garaycochea 1987: pers. com.)

Many political parties within Peru maintain development agencies, and they recently have begun to promote raised field agriculture in the Lake Titicaca region. Political groups see the introduction of raised fields as an inexpensive means of raising the standard of living, and thereby minimizing potential social discontent. The revitalization of traditional agriculture has been a goal of APRA, the political party presently in power, and several programs have proceeded with limited success. Many of these efforts are genuine, but fail because the technology is promoted without consideration of the existing socio-economic context of the Andean communities, as was the case in the Colca Valley (Treacy 1987, and this volume). Leftist groups commonly associate Andean "tradition" with communal "socialist" organization and land control, and their conceptions of the prehispanic Inca and Qolla States are often highly romanticized and idealized.

Possible Limitations to Raised Field Agriculture

We encountered some factors that may limit the use of raised field agriculture in the Lake Titicaca Basin. The most serious hindrance in many communities is the lack of large blocks of suitable land under the control of communal organizations. A solution to this problem was suggested by farmers in Coata, where individual families collaborate in farming contiguous private fields, with reciprocal labor exchanges in the traditional patterns of *ayni* and *minka*.[3]

Although we worked primarily with the *parcialidad* organizations in Huatta, we also worked with a few private groups, and noticed that there are some social mechanisms which can be used to coordinate group labor on private land (e.g. *ayni* and *minka*). Also, the "fictive kin" relationships (*compadrazco*) are often associated with economic partnerships which can include agricultural collaboration.

While the availability of communal labor and land permitted the rapid construction of large blocks of raised fields in Huatta, other communities around the lake lack these advantages. The diffusion and implementation of raised field agriculture in these communities would be much more difficult, but we believe that, once the advantages of the technology have been clearly demonstrated, Andean communities will be able to find ways to overcome these obstacles. While we can imagine some solutions to these problems, we feel that it would be important for each community to work out its own solution. The foreign researcher may be able to provide some suggestions and alternatives, but cannot dictate changes in social organization and land tenure to conform to technology.

A minor obstacle to raised field agriculture is the grazing of animals on the *pampa* and in harvested fields. We found that this was generally incompatible with raised field farming since sheep, pigs, and cows can easily destroy the raised fields if allowed to graze and root freely. More stringent control of the animals is necessary, either by caretakers of the fields (some groups selected raised field sites close to a member's house compound for this purpose) or by the shepherds. The cultivation of raised fields also reduces the amount of pasture land. The systematic harvest of aquatic plants in the canals, and the intensive production of forage crops on the platforms could be used to support confined animals. The carrying capacity of the native vegetation on the *pampa* is low, only approximately one sheep/ha. In contrast, an average of 10 metric tons of potatoes (which would feed 18.7 people for one year) can be produced on the same amount of land using raised fields. Forage crops such as winter wheat, oats, and barley also have been successfully grown on raised fields and could be used to support a large number of domestic animals (Erickson 1988). Cattle are often kept in corrals where they are given aquatic vegetation in areas near the lakeshore. As the *pampa* lands become more valuable for cultivation than for pasture this arrangement will probably become more widespread.

Potential Application: Raised Fields vs. Western Capital-Based Agriculture

The advantages of raised field agriculture over the modern introduced technologies promoted by the various development agencies have been demonstrated in the Andean highlands. "High tech" agricultural projects, such as those introduced by the Canadians (rapeseed) and New Zealanders (improved pasture crops and genetically improved sheep stock) in the 1970s and early 1980s failed because of their incompatibility with both the harsh physical environment of the *altiplano* and the limitations imposed by the existing socio-economic context. The capital invested by the SAIS Buenavista and local communities in these projects was lost. In contrast, the suitability of raised field agriculture to the environment of the lake basin was demonstrated in 1986 at the government experimental agricultural station of Illpa. Hundreds of hectares of mechanically prepared fields of winter wheat, improved seed potatoes, and other experimental crops were destroyed by floods, while the 2 hectares of experimental raised fields adjacent to them remained unaffected and produced a bumper crop.

Can raised field technology developed in the *altiplano* be successfully applied in other zones? Denevan (1982:190 Table 1) estimates a total area of 2,500 square kilometers of reported prehistoric raised fields in Latin America (excluding the Llanos de Mojos in Bolivia and the Basin of Mexico, where the total area of raised fields has not been accurately determined, but is expected to be quite extensive). Much of the vast *altiplano* of western Bolivia south of Lake Titicaca is either permanent wetland or seasonally inundated, especially the areas around Lake Poopo and along the Rio Desaguadero. Very little of these lands are currently under cultivation, although raised field remains indicate their past productivity. It is also possible that this technology could be introduced in seasonally and permanently waterlogged areas around other highland lakes, rivers, and springs where the remains of raised fields have not been found.

The most extensive raised field remains are located in the vast tropical lowlands of Latin America; over 150 square kilometers of raised field surfaces have been documented for the Llanos de Mojos in Bolivia (Denevan 1970, 1982) and experimental raised fields have proven successful in the lowlands of Veracruz and Tabasco of Mexico (Gomez-Pompa et al. 1982). Much of the knowledge and experience gained from the reconstruction of raised fields in the Lake Titicaca Basin could be useful in developing raised field agriculture in the tropical lowlands. Because of the social, economic, political, agronomic, and environmental differences between the Lake Titicaca Basin and these other areas, detailed multidisciplinary investigations will be necessary before the raised field technology could be implemented on a large scale. Our experience indicates that small-scale experimental and demonstration plots, which draw the interest and active participation of the local community, are the most effective way to initiate such development.

Conclusion: Andean Agriculture of
the Past for the Future

The Lake Titicaca Basin is a difficult agro-environment for present-day farmers. The current agricultural systems practiced by both small and large scale farmers under-utilizes the vast *pampa* lands and hastens the destruction of the fragile *cerro* lands. Centuries of poor farming practices have depleted the soil fertility, caused massive topsoil erosion, and denuded slopes of natural vegetation. Poor land management, in addition to other social, economic, and political factors, has severely reduced the carrying capacity of the land, promoting massive migration to coastal urban centers, and continuing the cycle of poverty in the *altiplano*.

In contrast, the widespread remains of prehistoric intensive agricultural features such as raised fields, terraces, and *qochas* document a successful adaptation to this difficult agro-environment by prehispanic peoples. Our archaeological and experimental investigation, combined with an applied project, indicates that raised field agriculture is 1) highly productive and sustainable, 2) ecologically sound in terms of both the cultivation of the *pampa* lands and as an effective means of relieving stress on the easily degraded *cerro* lands, and 3) a socio-economically appropriate technology.

The highly sustainable productivity of raised fields, in contrast to "modern" agricultural technologies presently used in the *altiplano*, could greatly improve the economic well-being of the indigenous communities. Because the raised fields are constructed on *pampa* lands currently under-utilized, raised field technology expands the agricultural frontier and permits fallowing of overused hill lands. Capital, rather than labor, is the limiting factor to agricultural expansion in most *altiplano* communities. Raised fields make efficient use of labor, and do not require capital investment. The most efficient social grouping for the construction and operation of these systems in Huatta is communal, based on traditionally defined local Andean social units (*ayllu, parcialidad*, or *communidad.*) This may not be practical in other situations where historical, social, and political factors have resulted in different forms of social organization and land tenure. In these cases, the family or some other social grouping may be more appropriate.

Many development projects currently in the *altiplano* are ecologically unsound, relying on introduced crops and farming practices developed for completely different environmental zones. More importantly, these systems are socially and economically inappropriate, relying on heavy capital inputs such as mechanization, petro-chemicals, and imported seed. Even if successful, these projects would benefit only a small portion of the local populations. Several of these projects proposed for developing the *pampa* would destroy vast areas of raised field systems. This might result in the tragic loss of the real agricultural potential of the *pampa* land which could be sustainably developed through the use of this indigenous technology.

Notes

1. All raised field production calculations include the canals, which comprise approximately 50% of the area used in the calculation. In addition, no fertilizers or insecticides were used on the raised fields, in contrast to the fields used to obtain the departmental and national averages.

2. Production along field boundaries is often less than in the interior of agricultural plots; this is called the "edge effect," and occurs regularly in raised field blocks. Although increased field area obviously increases perimeter, it reduces the proportion of edge to interior.

3. *Ayni* is a traditional form of symmetrically balanced reciprocity of labor between individuals who are equals. Labor or services performed by one individual for another are repaid in kind at a later date. *Minka* (also known as *faena*) is another form of reciprocal labor, and is usually practiced by groups larger than the family. It is asymmetrical and includes the exchange of goods (food, drink, gifts) for short-term labor or services for the benefit of an individual or the community.

References

Altieri, Miguel A. 1983. Agroecology: The scientific basis of alternative agriculture. Division of Biological Control, University of California, Berkeley.

Brinkmeier, Daniel A. 1985. A plan for disseminating information about traditional agriculture to indigenous farmers, Department of Puno, Peru. Unpublished Masters Thesis, Department of Journalism and Mass Communications, Iowa State University, Ames.

Browman, David L. (ed.). 1987. Arid land use strategies and risk management in the Andes. Westview Press, Boulder, Colorado.

Brush, Stephen & B. L. Turner II. (eds.) 1987. Comparative farming systems. The Guilford Press, New York.

Candler, Kay L. & Clark L. Erickson. 1987. Raised fields in the Lake Titicaca Basin: The indigenous community and agricultural expansion. Paper presented at the annual meetings of the Society for Applied Anthropology, April 8–12, Oaxaca, Mexico.

Christiansen, J. 1967. El cultivo de la papa en el Peru. Lima, Peru.

Darch, J. (ed.). 1983. Drained-field agriculture in the Americas. British Archaeological Reports, International Series, Oxford.

Denevan, William M. 1970. Aboriginal drained-field cultivation in the Americas. Science. 169:647–654.

Denevan, William M. 1980. Latin America. Pages 217–244 *in* Gary Klee (ed.), World systems of traditional resource management. Hasted Press, New York.

―――. 1982. Hydraulic agriculture in the American tropics: Forms measures and recent research. Pages 181–203 *in* Kent V. Flannery (ed.), Maya Subsistence. Academic Press, New York.

―――. & B. L. Turner II. 1974. Forms, functions, and associations of raised fields in the old world tropics. Journal of Tropical Geography. 39:24–33.

―――, Kent Mathewson, & Gregory Knapp (eds.). 1987. Pre-hispanic agricultural fields in the Andean region. British Archaeological Reports, International Series, no. 359 i and ii, Oxford.

Donkin, Robin A. 1979. Agricultural terracing in the aboriginal New World. University of Arizona Press, Tuscon.

Ellenberg, Heinz. 1979. Man's impact on the highland tropical environment. Journal of Ecology. 67:401–416.

Erickson, Clark L. 1985. Applications of prehistoric Andean technology: Experiments in raised field agriculture. Pages 209–232 *in* Ian Farrington (ed.), Prehistoric intensive agriculture in the tropics. British Archaeological Reports, International Series, no. 232, Oxford.

―――. 1986. Agricultura en camellones en la cuenca del Lago Titicaca: Aspectos tecnicos y su futuro. Pages 331–350 *in* Carlos de la Torre and Manuel Burga (eds.), Andenes y camellones en el Peru andino: Historia presente y futuro. CONCYTEC, Lima.

Erickson, Clark L. 1987. The dating of raised field agriculture in the Lake Titicaca Basin, Peru. Pages 373–383 *in* William M. Denevan, Kent Mathewson, and Gregory Knapp (eds.), Pre-hispanic agricultural fields in the Andean region. British Archaeological Reports, International Series, no. 359 i and ii, Oxford.

―――. 1988. An archaeological investigation of raised field agriculture in the Lake Tititcaca Basin, Peru. Unpublished Ph.D. dissertation, Department of Anthropology, University of Illinois, Champaign-Urbana.

――― & Ignacio Garaycochea Z. & Daniel A. Brinkmeier. 1986. Experiencias en la arqueologia aplicada: Recuperación de campos elevados en la comunidad campesina de Huatta. Paper presented in the VI Congreso Peruano del Hombre y la Cultura Andina, August 19–31, Lima Peru.

Farrington, Ian (ed.). 1985. Prehistoric intensive agriculture in the tropics. British Archaeological Series, International Series, no. 232, Oxford.

Flores, Jorge & Percy Paz. 1987. Cultivation in the qocha of the South Andean Puna. Pp. 271–296 *in* David L. Browman (ed.), Arid land use strategies and risk management in the Andes. Westview Press, Boulder, Colorado.

Garaycochea Z. Ignacio. 1983 Destrución y conservación de camellones en el Departamento de Puno. Paper presented at the third meeting of Las Jornadas Peruanos-Bolivianos, Puno (manuscript).

Garaycochea Z. Ignacio. 1986a. Potenciál agrícola de los camellones en el altiplano puneno. Pages 241–251 *in* Carlos de la Torre and Manuel Burga (eds.), Andenes y camellones en el Peru andino: Historia presente y futuro. CONCYTEC, Lima.

————. 1986b. Rehabilitación de camellones en la comunidad campesina de Huatta, Peru. Unpublished agronomy thesis, Department of Agronomy, Universidad Nacional del Altiplano, Puno, Perú.

————. 1987a. Agricultural experiments in raised fields in the Lake Titicaca Basin, Peru: Some preliminary considerations. Pages 385–398 *in* William M. Denevan, Kent Mathewson, and Gregory Knapp (eds.), Pre-hispanic agricultural fields in the Andean region. British Archaeological Reports, International Series, no. 359 i and ii, Oxford.

————. 1987b. Proyecto Rehabilitación de *waru-waru*. Proyecto de Investigación de sistemas agropecuarias, Puno. (manuscript).

Gomez-Pompa, A., H. Morales, E. Jimenez, & J. Jimenez. 1982. Experiences in traditional hydraulic agriculture. Pages 327–342 *in* Kent V. Flannery (ed.), Maya Subsistence. Academic Press, New York.

Harrison, Peter D. & B.L. Turner II (eds.). 1978. Pre-hispanic Maya agriculture. University of New Mexico Press, Albuquerque.

Kolata, Alan L. 1986. The agricultural foundations of the Tiwanaku state: A view from the heartland. American Antiquity. 51(4):748–762.

Lennon, Thomas J. 1982. Raised fields of Lake Titicaca, Peru: A pre-hispanic water management system. Unpublished Ph.D. dissertation, Department of Anthropology, University of Colorado, Boulder.

Morlon, Pierre, Benjamin Orlove, & Albert Hibon. 1982. Tecnologías agrícolas en los andes centrales: Perspectivas para el desarollo. Corporación Financiera de Desarollo (COFIDE), Lima, Peru.

ONERN-CORPUNO. 1984. Inventario, evaluación, e integración de los recursos naturales de la micro-región Puno. ONERN, Lima, Peru.

Ramos, Claudio. 1986a. Evaluación y rehabilitación de camellones o "kurus" en Asillo. Allpanchis. no. 27 (año XVIII): 239–284.

————. 1986b. Evaluación y rehabilitación de camellones en Asillo Puno. Paper presented at the V Congreso Internacional sobre la Agricultura Andina., March 10–14, Puno.

Smith, Clifford T., William M. Denevan, & Patrick Hamilton. 1968. Ancient ridged fields in the region of Lake Titicaca. The Geographical Journal. 134:353–367.

Treacy, John M. 1987. Building and rebuilding agricultural terraces in the Colca Valley of peru. Pages 51–57 *in* M. A. Works (ed.), Yearbook, Proceedings of the Conference of Latin Americanist Geographers, 13, Department of Geography and Anthropology, Louisiana State University, Baton Rouge.

Turner II, B. L. & Peter Harrison (eds.). 1983. Pulltrouser swamp: Ancient Maya habitat, agriculture and settlement in northern Belize. University of Texas Press, Austin.

Torre, Carlos de la & Manuel Burga (eds). 1986. Andenes y camellones en el Peru andino: Historia presente y futuro. CONCYTEC, Lima.

Wilken, Gene. 1987. Good farmers. University of California Press, Berkeley.

PART FOUR

A Strategy for Sustainable Agriculture on Desert Streambeds

15

Arroyos and the Development of Agriculture in Northern Mexico

William E. Doolittle

Introduction

The arid and semi-arid lands of northern Mexico, like those elsewhere, truly can be considered fragile. Indeed, they might well be the most fragile of all environments. Modifications of either the physical or the biological components of this region's landscape can produce scars that persist for centuries or even millennia. For example, because of moisture deficits, growth of perennial plants is slow and vegetation, once removed, takes a long time to recover (Hastings and Turner, 1965). The extended length of time over which it takes vegetation to regenerate itself results in the land being subjected to the forces of erosion. Lying bare, cleared desert lands tend to experience gullying that not only results in changes in topography and hydrology but also retards revegetation (Cooke and Reeves, 1976).

Although agriculture, in a general sense, is the trading of what might be called "natural" for "cultural" vegetation, its impact on arid lands can be as disastrous as the complete removal of all plants. Sustainable agriculture requires that crops and cropping practices mimic to some extent the vegetation indigenous to and the ecology of the area cultivated (Janzen, 1973; Beckerman, 1983). With the possible exception of the tepary bean (*Phaseolus acutifolius* var. *latifolius*), a grain amaranth (*Amaranthus hypocondriacus*), and a panic grass (*Panicum sonorum*) that were domesticated in northwest Mexico (Nabhan and Felger, 1978; Saver, 1976; Nabhan and de Wet, 1984), there are no food crops that can be substituted categorically for natural vegetation in Mexican dry lands without substantial amounts of labor and capital. Furthermore, these crops are of limited economic value and have not been grown profitably on anything other than a small scale. Other cultivars typically require large amounts of water that have to be either transported long distances from reservoirs in areas where rainfall is abundant, or extracted from reserves in the ground. Such irrigation can result in salinization and, hence, a condition whereby no vegetation, either cultural or natural, exists.

Large-scale irrigation as practiced today in some areas such as the coastal plain of the Gulf of California in southern Sonora and northern Sinaloa (Dozier, 1963; Henderson, 1965; Nir, 1974:150–154) appears to have no long-term future in the arid and semi-arid lands of northern Mexico (Dunbier, 1968:245–263; Hewitt de Alcantara, 1976:320–322). The supply of economically irrigable land has decreased from its peak in 1970 (Norton, 1982:104; Cartas Contreras, 1987:114), economically exploitable water resources are diminishing, and salinization is becoming a problem (Aguirre M. and Johnson G., 1981:24). This situation does not, however, mean that agriculture cannot be further developed. Sustainable agriculture is currently practiced in a few locales in northern Mexico (e.g., Nabhan, 1979), and it is expanding. Further development of such farming activities is feasible but will involve (1) young and unstable environments rather than those with ancient landforms, mature soils, and climax vegetation; (2) small rather than large landholdings; (3) spontaneous rather than planned expansion; (4) incremental or evolutionary rather than systematic or revolutionary change; (5) a great deal of tenacity, tolerance, and resiliency by the farmers themselves; and, (6) a rethinking on the part of Mexican agricultural policy-makers.

These issues are discussed in this paper. They are based on two seasons of intensive fieldwork in the eastern Sonora region and several survey trips throughout northern Mexico. Specific findings have been discussed elsewhere (Doolittle, 1983, 1984a, in press) and, therefore, will not be reiterated here. Rather, the broader implications and policy recommendations for arid land development are presented.

Arroyo Environments

The vast irrigated tracts developed concomitantly with the Green Revolution come to mind when one thinks of agriculture in northern Mexico (Wellhausen, 1976). Often overlooked, however, are the floodplains of small river valleys that are few and far between, but nevertheless found throughout the region. Although not highly conspicuous and important to the national economy, these areas have been farmed for centuries (e.g., Doolittle, 1984b), and they are crucial for sustaining local economies. Also overlooked are the floodplains of arroyos, or ephemeral stream valleys, of which there must be thousands in virtually every corner of the region (Plate 1).[1]

Plate 1 An aerial view of the Rio Sonora Valley south of the town of Baviacora (lower left). Note the full cultivation of the river floodplain and the few, isolated fields in the arroyos.

Unlike riverine floodplains that have long been cultivated to their fullest possible extent, arroyo bottoms are underutilized for agricultural purposes, and they are often used only intermittently. The principal reason for these conditions according to numerous farmers and local officials is the unpredictable nature of water, which comes mainly in the form of runoff.

A seasonal dichotomy of winter and summer rains exists in northern Mexico (Garcia, 1981). Although rainfall is variable across the region, approximately 60 percent is generated by convective and orographic thunderstorms during July and August. Another 20 percent falls in moderate but steady amounts during December and January. Severe drought conditions prevail during the late spring, and a more moderate drought occurs in the fall. Although winter rainfall is much less than that of summer, the effectiveness in the winter is much greater because of low rates of evapotranspiration. Cooler temperatures, however, hamper plant growth and curtail substantial crop production during this season. Summer rainfall in northern Mexico, as in most arid and semi-arid regions, is marked by temporal, quantitative, and spatial variations. Temporal variability tends to be greatest when the amount of rainfall is low but decreases as rainfall increases (Noy-Meir, 1973). Although the seasonality of the rainfall is predictable, the amount of rainfall is not. In Baviácora, Sonora, for example, the average July rainfall is 83.4 millimeters (Hastings, 1964). The total precipitation received during this month was 24.2 millimeters in 1958 and 130.3 millimeters in 1959. Large-scale temporal variations like these can just as easily lead to times of "boom" as times of "bust."

Spatial variations of precipitation are as unpredictable as temporal variations. For instance, Aconchi, Sonora, received 241.0 millimeters of rainfall in August, 1951, while 87.3 millimeters were recorded in Baviácora fourteen kilometers down the valley (Hastings, 1964). These spatial variations result in the destruction of crops in some fields by excessive rainfall, while nearby fields sometimes do not receive enough rainfall to produce even a marginal crop.

Agriculture in northern Mexico cannot, therefore, depend on direct precipitation. The practice of cultivating arroyos, although not perfect, is not only a solution to the problem of rainfall variability, but one that can be improved upon. Summertime thunderstorms, especially in higher elevations, often produce massive amounts of rainfall in periods of time so short that much of the water cannot be absorbed by either the vegetation or the soil. Excess water runs first into rivulets, then into gullies, and eventually into arroyos. While the chance of any one arroyo-bottom field receiving sufficient amounts of direct precipitation to produce a good crop is low, the probability of the field receiving runoff water in sufficient quantities is very high. This is particularly true if the field is located near the downstream end of the arroyo. Because arroyos with large drainage areas collect much runoff, the effects of rainfall variability there are reduced in comparison with arroyos that have small catchment areas. Hence, consistently productive arroyo-bottom fields are those located near the mouths of large arroyos.

In addition to runoff, arroyos also collect fertile sediment (Plate 2). Indeed, farmers acknowledge that arroyo lands are "better" than those of the river floodplains because the latter, having been cultivated for over 600 years (Doolittle, 1984b), are "tired." Most of the mountains of northern Mexico, especially those in the west, are volcanic. Accordingly, the materials that are eroded and deposited on the floors of the arroyos near their downstream ends, where the gradient decreases to less than one percent, tend to be deep, rock-free, and most productive. Arroyo soils are typically pale brown to brown Torripsamments of a loamy sand to sandy loam texture. At 1.3 percent on the average, the organic content is low. This deficiency is more than offset by high amounts of phosphorous (average 42 ppm), nitrate nitrogen (average 13 ppm), potassium (average 112 ppm), and alkaline condition (average 7.7 pH).

Plate 2 Silt deposited on an arroyo field by recent runoff.

Arroyo agriculture is not without problems, however. Droughts do occur and in some years no water flows. Conversely, in other years rainfall in the mountain catchment areas is so frequent that flooding damages crops, while sometimes it is so heavy that entire fields are destroyed by erosion or buried. These contrasting periods of drought and flood have resulted in environs that are highly unstable (Heede, 1986a). If there is any advantage to this condition, it is that agricultural development will not result in the destruction of valuable natural vegetation. Unlike both the much-discussed mature tropical rainforest and the extremely slow-growing desert flora, arroyo bottoms are dominated by relatively fast-growing mesquites, most of which are young.

Land Tenure Context of Arroyo Land Development

The lands of northern Mexico can be classified according to the type of user and the specific use. They are either owned privately or controlled by agricultural communities known as *ejidos,* and they are used for grazing or crop production (Soto Mora, 1980). Large, privately owned cattle ranches are typically located in the mountains but, in some cases, the more arid lowlands. Ejido-controlled grazing territory includes most of the remainder of the lower elevations that are not private ranches or under cultivation. The prime cropland involves the

floodplains of perennial rivers that provide water for gravity-flow irrigation. A wide variety of crops are grown throughout the year on
these irrigated lands, but alfalfa, marketed to neighboring ranchers
predominates in several locales. Average yields from floodplain fields
tend to be high with great predictability and dependability. For example,
in 1980 irrigated maize production in the Rio Sonora Valley averaged
2.28 metric tons per hectare (S.A.R.H., 1980), while in 1978, maize
production in Mexico as a whole averaged only 1.34 metric tons per
hectare (F.A.O., 1979:102).

Much of the irrigated land is privately owned. The Mexican revolution of 1910 resulted in the breakup of large privately owned estates
and the establishment of a system of usufructuary landholding (Ley de
Ejidos, 1921; Codigo Agrario, 1934). Haciendas throughout the country,
but especially in the arid north, tended to be both few and large. Many
had relatively little cropland; most of their land was used for grazing.
Current privately owned ranches are remnants of prerevolutionary
haciendas (Machado, 1981). Because the proportion of landless to landholding persons was not as great in the north as it was elsewhere in
Mexico, landowners were typically allowed to keep sizeable tracts of
cropland as part of the revolutionary land-reform program, in some
cases up to 10 hectares (Ley Agraria, 1920). Persons with small parcels
often were allowed to retain all their croplands. The remainder of the
land was divided among the landless so that each person received the
right to use a plot, characteristically no larger than three hectares. In
some municipalities, everyone who wanted cropland received an allot-
ment after the revolution. Leslie Hewes (1935), for example, found that
every farmer who participated in the land-reform program in Huepac,
Sonora, received a parcel of irrigated floodplain land.

Arroyo lands that are dependent on runoff for crop production
account for a small proportion of cropland in northern Mexico.[2] These
lands are almost entirely under the purview of ejidos. Summer-grown
maize is the principal crop on these lands. In an environment characterized by erratic rainfall and without benefit or irrigation, the average
annual yields from arroyo fields are low, variation great, and predictability minimal. According to local farmers, yields vary from zero in
years where rainfall is lacking or when floods destroy the crop to as
much as 5.60 metric tons of unshelled maize per hectare in years of
adequate rainfall without an excess of runoff. This great yield is, in
large part, attributable to the high fertility of arroyo soils.

As in the case of ejido-controlled irrigated floodplain lands, arroyo
holdings are rarely greater than three hectares. The yield from fields
this size appears sufficient to feed a family of five.[3] Also, given the

unstable nature of arroyo environments, it is highly unlikely that a farm family could effectively manage more than three hectares.

Prospects for Agricultural Expansion
on Arroyo Lands

Generally controlled by the ejido, arroyo lands can be brought under cultivation only by the approval of the agricultural community. In essence, there are two types of ejidos functioning in Mexico today. One involves the distribution of parcels of smallholdings to individuals to do with as they please. (McGuire, 1986:114–118), but with the provision that the tract cannot go unused for three consecutive years (Codigo Agrario, 1934; Chavez Padron, 1981). The other involves the collective usership of land (McGuire, 1986:111–114). In this system, each member contributes to the working of the land and, in turn, receives a share of the return. The success of this type of ejido has been questioned by some as yields tend to be lower than on either ejidos organized on the basis of individual parcels or private land holdings (Yates, 1981). These ejidos do, however, have the advantage of facilitating the use of large-scale mechanized techniques, but these appear to be poorly suited to arroyo environments (Freebairn, 1963:1158; Dovring, 1970:269).

The system involving the distribution of land by parcels to individuals appears to have the greatest future in the development of arroyo lands for agriculture and, indeed, is the prevailing system in places where arroyos are currently farmed (Doolittle, 1983). According to policy, any unused ejido land that is not farmed can be brought under cultivation by any member of the community. The normal procedure for a person wishing to farm is to choose a parcel and petition the ejido chief for the right to cultivate it. Once permission is granted, the farmer fences his parcel with barbed wire and begins to cultivate and make improvements.

The spontaneous rather than planned nature of this agricultural expansion has many advantages that help insure the success of development. First, rather than being conceived and implemented by either what might be considered "outsiders" (e.g., government agents) or local people who will not use the fields themselves (e.g., other members of the ejido who are already farming, in many cases prime irrigated floodplain fields), expansion is undertaken by people who know the local environments well. These are individuals who are best prepared to make decisions about field locations (e.g., Padoch, 1986), and where, when and how to construct water control devices that will ultimately affect only them. Second, spontaneous expansion onto arroyo land allows for farming strategies to be flexible, not predetermined by general agricultural policy. About the only political problem farmers encounter involves the permission to farm a parcel from the local chief. Third, as individuals, arroyo farmers are free to go into debt only as deeply as they wish. Collective schemes often involve sizeable capital investments that require large loans, the burden of which falls on all the members. Although data are unavailable for northern Mexico, evidence from planned developments in the southern part of the country (e.g. Ewell and Poleman, 1980) indicate that individuals could well be responsible for paying back greater amounts than they would if they were free to go into debt on their own.

In sum, spontaneous expansion of arroyo agriculture allows for independence not enjoyed by members of either collective ejidos or farmers who participate in projects planned by others. Although success is not guaranteed, decisions are made by those people who have the most to gain as well as the most to lose.

The freedom to do as one wishes does not come cheaply, however. For the most part, individuals who wish to begin cultivating arroyo lands do so with little money to invest (DeWalt, 1979), even less credit (Mogab, 1984), and no insurance (McGuire, 1986:116). Accordingly, arroyo land development is painstakingly slow (McGuire, 1986:117).

Establishment of viable and productive arroyo fields with minimal financial resources requires that work be undertaken in what has been identified as an "incremental" manner (Doolittle, 1984a). Normally, fields are envisioned as being cleared (e.g., rocks and trees removed) and improved (e.g., terraces built and canals excavated), prior to cultivation. Such a scenario requires substantial investments of money and time. In contrast to this "systematic" view, incremental change involves the gradual transformation of the arroyo landscape, through cumulative upgrading of fields using small units of cash and labor inputs over long periods of time in conjunction with cultivation activities. New fields and their associated agricultural features are not swiftly changed to a final form before cultivation takes place, but rather are transformed gradually through use. In this process, construction is not always distinguishable from other categories of agricultural inputs. Rather, construction is an ancillary by-product of cultivation and, in some cases, maintenance inputs. Incremental change does not necessarily involve formal planning, engineering, or organization beyond that within the domain of the individual farmer or farm family.

To illustrate, incremental development of a typical arroyo field first involves fencing, an activity that is carried out during the off season months (November through May) and involves the single greatest capital outlay. It also results in the clearing of some trees for use as posts. The next step usually involves plowing between remaining trees, followed by planting. During the crop-growing season, trees are removed from the fields. Branches are trimmed and woven into the fence where they assist in flood control by protecting the fields from rushing water that often overflows the arroyo channels (Plate 3). Brush removal during clearing is also used in the construction of water spreaders within the fields themselves. Over the course of a few years, these devices tend to collect sediment and, in turn, evolve into low, but distinctive, earthen terraces (Plate 4). Also, rocks removed during plowing and other cultivation activities such as weeding are often piled up in linear fashion across as well as around the perimeters of the fields. Like the brush water spreaders, rock alignments across the fields collect sediment deposited by runoff and flood waters. Those around the edges of fields often evolve into bunds after a number of years and become sufficiently high to protect the fields from channel overflow.

The time it takes for an arroyo field to be transformed incrementally from its natural state to a permanent and sustainable farming unit can take more than a decade. This might seem like a disproportionately long period of time to agricultural extension agents and others interested in short-term development. Indeed, everyone, especially the farmers themselves, would like to have the time involved shortened. There is, however, a notable advantage to such a long, drawn-out development process. Incremental change involves the farmers who will use the fields directly in the construction process. Unlike many large-scale, "revolutionary" schemes in which bulldozers reshape the land according to plans drawn up in some distant city, perhaps even outside the country, incremental development requires that the farmers themselves do their own engineering. In the process, these people not only gain a better understanding of the agricultural implications of their environment, but because arroyos are highly unstable, they can make necessary changes as work progresses. In effect, rather than having to live with rapidly constructed, inflexible field systems that are imposed on them, farmers who are developing lands incrementally are flexible—adaptive—and can rework their systems as needed. They also have a deeper sense of attachment to their land than they would have if someone else had done the work, especially if that work eventually proved to be a failure.

Farmer Behavior and Intermittent Use of Arroyo Lands

In part because of the highly unstable nature of arroyo environments, in part because of other opportunities, and in part because of lack of government support, arroyo fields are often cultivated intermittently. That is, they are brought into and taken out of cultivation frequently,

Plate 3   Brush removed from an arroyo field during initial clearing and woven into the barbed wire fence to help eliminate erosion and facilitate the deposition of silt during runoff events.

Plate 4   A typical arroyo field after several years of use. Improvements made incrementally involve the use of stake and brush water spreaders (left) that collect sediment and eventually contribute to the formation of low earthen terraces and embankments (right).

rapidly, and repeatedly for reasons other than fallow while they are undergoing development (Doolittle, in press). During the course of incremental change, many farmers abandon their fields. Because the process of developing an arroyo field into a permanent, sustainably productive unit can take more than a decade, few farmers actually complete their original plans. Their efforts, however, are not lost. Because some improvements typically have been made, abandoned fields are worth more than unimproved land. Accordingly, they are quickly claimed by new farmers who then continue the process of making improvements incrementally. Some parcels have been used, improved, and abandoned, then reused, and improved further by as many as three farmers.

Arroyo fields, by virtue of incremental development, are investments that increasingly take on a momentum toward permanence. The longer they exist, and the greater the improvements, the less the tendency for fields to be abandoned—over time intermittency becomes increasingly less common. In effect, as more improvements are made, the periods of cultivation become longer, and the periods of non-use become increasingly shorter. Eventually, fields are sufficiently modified to be permanently and continuously cultivated. Once completed, a field is an investment that is not quickly abandoned (Plate 5).

Most, perhaps all, beginning farmers have no intention of abandoning their fields and, therefore, contribute to the phenomenon of intermittent land use. Although they are well aware that numerous farmers do give up (a function of their taking over abandoned parcels), most feel that what befalls others cannot happen to them. Nevertheless, in some cases, arroyo farmers encounter better economic opportunities, such as jobs in urban areas, that they simply cannot afford to decline. In most cases, however, abandonment of agriculture is a function of the environmental vagaries (e.g., floods and droughts). These problems are coupled with a lack of support by the Mexican government. As it now stands, arroyo agriculture is undertaken only by the heartiest of characters who are tenacious, tolerant, and resilient. Such will continue to be the case in the future. Life can be made easier for arroyo cultivators, however, especially if the development of agriculture in these environments is facilitated by new governmental policies.

Conclusions and Recommendations

Farming in Mexico, especially that by smallholders in the arid northern half of the republic, has been historically limited by a shortage of land. In general, well-watered agricultural land is not abundant, and it is either owned by large-scale farmers or is held in collective ejidos

Plate 5   An arroyo field after a few decades of use. The farmer who used this field, improved incrementally, increased his yields annually. He also saved enough money after seven years to dig a tube well and irrigate a variety of crops year round. He now is one of the more prosperous arroyo farmers and will leave a great legacy to his successor.

(Hewitt de Alcantara, 1976). With the exception of one program that began in 1980 (Luiselli, 1982) but was abandoned early in 1983 because of funding problems resulting from the collapse of oil prices, the federal government has been guided by the prevalent belief that lands not currently under cultivation, in this case arroyos, cannot be economically improved. Preference has been given to the development of large-scale mechanized agriculture (Johnston, 1987:48). In the north, these so-called "planned" developments not only resulted in permanent damage to fragile desert plants and soil, but they were also poorly-conceived. For example, Mexican agricultural agents once devised a plan that involved water transfer from Cuatro Cienegas, Coahuila, to expansive fields 60 kilometers away near the city of Monclova. Initial tests indicated that the water to be used was acceptable for irrigation. Accordingly, the canals were excavated and water began to be moved. Unexpectedly, however, the water became increasingly saline during transit, in part because of evaporation. By the time it arrived at the fields, the water was unsuitable for crop production. The scheme failed within a year and, of course, was not publicized (Hendrickson, 1988).[4]

The improvement and cultivation of naturally unstable areas, such as arroyos, within the greater desert environment, and the expansion of cultivated hectarage by smallholders has not been supported financially by the Mexican government. It is however, the option pursued by many individual farmers. Because it will probably be used more frequently as the Mexican population continues to increase, the development of arroyos should be the focus of at least some government attention in the future.

Perhaps the single greatest contribution that the government could make to facilitate the development of arroyo agriculture involves the financing of the construction of small dams (Luiselli, 1987:338–339). Thus far, the government has focused mainly on building a few large dams, impounding millions of hectare meters of water, across river valleys in the mountainous areas (e.g., McGuire, 1986:38). Water from these reservoirs is used almost exclusively by large-scale producers on the desert coastal plains (S.A.R.H., 1979:55–84). Policies resulting in the construction of such features benefit relatively few large-holders and discriminate against a larger number of smallholders who live in proximity to the reservoirs but are not permitted to use the water (Sanderson, 1981). Furthermore, given the rate at which production has been declining on the large irrigated desert tracts due to environmental misuse, these dams will be obsolete early in the 21st century (Aguirre M. and Johnson G., 1981:24).

Future construction should not follow the path of the past and involve huge reservoirs that quite literally are hydrologic dinosaurs (see Erickson, this volume). Instead, it should follow the example set by the Israeli botanist Michael Evenari and his colleagues (1971). The next generation of dams should probably include the building of much smaller, technologically less complex, environmentally less damaging, and socially more equitable features (Johnston, 1987:48; Turrent Fernandez, 1987:308). Although engineering details have yet to be worked out, policies should be implemented to assist the construction of numerous reservoirs, each with the capacity of only a few hundred hectare meters of water (e.g. DeBano and Heede, 1987). These should not be built near the downstream ends of large arroyos where land that could be cultivated will be permanently inundated and all the water flowing throughout the arroyo drainage will be impounded. Instead, they should be built in the upstream reaches of the ephemeral drainages, and then not across every tributary of the first-order arroyo (Heede, 1986b). Building dams in the upstream sections of arroyo basins reserves the land in the downstream areas for cultivation. By not building dams across every tributary, some water is allowed to flow unregulated and, therefore, retain at least part of the natural hydraulics of arroyo systems.

Valuable sediment will continue to be carried downstream and, hence, made available to refurbish the fertility of arroyo fields (Heede, 1987). Constructing dams across only some of the streams will help reduce the impact of floods by retaining surplus flow before it gets downstream. This water later can be discharged slowly and harmlessly if supplies are adequate, or it can be used for irrigation purposes in times of drought.

The construction of such dams will not cure Mexico's agricultural woes. It will, however, assist in the development of ecologically sound agriculture in the fragile arid north. Rather than destroying, in a whole-sale fashion, fragile desert lands, the Mexican government needs to focus its attention on assisting *ejidotarios* who are allotted small parcels in arroyo bottoms.

Although detailed economic and environmental studies are few, it appears that arroyo agriculture is an acceptable practice, and a viable alternative to that promoted by the government. Fields have been identified in hundreds of arroyos across northern Mexico. Several thousand arroyos, however, remain unused. Undoubtedly, agriculture will expand into these areas as the demand for production increases.[5] With current practices and policies, farming arroyos is barely profitable. It is currently viable because other options are few. Agriculture in the arid half of Mexico is, therefore, at a crossroads. Future development can rely on attempts to convert the delicate desert into food factories that will function only at great cost and then for only a few decades before becoming obsolete as the environment is destroyed, or it can involve the management of unstable arroyo environments by small-holders at relatively little cost.

The 1980 Mexican census shows that a total of 38,242 people were unemployed in the 11 northern states which constitute 60 percent of the national territory. Assuming 50,000 to be a more realistic number, at three hectares per laborer, the government could solve unemployment here by developing 150,000 hectares of arroyo land. This is the equivalent of only two-thirds of the irrigated coastal plain at the mouth of the Rio Yaqui alone, but it would be distributed over the entire northern part of the country.

One final note. Arroyo fields will never produce large surpluses that will allow one farmer to feed several people. Currently arroyo fields are capable of supporting families only slightly above a subsistence level. Improvements in production will be modest. While this condition might not seem acceptable to planners in the "Developed World," it must be understood that agriculture, not agribusiness, pervades the attitudes of poor-farmers of the "Third World." In the specific case of Mexico, many people want to preserve the tradition of farming at the family level. Large-scale, mechanized, and commercial production techniques may "save labor," but it also drives people off the land. Promoting small-scale arroyo agriculture has a human dimension that must be preserved (Luiselli, 1987:339; Winder and Eade, 1987:376), and indeed can be at relatively little cost. In the process, the fragile environment of arid and semi-arid northern Mexico will be preserved.

Acknowledgments

This material is based on work supported by the National Science Foundation under grant SES-8200456, and by grants from the Biological and Physical Sciences Research Institute and the Vice-president for Graduate Studies and Research at Mississippi State University, the Tinker Foundation through the Institute of Latin American Studies at the University of Texas at Austin, and the Mellon Foundation through the Center for Latin American Studies at Tulane University. I thank Janis Alcorn, John O. Browder, William M. Denevan, and B.L. Turner, II, for their comments on an earlier draft.

Notes

1. Arroyos are defined as arid land or desert streambeds that are usually dry but carry water in short-lived torrents after intensive rainstorms in the upstream portions of their drainage basins. The term is of Spanish origin and is used widely throughout Latin America (e.g. Monkhouse 1965:20).

2. A survey of the middle Rio Sonora Valley in the northwestern state of Sonora revealed that nine of 1,800 square kilometers, or 0.5 percent of the total land area, involved arroyo lands that are suitable for cultivation and only a portion are actually farmed.

3. To illustrate, each person requires an average of approximately 2,400 calories per day, or 876,000 calories per year (Kirschmann 1975:233–234). At a rate of 3,400 calories per kilogram (Van Royen 1954:84), this requirement can be fulfilled by producing 258 kilograms or 0.258 metric tons, of maize per year. In exceptionally good years, a family of five should be able to live off approximately one hectare. In the poorest of years, however, no amount of land is adequate. Given the existing storage facilities, as well as marketing and banking opportunities, present-day arroyo cultivators in northern Mexico require a little more than 0.6 hectare per person.

4. Paradoxically, Cuatro Cienegas was the birthplace of Venustiano Carranza, president of Mexico during the revolution and the person most responsible for the Constitution of 1917, article 27 which involved the break-up of large holdings. It is also a biologically important, and fragile, area with numerous species endemic to each of the cienegas.

5. Assuming conservatively that arroyo lands suitable for agriculture constitute 0.3% of the total land area, then across the 11 arid states that encompass 1.2 million square kilometers a total of approximately 3,600 square kilometers of currently uncultivated arroyo land could be brought into production in northern Mexico. Less than nine percent of the total land area of Mexico, or approximately 170,000 square kilometers, are under cultivation today. Accordingly, if arroyo agriculture was developed to its fullest, the total cultivated area could be increased by at least two percent with minimal impact on fragile desert lands.

References

Aguirre M., R., and D. Johnson G. 1981. Current status of the natural resources in the northwest of Mexico. Pages 24–27 *in* D.R. Patton, et al. (coords.), Wildlife and Range Research Needs in Northern Mexico and Southwestern United States: Workshop Proceedings. Forest Service, U.S. Department of Agriculture, Washington, D.C.

Beckerman, S. 1983. Does the swidden ape the jungle? Human Ecology 11:1–12.

Cartas Contreras, C. 1987. The agricultural sector's contribution to the import-substituting industrialization process in Mexico. Pages 111–122 *in* B.F. Johnston et al. (eds.), U.S.-Mexico relations: Agriculture and rural development. Stanford University Press, Stanford.

Chavez Padron, M. 1981. Ley federal de reforma agraria, ley de fomento agropecuario. Editorial Porrua. Mexico City.

Código Agrário de los Estados Unidos Mexicanos del 9 de abril de 1934, Diario Oficial, 12 de abril de 1934.

Cooke, R.U. and R.W. Reeves. 1976. Arroyos and environmental change in the American South-west. Oxford Research Studies in Geography, Oxford, England.

DeBano, L.F., and B.H. Heede. 1987. Enhancement of riparian ecosystems with channel structures. Water Research Bulletin 22:463–470.

DeWalt, B.R. 1979. Modernization in a Mexican ejido: A study of economic adaptation. Cambridge University Press, Cambridge, U.K.

Doolittle, W.E. 1983. Agricultural expansion in a marginal area of Mexico. Geographical Review 73:301–313.

———. 1984a. Agricultural change as an incremental process. Annals of the Association of American Geographers 74:124–137.

———. 1984b. Cabeza de Vaca's land of maize: An assessment of its agriculture. Journal of Historical Geography 10:246–262.

———. in press. Intermittent use and agricultural change on marginal lands: The case of smallholders in eastern Sonora, Mexico. Geografiska Annaler, Series B.

Dovring, F. 1970. Land reform and productivity in Mexico. Land Economics 46:264–274.

Dozier, C.L. 1963. Mexico's transformed northwest: The Yaqui, Mayo, and Fuerte examples. Geographical Review 53:548–571.

Dunbier, R. 1968. The Sonoran Desert: Its geography, economy, and people. University of Arizona Press, Tucson.

Evenari, M., L. Shanan, and N. Tadmor. 1971. The Negev: The challenge of a desert. Harvard University Press, Cambridge.

Ewell, P.T. and T.T. Poleman. 1980. Uxpanapa: Agricultural development in the Mexican tropics. Pergamon Press, New York.

F.A.O. 1979. Production yearbook 32. Food and Agricultural Organization of the United Nations, Rome.

Freebairn, D.K. 1963. Relative production efficiency between tenure classes in the Yaqui Valley, Sonora, Mexico. Journal of Farm Economics 45:1150–1160.

Garcia, E. 1981. Modificaciónes al sistema de clasificación climática de Koeppen. Mexico City.

Hastings, J.R. (ed.) 1964. Climatological data for Sonora and northern Sinaloa. Technical Report on the Meteorology and Climatology of Arid Regions No. 15. University of Arizona, Institute of Atmospheric Physics, Tucson.

Hastings, J.R. and R.M. Turner. 1965. The changing mile: An ecological study of vegetation change with time in the lower mile of an arid and semiarid region. University of Arizona Press, Tucson.

Heede, B. 1986a. Balance and adjustment processes in streams and riparian systems. Pages 3–7 *in* Proceedings: Wyoming Water 1986 and streamside zone conference. Wyoming Water Research Center and University of Wyoming Agricultural Extension Service, Casper.

———. 1986b. Designing for dynamic equilibrium in streams. Water Research Bulletin 22:351–357.

———. 1987. Opportunities and limits of erosion control in stream and gully systems. Pages 205–209 *in* Erosion control: You're gambling without it, Proceedings of conference 18. International Erosion Control Association, Reno.

Henderson, D.A. 1965. Arid lands under agrarian reform in northwest Mexico. Economic Geography 41:300–312.

Hendrickson, J. 1988. personal communication

Hewes, L. 1935. Huepec: An agricultural village of Sonora, Mexico. Economic Geography 11:284–292.

Hewitt de Alcantara, C. 1976. Modernizing Mexican agriculture: Socioeconomic implications of technological change 1940–1970. United National Research Institute for Social Development. Geneva.

Janzen, D.H. 1973. Tropical agroecosystems. Science 182:1212–1219.

Johnston, B.F. 1987. The implications of rural development for employment and welfare: Experience in the United States, Mexico, Japan, and Taiwan. Pages 17–54 *in* B.F. Johnston et al. (eds.), U.S.-Mexico relations: Agriculture and rural development. Stanford University Press, Stanford.

Kirshmann, J.D. 1975. Nutrition almanac. McGraw-Hill, New York.

Ley Agraria del 27 de junio de 1919 (Sonora), Boletín Oficial del Estado de Sonora, No. 51, 6 de julio de 1920.

Ley de Ejidos del 30 de deciembre de 1920, Diario Oficial, 8 de enero de 1921.

Luiselli, C. 1982. The sistema alimentarion Mexicano (SAM): Elements of a program of accelerated production of basic foodstuffs in Mexico. University of California, San Diego, Center for U.S.-Mexican Studies, Research Report Series No. 22.

———. 1987. The way to food self-sufficiency in Mexico and its implications for agriculture relations with the United States. Pages 333–360 in B.F. Johnston et al. (eds.), U.S.-Mexico relations: agriculture and rural development. Stanford University Press, Stanford.

Machado, M.A. 1981. The north Mexican cattle industry, 1910–1975: Ideology, conflict, and change. Texas A&M University Press, College Station.

McGuire, T.R. 1986. Politics and ethnicity on the Rio Yaqui: Potam revisited. University of Arizona Press, Tucson.

Mogab, J. 1984. The Mexican experience in peasant agricultural credit. Development and Change 15:203–221.

Monkhouse, F.J. 1965. A Dictionary of Geography, Chicago: Aldine Publishing Co.

Nabhan, G.P. 1979. The ecology of floodwater farming in arid southwestern North America. Agro-Ecosystems 5:245–255.

Nabhan, G.P. and R.S. Felger. 1978. Teparies in southwestern North America: a biogeographical and ethnohistorical study of Phaseolus acutifolius. Economic Botany 32:2–19.

Nabhan, G.P. and J.M.J de Wet. 1984. Panicum sonorum in Sonoran Desert agriculture. Economic Botany 38:65–82.

Nir, D. 1974. The semi-arid world: Man on the fringe of the desert. Longman, London.

Norton, R.D. 1982. Future prospects for Mexican agriculture. Southwest Review 2:101–128.

Noy-Meir, I. 1973. Desert ecosystems: Environment and producers. Annual Review of Ecology Systematics 4:25–51.

Padoch, C. 1986. Agricultural site selection among permanent field farmers: An example from east Kalimantan, Indonesia. Journal of Ethnobiology 6:279–288.

Sanderson, S.E. 1981. Agrarian populism and the Mexican state: The struggle for land in Sonora. University of California Press, Berkeley and Los Angeles.

Saver, J.D. 1976. Grain amaranths. Pages 4–7 in N.W. Simmonds (ed.), Evolution of crop plants. Longman, London.

S.A.R.H. 1979. La ingeniería civil en el desarrollo agropecuario de México. Secretaría de Agricultura y Recursos Hidráulicos, Subsecretaría de Infraestructura Hidráulica. México, D.F.

S.A.R.H. 1980. Superficie agrícola en hectares. Secretaría de Agricultura y Recursos Hidráulicos, Oficina de Unidades de Riego para el Desarrollo Rural, Hermosillo, Sonora.

Soto Mora, C. 1980. Reforma agraria y tenencia de la tierra en México. Anuario de Geografía de la Facultad de Filosofía y Letras., U.N.A.M. 20:73–121.

Turrent Fernández, A. 1987. Research and technology for Mexico's small farmers. Pages 301–318 *in* B.F. Johnson et al. (eds.), U.S.-Mexico relations: Agriculture and rural development. Stanford University Press, Stanford.

Van Royen, W. 1954. The agricultural resources of the world. Vol. 1, Atlas of the World's Resources. Prentice-Hall, New York.

Wellhausen, E.J. 1976. The agriculture of Mexico. Scientific American 235:128–150.

Winder, D., and D. Eade. 1987. Agricultural issues in the United States and Mexico. Pages 361–378 *in* B.F. Johnston et al. (eds), U.S.-Mexico relations: Agriculture and rural development. Stanford University Press, Stanford.

Yates, P.L. 1981. Mexico's Agricultural Dilemma. University of Arizona Press, Tucson.

PART FIVE

Research in Progress

16

Developing the Chocó Region of Colombia

Gerardo Budowski

Introduction

The Chocó Region[1] of Colombia is possibly the world's most extreme case of a large area with very high rainfall. Although data on the precipitation are limited, the region ". . . represents the heaviest in all of the Americas and possibly the greatest for any equatorial area of the earth" (Trewartha, 1966. p. 14).

In many countries where there are areas of high annual rainfall, the prevalent opinion among development planners is that these areas have a definite potential for development, provided roads are built, settlements established, medical services supplied, and all the usual services linked with "development" are provided. There is indeed a long list of such "investments," with the large scale projects usually ending in failure. But again, rarely have such failures been clearly linked with the high rainfall pattern.

This brief report summarizes my ongoing research of the development potential of the Chocó region. I have personally visited the Colombian part on 6 occasions (and once in Northwestern Ecuador), 5 of them in the Department of Chocó, in response to missions requested by the Colombian authorities, all linked with land use and forestry research and training projects, and all of them intended to provide guidance for development projects. (Budowski et al., 1984; Budowski and Morales, 1987; Baquero and Budowski, 1987). A bibliography on the Province of Chocó is also available (CONIF, 1985).

The Remarkable Nature of the Chocó Forest

The forests of Chocó have an unusual degree of species endemism. It is generally considered that these lowland pluvial forests are the most species rich plant communities of the world (IUCN Conservation Monitoring Centre, 1988). The Chocó may possess the highest degree of bird endemism for a continental area, presumably with over 100 bird taxa, some of them endangered. It is estimated that in the Colombian Chocó there are 8,000–9,000 plant species, about one quarter of which are endemic with particular speciation of Araceae, Orchidaceae, Cyclanthaceae, Bromeliaceae, Melastomaceae. For instance, the genus *Trianaeopiper* (Piperaceae) has 17 endemic species. *Cremosperma* (Gesneraceae) has 16 and at least 17 ferns are endemic. There are also 56 endemic species of amphibians while 47% of the reptiles are considered endemic to the Chocó. In previous studies on species richness, Gentry (1987) compared different samples from different regions and found that the Chocó sample had the highest number of species and concluded that "community species richness increases with precipitation." The dominant families in Gentry's plots were Leguminosae, Rubiaceae, Palmae, Annonaceae, Melastomaceae, Sapotaceae, and Guttiferae. He also reports an unusual prevalence of Bombacaceae, especially of the genus *Quararibea*. He also emphasizes that the Chocó perhaps has the most diverse plant communities in the world and extremely high levels of local as well as regional endemism. He speculates that more yet-to-be discovered plant species are found there than anywhere else in the world.

Development in the Chocó

As in other regions of Colombia, several different agencies formulate development projects. Prominent among them is the Corporación de Desarollo del Chocó (Development Corporation of Chocó–CODECH-OCO). A number of these regional corporations cover either a province or other units such as large valleys (often encompassing several provinces). Another prominent organization, the Insituto de Desarollo de Recursos Naturales (INDERENA), located in Bogotá, is responsible for forestry, national parks, fauna and related fields.

Several reports have been recently produced proposing development alternatives for the Chocó (Budowski et al., 1984; Budowski and Morales, 1987; Baquero and Budowski, 1987; and Maya Copete et al., 1987). The major recommendations of these reports are outlined below.

Development Recommendations for the Chocó

1. Concentrate food production on alluvial river banks, including agroforestry combinations, with attention to native palms. Two palms are particularly promising in the Chocó: "chontaduro" *Bactris gasipaes*

and *Jessenia bataua,* locally known as "milpesos" (Anonymous, 1984; Ministerie van Buitenlandse Zaken, 1986). Both produce valuable fruits, those of "chontaduro" being cooked and eaten by local farmers as well as used as feed for hogs while "milpesos" provides a valuable oil. Both palms do not grow in the same site. "Chontaduro" grows best on the alluvial riverbanks, "mil pesos" on the "tierra firme" or on well drained hills following the swamps where it is exceptionally abundant in a number of sites.

Another tree typical of Chocó that is often mentioned as a valuable resource is "Borojó," *Borojoa patinoi,* a Rubiaceae, the fruits of which enjoy a reputation of being an aphrodisiac in the Chocó, and even more so in other Colombian provinces where they are sold at a relatively high price. Some commercial plantations have been established. Another product is medicinal plants. Investigations on these and other plants are just beginning and should yield interesting results although it is dubious that a large impact on local economies will result.

2. Promote sustainable forestry management schemes, especially in swamp forests and secondary forests, that include the planting of timber species on alluvial lands.

The management of primary natural mixed (heterogeneous) forests on well drained soils is another problem which has not yet been solved. These forests cover a very large part of the Chocó. There are experiences like those from Surinam (De Graaf, 1986) with the conclusion that the harvesting of 20 cubic meters per hectare every twenty years, a very conservative prescription, is economic, and apparently acceptable from the ecological (conservation-wise) viewpoint. Another more radical approach is being tried by Hartshorn et al. (1986, this volume) in Palcazú, Perú, and the results of these trials will be very significant. Here, large alleys simulating natural forest gaps are systematically opened in the forest and the products harvested for the benefit of local communities. The openings are then carefully tended to promote the best growth of valuable species. But it is dubious that these techniques can be transferred to the Chocó area without careful previous research. All the reports on forestry of natural mixed rain forests in the Chocó recommend the setting up of trials as indeed has already been the case (Bodegom, 1986). However, they take many years. Unfortunately, government initiatives are already being taken to "sell" timber to a large company for the benefit of local communities, but without due regard to sustained yields. This will undoubtedly lead to degradation and eliminate future options (Baquero and Budowski, 1987).

Concerning plantations, there are now data that planting in open areas on poor soils has resulted in complete failures as experimented by Bodegom and reported by Budowski and Morales (1987). But planting on the alluvial river banks ("diques") that are periodically replenished by alluvion from short term flooding of the rivers, has proven to be in several cases, a striking success (CONIF, 1986). Growth has been spectacular for various species, notably the valuable "roble" (*Tabebuia rosea*) that produces a cabinet wood. Over a short period of 4–5 years, roble trees reach annual diameter increments of 6–7 cm for the 25% best trees in some experimental plots. This is extraordinary in any part of the world. The form is very acceptable too. The results are also excellent for the valuable "laurel" trees (*Cordia alliodora*), very much in demand for construction and furniture for its valuable properties including resistance to termites. Here average diameters reach 3–4 cm a year for the 25% best trees coupled with a spectacular growth in height and an excellent form, typical of that fast growing and self-pruning species, making this tree extremely promising (Baquero and Budowski, 1987). Although *Cordia alliodora* is not native, it is well accepted by local farmers, and CONIF which launched the planting program is meeting large local demand for seedlings. It is likely that once the trees flower and fruit profusely, they will easily regenerate naturally as indeed has been the case in wet regions of Costa Rica and Ecuador (both Pacific and Amazonian) where natural regeneration has "exploded" into the open niches, provided soils are acceptable. What is more, laurel lends itself well to agroforestry combinations because of its small crown and self-pruning ability. The same can be said for a few other promising tree species. Many crops can be grown with trees as several experiments have shown (Leguizamo et al., 1985; Vega, 1985, Vega et al., 1985). However, it should be stressed again that success stories have been witnessed only on the best soils such as the alluvial river banks that are periodically replenished in nutrients from periodic flooding.

In conclusion, forestry offers some real options but for a rather limited set of conditions. These opportunities are presently not sufficiently exploited. For the majority of the forests on well drained soils, however, sustained yield is a problem that demands long-term research. It is likely that most of these forests at present offer little scope for sustained management.

3. Promote sustainable exploitation of freshwater fisheries. Research on tropical freshwater fisheries, like so many other fields, is just beginning. Most of the fish are unknown or not well-known. There is certainly some prospect to increase fresh water fishing practices on a sustainable yield basis, both for local consumption and for commercial purposes. Research leading to devices such as submerged traps, as well as careful management of certain lakes and rivers by local communities

should lead to various development schemes. Sport fishing is another distinct possibility.

4. Select a series of areas to be managed for conservation, scientific research, education and tourism based on the unique natural assets of the area.

The foregoing recommendations 1–3 on local resources show limited prospects to benefit the people of Chocó. But there is still another resource of very great potential, namely the uniqueness of Chocó as one of the world's extremes in rainfall and its by-products concerning flora, fauna, even its variety of people who have adapted to this unique environment. Conservation areas could to some extent follow and benefit from the experience of Costa Rica where a system of national parks and reserves has allowed development of a considerable industry concerning scientific, educational, and popular tourism based on its equally exceptional natural assets. What is more, such a policy could attract international funding that could make the difference (ISTF, 1986).

A promising strategy for conservation has been described in detail by Budowski and Morales (1987) and was based on previous suggestions (García Kirkbride, 1986 a and b). These studies include identification of areas that should be protected and establishment of a network of biological stations to become centers for research and training for the people of Chocó, Colombians and of course scientists and students from outside. This proposal would require the creation of a mixed organization of Colombians and foreign scientists to help supervise development projects and channel resources towards this aim. In early 1987, a team of four prominent Chocoans were invited to visit various parks and other protected areas in Costa Rica and Panamá. Their report (Maya Copete et al., 1987) shows how well they perceived how much the experiences from these countries could be transferred to the Chocó.

5. In each of these recommendations, make certain that the local population and authorities are involved in the planning and execution stages.

Notes

1. The term Chocó in Colombia applies to a Department in the northwestern part of the country bordering both with the Atlantic and Pacific Oceans. But the term also applies to a much larger area covering the wet areas along the whole Pacific side of Colombia including northwest Ecuador, always with high rainfall. It is sometimes referred to as the phytogeographic province of Chocó.

References

Anonymous. 1984. Diagnóstico agropecuario forestal del Departamento del Chocó. Unidad Regional de Planificación Agropecuaria URPA-CHOCO. Quibdó, Colombia. p.278. + annexes.

Baquero, Irma and Budowski, Gerardo. 1987. Informe de la Misión técnica de orientación al convenio CONIF/HOLANDA/ Corporaciones Regionales. Bogotá, CONIF. p.35.

Bodegom, Arend Jan Van. 1986. Manejo del bosque en Tanandó. CONIF. Quidbó. p.12. (Typewritten).

Budowski, Gerardo et al. 1984. Informe de la Misión técnica de orientación al convenio CONIF/HOLANDA/CORPORACIONES. Bogotá, CONIF. p.70. (mimeographed).

_____. and Morales, R. 1987. En busca de alternativas viables para el manejo sostenido de los recursos renovables del Chocó, Colombia. Informe de una misión técnica. San José, Universidad para la Paz. p.66. (Mimeographed).

CONIF. 1985. Región del Chocó (Colombia). Bibliografía (1951–1984). Serié de Documentación No. 7, Bogota. p.92.

_____. 1986. Programa integral de investigaciones silviculturales y agroforestales CONIF/HOLANDA. Plan Anual. Bogotá, CONIF. pag. irr. (Mimeographed).

De Graaf, N.R. 1986. A silvicultural system for natural regeneration of tropical rain forest in Surinam. Wageningen, Netherlands, Agricultural University. p.250.

García Kirkbride, Cristina. 1986. a. Biological evaluation of the Chocó phytogeographical region in Colombia. First draft. p.18.

_____. 1986. b. Conserving the Chocó threatened plants newsletter (UICN) 17:4–7.

Gentry, Alwyn H. 1987. Species richness and floristic composition of Chocó region plant communities. Manuscript. Presented to "Caldasia," Colombia. p.29.

Hartshorn, G.S., Simeone R., and Tosi, J. A. 1986. Manejo para rendimiento sostenido de bosques naturales: un sinopsis del proyecto de desarollo del Palcazú en la selva central de la Amazónia peruana. Centro Científico Tropical (Costa Rica) p.10. (Mimeographed).

ISTF. 1986. World Bank adopts wildland policy. ISTF News 7(4):1.

IUCN Conservation Monitoring Center. 1988. Colombian Chocó. Conservation of biologic diversity and forest ecosystems. A briefing document prepared by the IUCN Tropical Forest Programme. p.12. (Mimeographed).

Leguizamo, A. et al. 1985. Asociacion de *Cedrela adorata, L. Borojoa patinoi* y *Pouteria cainito* en rotación con barbecho y cultivos agrícolas en Bajo Colima, Colombia. CONIF, Serie Técnica No. 14 p.22.

Maya Copete, Antonio: Ortiz Saavedra, Consuelo; Caicedo Licona, Carlos A.: and Serna Alvarez, Oscar. 1987. Informe de comisión de estudios e investigación en Costa Rica y Panamá. Bogotá, Colombia. (Typewritten). p.20.

Ministerie Van Buitenlandse Zaken. 1986. Chontaduro (*Bactris gasipaes* H.B.K.) Mil pesos (*Jessenia bataua* (Mart) Burret), Achiote (*Bixa orellana L.*) and the world market projections for oils and fats 1980–1990. IDECO, Wageningen, p.123.

Southeast Consortium for International Development. 1984. Fragile lands. A theme paper on problems, issues and approaches for development of humid tropical lowlands and steep slopes in the Latin American region. Development Alternatives, Inc. Washington D.C. pp. irregular.

Trewartha, Glenn T. 1966. The earth's problem climates. Madison, The University of Wisconsin Press. p.134.

Vega, L.E. 1985. Resultados de la Asociación de *Apeiba aspera* Aub. y *Manihot esculenta,* Bajo Colima, Buenaventura, Colombia. CONIF., Bogotá. 15 p. Serie Técnica No. 15.

———. et al. 1985. *Apeiba aspera* y *Cordia alliodora* en el asocio inicial con *Manihot esculenta* y *Musa* sp. en Bajo Colima, Colombia. CONIF, Informe No. 3 p.12.

17

Socioeconomic Analysis of Agroforestry Systems Applied on Demonstration Farms in Central America

Carlos Reiche

Introduction

Tropical Forests in Central America have traditionally supplied many different wood products. The majority of low income rural residents have relied on forests as a source of timber, fuel-wood, charcoal, poles for roundwood construction, stakes to support crops, fence posts, and fodder for farm animals. However, the cumulative effect of recent deforestation and deterioration of natural resources has been land degradation and an acute wood shortage.

For the majority of small farmers, the current increase of pressure upon their land and their shrinking resource base makes it difficult for them to apply adequate practices to manage trees, without a corresponding increase in their technical knowledge. Also, smallholder silviculture has received little research attention, until recently, and socioeconomic information has been lacking.

In response to the increasing demand for tree products, the Centro Agronómico Tropical de Investigación y Enseñanza (CATIE) and its Tree Crop Project have developed an innovative multidisciplinary agroforestry strategy to transfer tested species and techniques for growing multipurpose trees, within the framework of farmers' needs and the potential of their land use systems.

Farms are selected by a multidisciplinary method for rapid rural appraisal. Agroforestry systems are designed for each farm which correspond not only to the ecology of the site, but also to the diverse objectives, restrictions, and needs felt by the farmers.

By developing over time sustained production from a tree crop component, the aim of the Project is to create clusters of demonstration farms on representative areas. This implies conducting an initial and dynamic assessment of socio-economic variables.

The work is being conducted in five Central American countries. (Appendix A) Early results show positive results from applying this innovative approach.

Agroforestry Development Options for Small Farms

During the period 1980–85 silviculture research was initiated at CATIE involving more than 150 tree species of rapid growth, native and exotic, in different locations in Central America. The results of this research indicate that 24 species were considered promising for immediate use in agroforestry systems. Of these, 14 species are receiving priority attention (Table 1).

The development of production options requires the definition of a "minimum set" of agroforestry systems which considers multiple use of trees as part of the integrated production plans for a farm. At present the prevailing production systems, family needs, size limitations and other characteristics of the demonstration farms selected in Central America show the feasibility, and the interest of small farmers, to include trees as one of the components of multiple use. In accord with the production plans, four groups of agroforestry systems are proposed (Table 2).

Some Observations on Results

The technical feasibility of the proposed agroforestry systems are supported by silvicultural research carried out in Central America. A limiting factor in the financial analysis is the lack of information on the costs of planting, maintenance, management, and harvesting, as well as market prices for some of the products of these systems. With regard to these limitations, the Project is making efforts to systematically obtain information on inputs, market prices, and labor productivity in each system. Preliminary results of these and others studies allow one to estimate, *ex-ante,* some financial indicators of production, such as those shown on Table 3.

Although the majority of the agroforestry systems show positive financial returns, indirect costs and benefits generated by these systems have yet to be accurately measured. It is also necessary to demonstrate the effects not just from the point of view of the individual farmer, but also in relation to society or the community. Among these aspects, the preliminary observations indicate that more attention should be given to considering the possible benefits, especially the contributions

Table 1
Categories of Products, Species, and Production Systems for Selected Tree Species

Species	Categories of Products	Plantation Systems	Rotation
Bombacopsis quinatum *Cupressus lusitanica* *Gmelina arborea* *Pinus caribaea* var hon. *Tectona grandis*	Timber for industrial and sub-products uses (fuelwood and posts)	Pure plantation or associated with crops	Less than 15 years
Acacia mangium *Caesalpinia velutina* *Casuarina equisetifolia* *Eucalyptus camaldulensis* *Eucalyptus saligna* *Leucaena leucocephala* *Mimosa scabrella*	Timber and posts for rural uses and firewood	Pure plantation or associated with crops in soils with few limitations	5 to 15 years
Gliricidia sepium *Guazuma ulmifolia*	Protection posts, firewood forage, green fertilized or combinations	Plantation associated with crops or livestock activities	Less than 8 years

Source: Centro Agronómico Tropical de Investigación y Enseñanza (1986).

Table 2
Grouping of Possible Agroforestry Systems in the Demonstration Farms of the MADELEÑA Project

Group 1	Trees with crops Separated Mixed In allies Alternated rows Nitrogen-fixing Taungya system	*Group 2*	Trees for protection Live fences Windbreaks Contour plantings Hedges
Group 3	Trees in compact stand Fuelwood Forage Orchards	*Group 4*	Trees in pastures Individual trees Trees in groups

Source: Martínez (1988).

Table 3
Preliminary Financial Assessment of Selected Agroforestry Associations in Central America

Species	System	Cost of System Establishment		Type of Product	Cash Flow Period (years)	Discount Rate (%)	Net Present Value from Production/ha (US$)	Projected Internal Rate of Return (%)
		US$/ha	Mandays/ha					
Bombacopsis quinatum	Plantation	285.35	32	Sawn wood Posts for construction	26	12	135.80	12.17
Cupressus lusitanica	Plantation	373.32	46	Sawn wood	24	8	1,612.06	10.00
Eucalyptus with *Zea mays*	Taungya	356.50	124	Fuelwood	4	10	54.62	20.15
Gliricidia sepium	Plantation	493.05	68	Posts Fuelwood	4	8	377.74	28.20
Gliricidia sepium	Live fence	259.64[a]	21	Live posts Forage	20	12	988.30	33.66
Coffee, *Cordia* and *Erytrina* p.	Coffee with trees	23.67	168	Coffee Timber Shade	20	12	5,753.63	33.93
Guazuma ulmifolia	Plantation	392.20	63	Fuelwood Posts Forage Sawn wood	24	8	1,312.42	25.00

(Continued)

Table 3 (Continued)
Preliminary Financial Assessment of Selected Agroforestry Associations in Central America

| Species | System | Cost of System Establishment | | Type of Product | Cash Flow Period (years) | Discount Rate (%) | Net Present Value from Production/ha (US$) | Projected Internal Rate of Return (%) |
		US$/ha	Mandays/ha					
Acacia mearnsii	Protection	405.00	50	Fuelwood Protection of soil	18	10	897.00	27.55

[a] Cost per km.

Sources: Bonilla et al. (1986); Navarro (1987); Organización para Estudios Tropicales y Centro Agronómico Tropical de Investigación y Enseñanza (1986); Oyuela (1987); Salazar (1985); Smits (1988).

of these systems to resource conservation, environmental protection, financial security, and the improvement in the quality of life that comes as a result of sustained production of goods and services from trees of multiple uses.

References

Bonilla, H. et al. 1986. Diseño de sistemas agroforestales para el área de Taque-Taque, Pejiballe. CATIE, Turrialba, Costa Rica. (Working paper).

Centro Agronómico Tropical de Investigación y Enseñanza. Proyecto cultivo de arboles de uso múltiple. 1986. Plan de investigación silvicultural 1986–1991. CATIE, Turrialba, Costa Rica. 41 p.

Centro Agronómico Tropical de Investigación y Enseñanza. Proyecto cultivo de arboles de uso múltiple. 1988. Manual para toma de información y análisis de situación inicial en fincas demostrativas; Análisis Estático. Turrialba, Costa Rica, CATIE.

Martínez, H. 1988. Combinaciones agroforestales con especies de AUM en las fincas demostrativas. Turrialba, Costa Rica, CATIE. 18 p.

Navarro P., C.M. 1987. Evaluación del crecimiento y rendimiento de *Bombacopsis quinatum* (Jacq) Dugand en 14 sitios de Costa Rica. Indices de sitio y algunos aspectos financieros de la especie. Tesis Mag. Sc. Turrialba, Costa Rica, UCR-CATIE. 136 p.

Organización Para Estudios Tropicales y Centro Agronómico Tropical De Investigación y Enseñanza. 1986. Sistemas agroforestales; principios y aplicaciones en los trópicos. San José, Costa Rica. 818p.

Oyuela, O. 1987. Los sistemas de producción agrícola y la determinación de posibles fuentes de contaminación en la sub cuenca del río Guajire, cuenca Guacerique. Tesis MS., Sistema de Estudios de Posgrado Universidád de Costa Rica-CATIE. Turrialba, Costa Rica. 190 p.

Salazar, Rodolfo (ed.). Técnicas de produccion de leña en fincas pequeñas y recuperación de sitios degradados Por medio de la silvicultura intensiva, 1985, Turrialba, Costa Rica. 1986. Actas de los simposios sobre técnicas de producción de leña en fincas pequeñas y recuperación de sitios degradados por medio de la silvicultura intensiva. Turrialba, Costa Rica, CATIE, p. 459.

Smits, M. 1988. Cercas vivas en la Zona Atlántica de Costa Rica. Un análisis económico del sistema silvopastoril cercas vivas de Erythrina berteruana (Urban) y Gliricida sepium (Jacq.) Steud, and la zona Atlántica de Costa Rica. Universidad de Wageningen, Holanda/CATIE. Turrialba, Costa Rica, CATIE. Working paper.

Appendix A
Locations of the CATIE Tree Crop Projects[a]

Country	Working Areas	Communities
Costa Rica	Dry Pacific	Peníns de Nicoya, Guanacaste
	South Pacific	Pérez Zeledón, Buenos Aires
	Central Valley	San Ramón, Puriscal, San José
El Salvador	Region I	Ahuachapán, Sonsonate, Armenia
	Region II	La Libertad, San Salvador
	Region III	La Paz
	Region IV	S. Miguel, Usulután
Guatemala	West Highland	Quezaltenango, Huehuetenango, Totonicapan, San Marcos
	Central Highland	Chimaltenango, Sacatepequez, Guatemala
	Pacific coast	Suchitepequez, Escuintla
	Dry Oriental zone	El Progreso, Zacapa, Jutiapa, Jalapa, Santa Rosa
Honduras	North zone	San Pedro Sula, S. Omoa
	Central zone	El Zamorano, Tegucigalpa, Valle de Talanga, Comayagua, Siguatepeque
	Southern zone	Valle y Choluteca
Panama	P. Azuero	Herrera, Macaracas, Tonosí, Los Santos
	Central zone	Coclé, Rio Hato
	Watershed canal zone	
	Chiriqui area	

[a] These areas present the greatest challenges to resolving the problems of deforestation, soil erosion, population pressure, and intensive use of forest products and, as a result, their scarcity.

Source: Centro Agronómico Tropical de Investigación y Enseñanza (1988).

Index

Abaetetuba (Brazil), 119, 120(fig.)
Açai Market (Belém, Brazil), 118, 121
Açai palm, 3, 69, 114, 115, 119
  beverage, 118
  distribution, 117
  fruit, 118, 119, 122, 124, 125
  heart, 117, 118-119, 122, 123, 124(fig.),
    125
  income from, 123-124
  labor inputs, 123
  productivity, 122, 123, 124, 129(tables)
  pruning, 119, 121, 122, 123, 124(table),
    129(tables)
  regeneration, 118, 119
  thinning, 119, 121, 122, 123, 124(table),
    129(tables)
  uses, 117, 118, 121, 125, 127-128(table)
Acerola, 65
Aconchi (Sonora, Mexico), 254
Acre state (Brazil), 72, 150-152, 155
Africa, 28, 92
African oil palm, 140
Agency for International Development
  (AID), 4, 25, 31, 37, 38, 130, 131,
  146, 233
Agoutis, 140, 145, 146, 174
Agriculture
  colonization, 2, 6, 130, 133. *See also*
    Amazonian rain forests, colonized
  dual sectors, 48
  investment return, 2, 3
  See also Amazon floodplains, farming;
    Pre-Columbian agricultural methods;
    Resource management strategies;
    under Kayapó Indians; *individual*
    countries
Agrochemical inputs, 28, 168
Agroecosystems, 6, 23, 24, 50
  properties of, 26-27
  and terrace farming, 215-217
Agroforestry systems, 5, 21, 32, 47, 64-
  65, 68, 102, 171, 184, 199-200
  in Amazon floodplains, 81, 92-93, 104-
    110, 274-277
  Andean, 224

Central American, 280-285
labor input, 109, 199
Aguajal. See Palm swamp
Aguaje palm, 65, 78, 84, 117
AID. *See* Agency for International
  Development
Air pollution, 1
Alcorn, Janis B., 5, 6, 7, 185
Alfalfa, 215, 217, 218(table), 224, 256
Alfisol, 169
Alluvial river banks, 274, 275, 276
Alternative agriculturalists, 27
Altiplano, 233, 236, 241, 245
Altura, 77, 80, 84, 87, 92
Aluminum, 132, 167
Amapá state (Brazil), 62
Amaranth, 251
Amaranthus hypocondriacus. See
  Amaranth
Amazonas state (Brazil), 62, 68
Amazon floodplains, 2, 3, 4, 6, 18(fig.),
  103
  climate, 77, 120
  communication, 77
  erosion, 77
  farming, 64, 76, 78, 79, 80, 81-85, 90-
    91, 94-95, 103, 104, 107, 115. *See*
    also Ribereños
  fauna, 78, 79, 82, 94, 95-96, 100(table)
  fish, 94
  fishing, 76, 77, 78, 79, 82, 87, 94
  forest products gathering, 76, 77, 78,
    80, 81, 82, 84, 87, 93, 94, 100(table),
    107, 115, 118, 122
  forest species, 65, 78, 80, 115-117, 127-
    128(table)
  geology, 77
  growing season, 84, 95
  hunting, 76, 77, 79, 82, 84, 94
  landform, 77, 91
  precipitation, 77, 79, 120
  and protein production, 95, 96
  sediments, 76, 77, 79, 84, 85, 90
  size, 77
  soils, 87, 90, 92, 95, 101(table), 120